1995

THE LAW OF THE WORKPLACE

Rights of Employers and Employees

Third Edition

THE LAW OF THE WORKPLACE

Rights of Employers and Employees

Third Edition

James W. Hunt
Patricia K. Strongin

The Bureau of National Affairs, Inc. Washington, D.C.

Co-author James W. Hunt writes in his
private capacity. No official support or
endorsement by the U.S. Government is
intended or should be inferred.

Library of Congress Cataloging in Publication Data

Hunt, James W.
  The law of the workplace : rights of employers and
employees / James W. Hunt and Patricia K. Strongin.
— 3rd ed.
    p. cm.
  Includes index.
  ISBN 0-87179-841-7
  1. Labor laws and legislation—United States.
I. Strongin, Patricia K.   II. Title.
KF3319.H83   1994
344.73'01—dc20
[347.3041]   94-38145
                                    CIP

Published by BNA Books
1231 25th Street, N.W., Washington, D.C. 20037

International Standard Book Number: 0-87179-841-7
Printed in the United States of America

INTRODUCTION

Since publication of the second edition of this book in 1988, five major new federal employment-related laws were enacted having a profound impact on workers and their employers. The law requiring employee notification of a plant closing and the one prohibiting discrimination against persons with disabilities were followed by legislation in many states using the federal law as a model. The other new federal statutes on family and medical leave, protection for "whistleblowers," and restrictions on the use of poly-graphs (lie detectors) extended nationally the laws that a number of states had already enacted.

In addition to these five laws, another federal law—the Clean Air Act, which normally affects only the environ-ment—mandated changes for employers in the commuting or transportation programs they underwrite or sponsor. At the same time, there has been a significant increase in the number of state laws that have an impact on many other segments of the workplace. Legislation is not the only route for changing the existing "law of the workplace." Federal and state regulations, as well as decisions from federal and state courts, impact on the rights and responsibilities of employers and employees.

Staying on top of these developments, and understand-ing their interaction, is a daunting task for the employer and employee. This is particularly true in light of the fact that there is no centralized government source for working people or their employers to contact for information about the overall scope of the laws and programs that affect them, largely because of the specialization of each of the federal and state agencies involved with employment-related mat-ters.

The purpose of this book is to fill this information gap for employers and employees by providing them with a summary of current workplace laws, the ways these laws affect them, and the agencies and programs involved. In some cases, the summaries and explanations provide some insight into the way the requirements of the myriad of laws overlap or intersect.

The laws that directly affect the approximately 120 million Americans who work for a living and their employers extend to all types of jobs and all aspects of employment and indeed affect most working men and women from the time before they are hired until after they retire.

These laws generally fall into one of two categories. The first covers on-the-job occurrences, such as employment discrimination, union activity, and health and safety practices. Laws relating to these matters, and the regulations issued by the government agencies charged with enforcing these laws, establish ground rules that govern the conduct and practices of employers, employees, and unions in the workplace.

The other general category of employment law covers those programs providing services for persons seeking work, or benefits for former job holders, such as training for job seekers, and unemployment and Social Security benefits for the jobless, disabled, or retired worker.

More specifically, these work-related laws:

- Expand employment opportunities for job seekers through job training programs.
- Provide persons who are out of work with assistance in finding jobs.
- Regulate entry into certain occupations.
- Require nondiscriminatory hiring, pay, and other employment practices.
- Provide for the rights of employees to take leave under certain circumstances.
- Restrict the circumstances in which employees can be terminated.
- Protect the privacy of individuals in the workplace.

- Regulate the testing of job applicants and employees.
- Allow workers to join or form unions.
- Provide financial assistance to workers who lose their jobs or become disabled.
- Establish minimum wage rates and job safety standards.
- Regulate private pension plans and provide workers with a basic retirement income through Social Security.

This book summarizes these requirements and offers only broad guidance. It does not intend to make any claim to answer the vast number of legal questions that can and may arise relating to employers' and employees' rights and responsibilities. Legal counsel or other professional help should be sought for advice and guidance in specific situations.

October 1994
Washington, D.C.

THE DEVELOPING LAW OF THE WORKPLACE

Today's far-reaching workplace laws have their origin in federal and state labor laws dating back to the last century.

Indeed, the states, rather than the federal government, were the first to enact labor laws, starting with Massachusetts' 1836 statute regulating child labor. Massachusetts was also the first state to adopt a minimum wage law (1912). Wisconsin also had two "firsts": It was the first state to put into effect a workers' compensation program (1911), and the first to enact an unemployment insurance law (1932).

The federal government began enacting most of its labor laws in the last 50 years. These laws, as well as laws in other subject areas referred to in this book, are listed below according to the year in which they became law. The title and section numbers of the U.S. Code where these laws are codified are also noted.

1866 Civil Rights Act, 42 U.S.C. §1981

1883 Civil Service Act, 5 U.S.C. §2101

1926 Railway Labor Act, 45 U.S.C. §151

1934 Copeland Anti-Kickback Act, 18 U.S.C. §874

1935 Davis-Bacon Act, 40 U.S.C. §276a

1935 National Labor Relations Act, 29 U.S.C. §151 (amended by the Labor Management Relations Act in 1947)

1936 Social Security Act, 42 U.S.C. §301

1936 Walsh-Healey Public Contracts Act, 41 U.S.C. §35

1938 Fair Labor Standards Act, 29 U.S.C. §201 (amended by the Equal Pay Act in 1963)

1947 Portal-to-Portal Act, 29 U.S.C. §251

1959 Labor Management Reporting and Disclosure Act, 29 U.S.C. §401

1962 Work Hours and Safety Act, 40 U.S.C. §327

1964 Title VII, 1964 Civil Rights Act, 42 U.S.C. §2000e

1965 McNamara-O'Hara Service Contract Act, 41 U.S.C. §351

1965 Executive Order 11246

1966 Freedom of Information Act, 5 U.S.C. §552

1967 Age Discrimination in Employment Act, 29 U.S.C. §621

1968 Consumer Credit Protection Act, 15 U.S.C. §1671

1970 Family Educational Rights and Privacy Act, 20 U.S.C. §1232g

1970 Occupational Safety and Health Act, 29 U.S.C. §651

1971 Fair Credit Reporting Act, Title III, 15 U.S.C. §1681
(also known as Consumer Credit Protection Act)

1972 Vietnam Era Veterans' Readjustment Assistance Act, 38 U.S.C. §2011
(also known as Veterans Reemployment Rights Act)

1973 Vocational Rehabilitation Act (handicapped employment amendment), 29 U.S.C. §793

1974 Employee Retirement Income Security Act, 29 U.S.C. §1001

1974 Federal Privacy Act, 5 U.S.C. §552a

1978 Civil Service Reform Act, Title VII, 5 U.S.C. §5596

1978 Pregnancy Discrimination Act, 42 U.S.C. §2000e

1982 Job Training Partnership Act, 29 U.S.C. §1501

1984 Child Support Enforcement Act, 42 U.S.C. §666

1986 Consolidated Omnibus Budget Reconciliation Act, 29 U.S.C. §1161

1986 Immigration Reform and Control Act, 8 U.S.C. §1324A

1988 Employee Polygraph Protection Act of 1988, 29 U.S.C. §2001

1988 Worker Adjustment and Retraining Notification Act, 29 U.S.C. §2101

1989 Whistleblower Protection Act, 5 U.S.C. §1213

1990 Americans With Disabilities Act, 42 U.S.C. §12101

1990 Clean Air Act, 42 U.S.C. §7401

1993 Family and Medical Leave Act of 1993, P.L. 103-141

This list, while current, is not complete. The laws of the workplace continue to evolve and develop. Each year federal and state legislators make changes to the laws, ranging from modifications of existing statutes, such as changes in the minimum wage, to the enactment of entirely new laws, such as those regulating smoking in the workplace, providing for extended family and medical leave, prohibiting the use of polygraph testing, providing for drug testing in the workplace, protecting whistleblowers, prohibiting discrimination against individuals with disabilities, and other provisions promoting the safety and health of workers. Still other areas are being considered by federal and state lawmakers as the subjects of proposed future legislation. Matters under consideration include proposals to prohibit employers from permanently replacing economic strikers and measures requiring mandatory health insurance for all employees. Rulings and decisions by administrative agencies and courts also frequently have a profound impact on the law.

Keeping current with these frequent changes is not always an easy task, but there are various sources available for this purpose. The publisher of this book, The Bureau of National Affairs, is one of several private companies providing up-to-date information on changes in workplace laws by legislators, agencies, and courts. In January of each year, BNA's *Daily Labor Report* publishes a summary of all newly enacted state labor laws and BNA's *Labor Relations Reporter* publishes the full text of all the federal and state labor laws.

In addition, an excellent source of information on legislative activity in the states is the *Monthly Labor Review*, a publication of the U.S. Department of Labor. Its annual January issue contains a complete summary of the workplace laws enacted by state legislators in the preceding year. The *Monthly Labor Review* is available in most libraries.

ACRONYMS

AAP	Affirmative Action Program
AFDC	Aid to Families With Dependent Children
AFL-CIO	American Federation of Labor-Congress of Industrial Organizations
AIDS	Acquired Immune Deficiency Syndrome
ALJ	Administrative Law Judge
BFOQ	Bona Fide Occupational Qualification
CETA	Comprehensive Employment and Training Act
CFR	Code of Federal Regulations
CLEP	College-Level Education Program
COBRA	Consolidated Omnibus Budget Reconciliation Act
CODA	Cash or Deferred Account
DHHS	Department of Health and Human Services
DIB	Disability Insurance Benefits
DOL	Department of Labor
DUA	Disaster Unemployment Assistance
EEO	Equal Employment Opportunity
EEOC	Equal Employment Opportunity Commission
EPA	Equal Pay Act
ERISA	Employee Retirement Income Security Act
ESA	Employment Standards Administration
ETA	Employment and Training Administration
FEP	Fair Employment Practices
FICA	Federal Insurance Contribution Act
FLRA	Federal Labor Relations Authority
FLSA	Fair Labor Standards Act
FMCS	Federal Mediation and Conciliation Service

FMLA	Family and Medical Leave Act
GED	General Education Development
GS	General Schedules
INS	Immigration and Naturalization Service
IRA	Individual Retirement Account
IRCA	Immigration Reform and Control Act
IRS	Internal Revenue Service
JTPA	Job Training Partnership Act
LMRA	Labor Management Relations Act
LMRDA	Labor Management Reporting and Disclosure Act
LMSA	Labor Management Services Administration
MSDS	Material Safety Data Sheet
MSPB	Merit Systems Protection Board
NLRA	National Labor Relations Act
NLRB	National Labor Relations Board
NMB	National Mediation Board
OFCCP	Office of Federal Contract Compliance Programs
OPM	Office of Personnel Management
OSHA	Occupational Safety and Health Administration
OWCP	Office of Workers' Compensation Programs
PIC	Private Industry Council
RIB	Retirement Insurance Benefits
RIF	Reduction in Force
RLA	Railway Labor Act
SDA	Service Delivery Area
SEP	Simplified Employee Pension Plan
SES	Senior Executive Service
SSA	Social Security Administration
SSI	Supplemental Security Income
TAA	Trade Adjustment Assistance Act
UC	Unemployment Compensation
UEP	Unfair Employment Practice
UI	Unemployment Insurance
ULP	Unfair Labor Practice

USES U.S. Employment Service
WARN Worker Adjustment and Retraining
Notification Act
WC Workers' Compensation
WIN Work Incentive Program

CONTENTS

1

PROGRAMS FOR JOB SEEKERS

An obvious requirement for employment is the ability to perform the work required. Although many entry-level positions require only that a person be able to perform simple tasks, greater qualifications are needed to advance to more responsible and better paid positions.

Most job training for these positions is provided by employers to those employees having the aptitude and willingness to do the work. But federal and state governments, often through joint efforts, also offer a variety of programs to equip both job holders and job seekers with the means to qualify for higher level positions.

Job Information Services

Many persons, whether young workers new to the labor market or experienced workers looking for a new line of work, are unfamiliar with the range of available career opportunities that they may be qualified to pursue with the necessary education and training. An information source that can help is the U.S. Department of Labor's *Occupational Outlook Handbook*, which describes different jobs, the education and training requirements needed for these jobs, expected earnings, and career potential in these positions.

The *Handbook* provides detailed information on more than 250 occupations—from production and service jobs to administrative, managerial, and professional positions—summarizes 80 others, and lists the names and addresses of state agencies to contact for information about each

1

state's job market and career opportunities, as well as the names of public and private organizations covering a wide range of jobs and careers. Suggestions on how to look for a job, how to interview, and where to find additional information are also included.

A related Labor Department publication, the *Dictionary of Occupational Titles,* while not providing the comprehensive job descriptions contained in the *Handbook,* does list and define the nearly 20,000 jobs that exist.

Most public libraries have the *Handbook* and the *Dictionary.* They can also be bought from:

United States Government Printing Office
Washington, D.C. 20402

U.S. Employment Service

The U.S. Employment Service, a federal-state system of almost 2,000 local Job Service (or Employment Service) offices nationwide, offers "no fee" job placement and job counseling assistance to all job seekers and applicant assessment and screening services to interested employers. Local Job Service offices, through the Interstate Job Bank, a job matching system that is computerized in many cities, provide up-to-date information on jobs currently in demand, from entry-level positions to technical and professional occupations, and information on where such jobs are located, the training needed, and their rates of pay. In some instances even out-of-state jobs are listed. During any given week the Job Bank may contain over 20,000 job openings.

The Job Service also helps employers obtain workers for their general work force as well as for jobs requiring special skills and experience. Top priority is given to veterans under the Veterans' Readjustment Benefits Act and the Vietnam Era Veterans' Readjustment Assistance Act to provide them with job training and counseling and placement services. The Job Service is listed in the telephone directory under that name, or as the Employment Security Commission, or Employment Service, depending on what each state calls its service. A Job Service office can also provide information on the training programs referred to in this chapter.

Education Assistance

In today's competitive labor market the lack of a high school diploma or college degree can frustrate the career advancement of many otherwise qualified workers. Therefore, local school systems have developed programs for working adults to give them the opportunity to obtain the formal educational qualifications they lack without spending long hours in the classroom. Some programs, for example, allow adults to earn high school equivalency certificates through the General Educational Development (GED) program, while college credit can be obtained through such systems as the College-Level Education Program (CLEP). More information about these and other programs can be obtained through a local school system or by writing to:

GED Testing Service
One Dupont Circle, N.W.
Washington, D.C. 20036

CLEP College Board
Programs Service Office
45 Columbus Avenue
New York, N.Y. 10023–6917

College-Level Examination Program
Educational Testing Service
Princeton, N.J. 08541

Apprenticeships

Apprenticeship programs operated under federally approved standards provide combined on-the-job and classroom training to persons learning to perform the work of a highly skilled occupation, such as automotive mechanic, electrician, or carpenter. There are literally hundreds of apprenticeship trades, with the training lasting from one to six years, depending on the trade, until the worker becomes a full-fledged journeyman.

The programs are usually employer-sponsored, with many cosponsored by labor unions. Qualifications generally require that an applicant be at least 16 years old and have a high school diploma or GED certificate, although the specific requirements are determined by the sponsor. The programs, under written agreements, must be open to both men and women and must conform to equal employment opportunity (EEO) requirements. Some receive government funding, and many are operated in correctional institutions to provide inmates with a legitimate trade they can practice upon their release. Apprentices are paid on an increasing schedule consistent with skill acquired. The term of these federally approved apprenticeships is at least 2,000 hours of work experience and a minimum of 144 hours of organized and related instruction.

National standards governing the scope of the training, instruction, and pay are approved by the federal government's Bureau of Apprenticeship and Training or by a state apprenticeship council.

For more information, contact a local Job Service office or write to:

Bureau of Apprenticeship and Training
U.S. Department of Labor
200 Constitution Avenue, N.W.
Washington, D.C. 20210

Youth Programs

Under the federal Job Corps program, disadvantaged youths aged 16–21 are provided with a broad range of work experience, training, and services, including basic education, health, residential, and other support services, to enhance their employability in what job specialists call the "world of work." The services are provided through full-time residential centers located in both rural and urban areas. Other youth programs include short-term summer employment for disadvantaged young people.

Work Incentive Program

Persons 16 years of age or older who receive or apply for Aid to Families with Dependent Children are required to register for the Work Incentive (WIN) program at a local Job Service office. The WIN program, operated jointly by the U.S. Departments of Labor and Health and Human Services, provides various services to the registrants to help them find and hold jobs, including social services allowing eligible individuals to participate in job-related activities, relocation assistance, and training.

Job Training Partnership Act

The Job Training Partnership Act (JTPA) provides job training and assistance for economically disadvantaged youth and adults and others who may face employment barriers, such as Native Americans, seasonal and migrant farm workers, and veterans, to assist their entry into the labor market. Through a public/private partnership it also provides training and other employment services to dislocated workers—those laid off due to plant closings, the long-term unemployed, and those unable to return to the same industry or occupation. State governments provide matching funds for the programs for dislocated workers.

Under JTPA the governors of each state designate Service Delivery Areas (SDAs) within their states where local government units and Private Industry Councils (PICs) develop job training plans tailored to their areas. SDAs can be composed of one or more cities or counties, while PICs are made up mostly from representatives from private industry, together with representatives from labor unions and other community-based organizations. JTPA employment programs are also coordinated with the local Job Service.

Rehabilitation Services for Handicapped Persons

A federal-state system of local vocational rehabilitation agencies provides services to persons 16 years of age or older having a physical or mental disability that hinders their ability to find work. Rehabilitation services, which are provided if the individual can reasonably be expected to benefit from them, are tailored to the individual and can include corrective surgery, artificial limbs, transportation to receive services, education, on-the-job training, vocational training, and counseling.

Federal law also reserves the opportunity for the blind to run vending facilities in federal buildings, and employers with workshop programs providing training and jobs for blind and handicapped individuals receive preference in bidding on government contracts for products and services.

Bonding Program

Some employers require that their employees be bonded, a form of insurance protecting the employer against employee dishonesty, theft, or embezzlement. Insurance companies, however, often refuse to bond individuals with a criminal record, a history of alcohol or drug abuse, or a poor credit record. These persons consequently are not hired when a bond is required even though they may have been rehabilitated. Under the federal bonding program a person not commercially bondable because of one of the above reasons, but otherwise qualified for an available job, can apply for and receive a bond at a Job Service office.

Other Programs

Somewhat lower on the scale than the others, but nevertheless important to the persons they serve, are programs for older workers, Native Americans, and migrant workers. As with most government-sponsored programs, the Job Service is the agency to contact for information.

There are, of course, many nongovernmental, privately operated programs providing training for occupations ranging from secretarial positions to truck driver and computer operator. And there are also private job counseling and placement agencies. Like the government-sponsored employment programs, private sector activities serve job seekers by providing them with the qualifications and assistance needed to get hired for, and advance in, the jobs they want.

Private employment agencies provide job placement services for both employers and applicants. Some of the activities of these agencies are regulated by state law. A number of states limit the fees that agencies can charge individuals, while others require agencies to be licensed. State laws may also provide that agencies refund fees that applicants have paid if the job does not last beyond a specified length of time, require posting of surety bonds, or prohibit agencies from making false or misleading statements.

Tax Credits

The Targeted Jobs Tax Credit program gives employers an incentive to hire individuals from targeted groups with high unemployment rates or other special employment needs. Employers hiring these workers can receive a tax credit of up to $2,400 during the first year of employment for each person they hire. For economically disadvantaged young summer-job employees, the maximum credit is $1,200. There are 10 target groups, including:

- Welfare recipients;
- Persons with disabilities;
- Young workers (14–18 years old) from economically disadvantaged families;
- Economically disadvantaged Vietnam-era veterans; and
- Economically disadvantaged ex-offenders.

An employer interested in obtaining a tax credit can contact a local Internal Revenue Service office for more information.

Workers are also allowed tax credits (earned income credit) for the actual expense incurred for child or dependent care when the expense is necessary to enable the worker to be gainfully employed. More information about the credit is provided in the instructions the IRS sends to individual taxpayers with their tax forms.

EMPLOYEE TAX DEDUCTIONS

An employee who itemizes deductions on his or her federal income tax return is allowed to deduct certain employment-related expenses, but only to the extent that the employee was not reimbursed for the expense. To be eligible, 1994 income must be less than $23,760 for taxpayers with one child. In 1993, eligible employees could get up to $1,434 in credit. The basic credit is 30 percent on the first $8,425, with a reduction in the credit for workers with larger incomes. These deductions include:

- Moving costs if there was a change in the commuting distance for the employee of at least 50 miles from the former location to the new location and the move takes place within one year after the employee starts work at the new location;
- Expenses for business travel, parking, tolls, transportation (but not commuting expenses to and from work), meals and lodging;
- Union or professional dues;
- Tools, employer-required uniforms, and safety equipment used in the employee's work;
- Costs for education required by the employer, or by law or regulation, in order to keep a present job or salary; and
- Fees paid to employment agencies and other costs to get a new job in the employee's present trade or profession.

Either a local office of the Internal Revenue Service or a public library has publications explaining these deductions in more detail.

2

EMPLOYMENT RESTRICTIONS

Americans have a basic right to pursue any legitimate business, occupation, or profession as a means of earning a living. The laws of the federal and state governments have generally been intended to promote that right by expanding job opportunities through various employment services.

A government, however, also has the power to impose in the public's interest reasonable restrictions on a individual's right to operate a business or perform some types of work. When this power has been exercised, it has been used to place restrictions on the employment of women, ex-offenders, young workers, and aliens. It also has been used to restrict entry by all persons into certain jobs through occupational licensing laws.

Women

Many states in the past adopted laws to protect women from the hazards of industrial work by restricting the type of work they could perform, the number of hours they could work, night-work, and the maximum weight they could be required to lift.

These laws, however, are now generally considered to limit job opportunities for women rather than protecting them. Although they are still on the books in some states, the federal Equal Employment Opportunity Commission (EEOC), which enforces the law prohibiting job discrimination, does not consider an employer's reliance on such laws

9

in denying a woman a job to be a valid defense to a charge of unlawful sex discrimination.

State Occupational Licensing Laws

Occupational licensing is in effect permission from a government-created board or commission to engage in some job, trade, or profession. All states have enacted laws that make it illegal for an unlicensed person to work in an occupation that requires government licensure or certification. The basis for the government's licensing authority is that certain jobs affect the public in such a way that the government can require that persons wanting to work in these jobs have a minimum level of competency to protect the public's health, safety, or welfare.

The occupations regulated by licensing laws vary from state to state and cover a variety of vocations, trades, and professions, ranging from, in some states, fortune-teller and junk dealer, to, in all states, doctors, lawyers, and teachers. Some jobs, such as taxicab operator, are licensed by cities. Nationwide, more than seven million persons work in occupations or for businesses requiring a government license or certification.

Information about a state's occupational licensing requirements can be obtained from the licensing agencies listed in the telephone directory under the state government listing.

Federal Licensing Laws

Federal laws provide for the licensing, in one form or another, of persons engaged in certain food industries, such as dealers and brokers who buy and sell produce. Meat and poultry food processors, on the other hand, do not need a license but they are regulated as though they do need one by being barred by law from selling their products unless they have applied for and been granted federal meat inspection services. The Department of Agriculture, which regulates these industries, will suspend or revoke the license, or inspection service, of anyone failing to comply with its regulations governing the practices of these industries.

Other forms of licensing apply to airlines, railroads, and truck companies engaged in interstate activities.

Ex-Offenders

The occupational licensing laws of some states expressly prohibit the issuance of a license to a person with a criminal record, while others contain indirect restrictions, such as the requirement that an applicant for a license be of "good moral character," which has often been used to exclude anyone with a police record. Some state laws also prohibit the employment of ex-felons in state jobs.

In recent years, however, about half the states have adopted laws which provide that an ex-offender is not to be automatically denied a license or a government job and that, in determining the applicant's fitness for a job or a license, consideration be given to the nature of the crime, its relation to the job the individual wants to perform, and his or her rehabilitation efforts.

The federal government applies essentially the same standards in considering whether ex-offenders applying for civil service jobs should be hired. The federal Landrum-Griffin Act, however, also prohibits persons convicted of certain offenses from holding office in a labor union and indirectly limits jobs and job training for offenders by prohibiting goods made in prison from being shipped across state lines or from being used on federally funded highway projects.

The Drug-Free Workplace Act of 1988 restricts employment by a federal contractor of workers convicted of drug-related activity by requiring the employer to:

- Notify employees that they must report any criminal convictions for unlawful drug activity in the workplace within five days after a conviction;
- Notify the federal contracting or grant agency of any such criminal convictions; and
- Take "appropriate" personnel action against any employee convicted, ranging from termination to requiring participation in an approved drug abuse assistance or rehabilitation program.

Young Workers

All states and the federal government have adopted child labor laws restricting the types and hours of work for young workers. These laws generally require that young workers obtain work permits from their local school system and that employers hiring young people observe the following standards:

- An 18-year minimum age for hazardous work;
- A 16-year minimum age for factory work;
- A 14-year minimum age for nonfactory work outside school hours (except for work on farms and such work as delivering newspapers);
- A maximum 40-hour work week for children under 16 years of age;
- Limitations on working time outside school hours for youth still in school (the limitations vary from state to state); and
- Restrictions on working at night.

More information about a state's child labor laws can be obtained from the state's labor department. The addresses of these departments are listed in Appendix A. Chapter 8 covers in more detail the federal child labor law.

Aliens

Aliens living in the United States do not have the right to work while here unless they fall into one of the categories of aliens allowed to work by the federal Immigration Reform and Control Act (IRCA). Indeed, it is unlawful for an employer to hire an alien who lacks authorization to work (referred to as an "undocumented alien") and has not fulfilled the requirements of employment eligibility verification procedures under IRCA. An employer may be fined up to $2,000 for a first offense, $5,000 for a second offense, and up to $10,000 for any subsequent offenses. Failure to comply with other requirements of the law, is punishable with a fine of $100 to $10,000, depending on the offense.

Aliens allowed by law to work include lawful permanent resident aliens, certain political refugees, lawful temporary residents, asylum grantees, and family members (including fiancee) of lawful aliens. Other aliens who are lawfully admitted into this country, including nonimmigrant students studying at American schools, foreign government officials and their relatives and employees, personal employees of officials or representatives of international organizations, and certain temporary workers or trainees, must obtain authorization to work from the Immigration and Naturalization Service.

Other foreign workers may also be allowed to work temporarily or permanently in the United States, but only if qualified Americans are not available to do the work and the terms of employment for the foreign workers will not adversely affect the wages and working conditions of American workers. The conditions under which foreign workers are allowed to work depend on whether temporary or permanent work is sought.

For immigrants to gain access to the United States and to lawfully work in this country, two categories of visas are issued: immigrant and nonimmigrant.

Immigrant Visas. Often called "Green Cards," immigrant visas are allocated each year according to a predetermined order of preference. The first, second, fourth, and fifth preference categories are family preference categories, while the third and sixth preferences are employment-based. The third preference is assigned to professionals of "exceptional ability" in the arts, sciences, or business, education, or athletics. Sixth preference is for unskilled laborers, capable of performing work not of a temporary or seasonal nature and for which a shortage of employable and willing persons exists. Persons in this category have less than two years of experience on the job.

Nonimmigrant Visas. These are visas issued to foreign nationals coming to the United States for a limited time to accomplish a specific purpose. Such visas may or may not include work authorization. Persons with nonimmigrant visas are required to complete and retain in their possession a white "I-94" identification card. These nonimmigrant visas, sometimes referred to as "temporary visas," have been used to permit foreign registered nurses to perform services as registered nurses at certain certified health care facilities and to fill "specialty occupations," defined as jobs requiring theoretical and practical application of highly specialized knowledge and an academic degree from an accredited college or university in a field related to the position to be filled.

Temporary Employment. An employer, or his agent, anticipating a labor shortage not caused by a strike or lockout may apply for a "temporary labor certificate" for temporary foreign workers (ETA form 575-B). The application, filed with the Job Service office serving the area where the work is to be performed, must, among other requirements, document the employer's attempt to recruit Americans and show that it made job offers to Americans without regard to their race, color, religion, sex, age, or nationality, including offers to handicapped workers qualified to perform the work.

The Job Service will then attempt to recruit Americans for the jobs. If all conditions are met and there are still no qualified Americans available, the employer may be allowed to hire foreign workers. However, they can perform only the work indicated in the application.

Permanent Employment. An employer may apply for a labor certification to allow an alien to work permanently in the United States. An alien also may apply. The application for permanent employment (ETA form 750) can be obtained from the local State Employment Service or a Job Service office, which is where an employer files the application. An alien, however, files the application with a U.S. Consular office if he or she is living abroad, or with an office of the Immigration and Naturalization Service if he or she is living in the United States. Both employers and aliens may have an agent do the filing for them.

The government has facilitated the process for obtaining permanent employment applications by preparing two lists of occupations, called Schedules A and B. Schedule A lists the occupations for which there are not a sufficient number of qualified American workers; Schedule B lists the jobs for which there are a sufficient number. Aliens can apply only for Schedule A jobs, while employers can apply to have an alien hired to do a job listed in either Schedule A or B.

An employer applying for an alien's certification for an occupation not listed in Schedule A must document its efforts to recruit Americans for the job. The Job Service will still conduct its own job search to try to fill the position with an American before approving the certification.

In the event an employer wants to hire an alien of "exceptional ability in the performing arts," it is permitted to reject applications for the job from Americans who are less qualified than the alien. The government, however, makes the final determination whether to grant any request for a certification to allow an alien to work here.

More information about the employment of aliens can be obtained from:

Division of Labor Certification
U.S. Employment Service
200 Constitution Avenue, N.W.
Washington, D.C. 20210

Undocumented Aliens. It is unlawful for an employer to hire aliens lacking the necessary documentation showing that they are authorized to work. The documents that aliens can use for this purpose, and to prove their identity, include a United States passport, an Alien Registration Card with a photograph, or an unexpired foreign passport with attached employment authorization.

Although employers are required to verify an alien's employment authorization and are prohibited from hiring undocumented aliens, they are also prohibited by the Immigration Reform and Control Act of 1986 from discriminating in the hiring of aliens because of their national origin and discriminating against aliens because of their citizenship when they intend to become American citizens. A separate federal law, Title VII of the 1964 Civil Rights Act, also prohibits discrimination on the basis of national origin.

3

CREATING THE EMPLOYMENT RELATIONSHIP

Americans have a basic right to seek work. This does not, however, guarantee that all persons will find or be hired for the jobs they want. With the exceptions noted below, employers generally have the right to decide which applicants to hire, or to refuse to hire, as long as they do not discriminate on the basis of race, religion, sex, disability, or one of the other grounds discussed in later chapters on equal employment opportunity and discrimination.

During the hiring process employers often use a variety of selection tools, including preemployment tests, to screen prospective employees and to identify qualified job applicants. As discussed in later chapters, federal and state laws restrict the use of these screening practices to the extent that they may be discriminatory.

Most exceptions to the general rule that an employer can decide which employees to hire extend to certain categories of former employees. Workers whose employment was terminated because of federal military service or because of being called to active duty in the National Guard in some states have the right to be rehired. Employees who were unlawfully discharged from their jobs have the right to be reinstated, and striking employees have a preferential right to employment in circumstances covered later in the discussion on strikes. Unionized employees protected under a collective bargaining agreement who were laid off or lost their jobs because of plant removal may also have the right to be rehired.

Job seekers, on the other hand, have the right to refuse jobs they do not want, to refuse to work for an employer for whom they do not wish to work, and to quit jobs they do not like. Americans, for that matter, have the right not to work at all.

Unemployed workers, however, can lose their entitlement to benefits under an unemployment compensation program if they refuse to look for work or refuse to accept suitable job offers. "Workfare" programs in all the states condition payment of welfare benefits to recipients on their participation, if able-bodied, in the Job Opportunities and Basic Skills Training Program, as long as the states have the resources to serve them.

Work Eligibility

The Immigration Reform and Control Act of 1986 requires all employers, both in the private and public sectors, to verify the legal employment status of all new hires, including American citizens. In short, an employer must verify a person's eligibility to work before entering into an employer-employee relationship with the person. Generally, a U.S. passport, a certificate of U.S. citizenship, or an alien registration receipt is sufficient to establish both the person's identity and work eligibility. Similarly, a Social Security card or birth certificate with accompanying verification of the person's identity, such as a driver's license containing a photograph, can be used. Employers must receive this documentation within three days of the person's start of employment, must examine the documents, and then complete a form called "Employment Eligibility Verification" (Form I-9). Section 1 of the I-9 form must be filled out by the employee at the time of hire, and the employer must complete Section 2 within three business days. Employers do not need to complete a Form I-9 for independent contractors or leased employees. The employer must retain the I-9 form for three years after hiring or for one year after the individual's termination, whichever is later. The form reproduced on page 19 is largely self-explanatory. The same form is also used when an employer hires an alien as covered in the preceding chapter.

Social Security Card

A Social Security card is now virtually a prerequisite for employment. It is obtained by applying for one at a local Social Security office. It can be obtained any time after a person is born either by that person or someone serving as his or her representative, such as a parent. A copy of the applicant's birth certificate or religious hospital record of birth made before five years of age together with a document showing the person's identity must accompany the application. Since 1991, a Social Security card is required for any person being claimed as a dependent by a taxpayer. The person to whom a card is issued will receive an exclusive lifetime Social Security number. This number will be used thereafter by the government to credit payments to the person's Social Security account and will also serve as an identification number for income tax purposes.

Tax Information

At the time of hiring, the employer must ask each new employee to complete the income tax withholding form (Form W-4). The employer also must record each new employee's name and number from his or her Social Security card.

Employers and Employees

An employer-employee relationship is created when a job seeker (prospective employee) agrees to work or perform services for someone else (prospective employer), under circumstances where the employer has the right to control both the results the employee is to accomplish and the method or means by which the employee is to achieve those results. It is this control, not an employee's job title, that determines whether an employer-employee relationship

INS I-9, EMPLOYMENT ELIGIBILITY VERIFICATION

U.S. Department of Justice
Immigration and Naturalization Service

OMB No. 1115-0136
Employment Eligibility Verification

Please read instructions carefully before completing this form. The instructions must be available during completion of this form. **ANTI-DISCRIMINATION NOTICE.** It is illegal to discriminate against work eligible individuals. Employers **CANNOT** specify which document(s) they will accept from an employee. The refusal to hire an individual because of a future expiration date may also constitute illegal discrimination.

Section 1. Employee Information and Verification. To be completed and signed by employee at the time employment begins

Print Name: Last	First	Middle Initial	Maiden Name

Address (Street Name and Number)	Apt. #	Date of Birth (month/day/year)

City	State	Zip Code	Social Security #

I am aware that federal law provides for imprisonment and/or fines for false statements or use of false documents in connection with the completion of this form.

I attest, under penalty of perjury, that I am (check one of the following):
☐ A citizen or national of the United States
☐ A Lawful Permanent Resident (Alien # A _____)
☐ An alien authorized to work until ___ / ___ / ___
(Alien # or Admission # _____)

Employee's Signature	Date (month/day/year)

Preparer and/or Translator Certification. (To be completed and signed if Section 1 is prepared by a person other than the employee.) I attest, under penalty of perjury, that I have assisted in the completion of this form and that to the best of my knowledge the information is true and correct.

Preparer's/Translator's Signature	Print Name

Address (Street Name and Number, City, State, Zip Code)	Date (month/day/year)

Section 2. Employer Review and Verification. To be completed and signed by employer. Examine one document from List A OR examine one document from List B **and** one from List C as listed on the reverse of this form and record the title, number and expiration date, if any, of the document(s)

	List A	OR	List B	AND	List C
Document title:					
Issuing authority:					
Document #:					
Expiration Date (if any): ___/___/___		___/___/___		___/___/___	
Document #					
Expiration Date (if any): ___/___/___					

CERTIFICATION - I attest, under penalty of perjury, that I have examined the document(s) presented by the above-named employee, that the above-listed document(s) appear to be genuine and to relate to the employee named, that the employee began employment on (month/day/year) ___/___/___ and that to the best of my knowledge the employee is eligible to work in the United States. (State employment agencies may omit the date the employee began employment).

Signature of Employer or Authorized Representative	Print Name	Title

Business or Organization Name	Address (Street Name and Number, City, State, Zip Code)	Date (month/day/year)

Section 3. Updating and Reverification. To be completed and signed by employer

A. New Name (if applicable)	B. Date of rehire (month/day/year) (if applicable)

C. If employee's previous grant of work authorization has expired, provide the information below for the document that establishes current employment eligibility.

Document Title: _____   Document #: _____   Expiration Date (if any): ___/___/___

I attest, under penalty of perjury, that to the best of my knowledge, this employee is eligible to work in the United States, and if the employee presented document(s), the document(s) I have examined appear to be genuine and to relate to the individual.

Signature of Employer or Authorized Representative	Date (month/day/year)

Form I-9 (Rev. 11-21-91) N

exists. It also does not matter how an employee is paid, whether hourly, salaried, or commissioned, or whether the employee works full- or part-time.

The agreement between the employer and employee does not have to be actually expressed; it can be shown by the conduct of the parties indicating that one agrees to perform work for the other with the understanding that he or she will be paid for the work performed. This arrangement is legally a contract whether written or not and imposes certain duties on both the employer and the employee.

Duties of Employers and Employees

An employee has a duty to follow his or her employer's instructions, work diligently, be loyal, and perform work only for the employer during the hours of employment. Otherwise, the employee can have a second job ("moonlight"), or engage in self-employment, as long as it does not adversely affect the duties owed to the employer.

Any invention the employee develops on his or her own time belongs to the employee, unless there is an agreement to the contrary with the employer, or unless the employee was expressly hired to develop inventions. The employee, however, has no right to disclose secret processes or methods developed by the employer, even if the employee should leave the employer to work for someone else. The employee does, on the other hand, have the right to use the technical knowledge or skills in a new position that he or she learned in the prior job.

An employer, for its part, has a duty to an employee to:

- Pay for the work performed.
- Refrain from discriminating in pay, promotions, benefits, and working conditions because of the employee's race, sex, religion, national origin, disabilities, union activity or membership, or for other reasons covered in later chapters.
- Provide a workplace free from recognizable hazards to the employee's safety or health.

- Make required contributions for workers' compensation, unemployment insurance, and Social Security.
- Make required deductions from the employee's pay for the worker's income tax and Social Security payments.
- Not divulge to other persons any confidential or medical information in the employee's personnel file.
- Comply with federal, state, and local laws covering other aspects of employment.
- Comply with the terms of any employment contract with the employee or with any contractual obligations under a collective bargaining agreement with a union representing the worker.

The enforcement of an employer's duty to an employee varies according to the nature of the duty. Some duties may be enforced through court action, while others are enforced through action by government agencies. Later chapters cover these matters in more detail.

An employer-employee relationship can also be created even though the employee is not legally eligible to work, such as an alien lacking work authorization. The alien as an employee is entitled to many of the legal protections to which work-eligible workers are entitled.

Independent Contractors

Not all arrangements in which one person agrees to perform services for another creates an employer-employee relationship. It largely depends on whether the person for whom the work is being performed controls the method or means by which the work will be performed and the result to be accomplished. A person having such control over the relationship becomes the employer and the worker the employee. However, if the person doing the work has the right to decide how to provide the promised work or services, he or she may be considered an independent contractor rather than an employee. Self-employed electricians, plumbers, and carpenters are examples of independent contractors when they control how they will perform the work, can hire their own employees, are answerable to the person for whom they do the work only as to the final product or result, and receive their pay (or profit) on the basis of the difference between their contract price and the cost of doing the work.

Keep in mind, however, that there is a complex set of factors that determine whether a worker is an employee or an independent contractor and that no one factor or set of factors is automatically controlling. All the facts and circumstances of a particular situation must be taken into account in determining whether an individual worker should be treated as an employee or as an independent contractor. Advice of legal counsel in specific cases may be necessary.

A person employing an independent contractor does not have to withhold income or Social Security taxes from the contractor's pay or to pay Social Security and unemployment taxes and does not have to negotiate with any union that may represent the contractor or its employees. Independent contractors also are not considered employees under federal equal employment opportunity law. An employer who is unsure about an individual's status can request a ruling by the Internal Revenue Service by filling out IRS Form SS-8.

Agents

An agent is a person authorized to act on another person's behalf with a third person. An employee is generally not an employer's agent unless given that authority by the employer, expressly or impliedly. On the other hand, an employer can give another person the authority to act as its agent for specific purposes without making that person an employee.

Even though an employee has not been authorized by the employer to be its agent and therefore cannot bind it in business dealings with another person, the employer can still be held responsible for an employee's actions when the employee injures a third person during the course of employment, regardless of whether the employer actually authorized the employee's misdeed. An employer, however, is generally not liable if the employee inflicts the injury while acting outside the scope of employment.

Whether an injury was inflicted in "the scope of employment" is often a difficult question requiring the advice of legal counsel in specific cases.

Leased Employees

Leasing employees is a form of employment arrangement that came into more frequent use after a 1982 tax law change. Under a leasing arrangement, a business seeking workers contracts with a work force leasing company to provide it with one or more workers. The leasing company agrees to become the workers' employer of record for tax and insurance purposes while the business continues as the owner and operator of the enterprise. Complicated tax requirements, as well as potential union and collective bargaining implications, make it important that one receive legal advice when pursuing a leasing arrangement.

4

EMPLOYMENT TESTING AND SCREENING

Testing

Preemployment testing is one of a number of screening tools an employer can use to select qualified workers. Employers, however, are required by law to make sure that any tests they administer are valid and job-related so that the tests do not screen out persons in "protected classes," that is, persons in those classifications identified in equal employment opportunity laws as being protected against employment discrimination.

In other words, while tests are not prohibited, there are restrictions on their use to try to ensure that they will not have a disparate impact on members of a protected classification.

Test Validation

If an employer gives a test as part of the selection process, state and federal equal opportunity laws provide that the test

- Be job-related;
- Accurately predict an applicant's job performance; and
- Require uniform passing scores.

The employer has the burden of proving the appropriateness of the test and may have to produce records as proof.

The U.S. Employment Service, a federal-state system of almost 2,000 local Job Service (or Employment Service) offices nationwide, offers "no fee" job placement and job counseling assistance to all job seekers and applicant assessment and screening services for employers who request it.

Testing and the Americans With Disabilities Act

Under the Americans With Disabilities Act (ADA), an employer may test so long as persons with disabilities who can do the job are not screened out. If a test screens out a person because of a physical or mental impairment, the employer may be required to show that the test is job-related and consistent with business necessity. An employer may also have to provide, upon request, an alternative "accessible" test format for persons with impaired sensory, manual, or speaking skills when the test used by the employer is not designed to measure those skills. For example, an employer may have to:

- Substitute a written test for an oral test for persons with impaired speaking or hearing skills;
- Administer the test in large print or Braille, or by a reader, or on a computer for individuals with visual or other reading disabilities;
- Allow an individual to record test answers by tape recorder, dictation, or computer if he or she has a visual or learning disability;
- Provide extra time;
- Simplify test language;
- Schedule rest breaks; or
- Provide a separate, isolated setting for the test.

If the test cannot be given in an alternative accessible format, the employer may have to evaluate the skill or ability being tested through some other means, such as an interview; by evaluating education or work experience; or a job demonstration for a trial period.

Medical Examinations and Inquiries

Medical examinations are often requested or required as one of the steps in the hiring process. While regulating the use of examinations, the ADA does not prohibit their postemployment use.

Federal laws also do not prohibit employers from requiring applicants to pay for examinations done at the employer's request, but a number of states do prohibit or restrict their use, including Arkansas, California, Colorado, Hawaii, Illinois, Kentucky, Louisiana, Maine, Massachusetts, Michigan, Minnesota, Montana, Nebraska, New Hampshire, New York, Oklahoma, Oregon, Pennsylvania, Rhode Island, South Dakota, Utah, Vermont, Virginia, Washington, West Virginia, and Wisconsin.

Under ADA, employers are prohibited from requiring applicants to undergo medical examinations before hiring, but they can make employment conditional on the results of a postemployment examination.

Examinations, if given, must be given to all individuals being considered for employment in the same or similar job category. The examination results must be kept confidential.

An employer withdrawing a job offer as the result of a medical examination may be required to show that the individual does not meet necessary, job-related physical or psychological employment criteria. The employer, furthermore, must also show that there is no reasonable accommodation that will enable the individual to perform the essential functions of the job.

Voluntary medical examinations that are included in employee health programs, such as screening for high blood pressure, are permitted, but the results must be kept confidential and cannot be used to adversely affect the employment of a person who is capable of performing the required work.

AIDS Screening

Some employers who have required routine screening for AIDS or HIV have had their practices challenged in court.

The Americans With Disabilities Act also classifies such infections as disabilities under that law. Thirty-nine states, either through laws, regulations, or other means, also directly or indirectly restrict the employer's ability to require testing of applicants or employees to obtain HIV-related information. These states include Alabama, Arizona, Arkansas, California, Colorado, Connecticut, Delaware, Florida, Georgia, Hawaii, Illinois, Indiana, Iowa, Kansas, Kentucky, Maine, Massachusetts, Michigan, Minnesota, Missouri, Montana, Nebraska, New Hampshire, New Mexico, New York, North Carolina, North Dakota, Ohio, Oklahoma, Oregon, Rhode Island, Texas, Vermont, Virginia, Washington, West Virginia, Wisconsin, and Wyoming.

Drug and Alcohol Testing

Federal Law. The ADA does not bar preemployment testing for illegal drug use. For that matter, the law does not encourage, prohibit, or authorize drug testing, which under the law is not considered a medical examination. As federal law now stands, an applicant or employee can be required to take a drug test whether or not it is job-related. On the other hand, a test to determine blood-alcohol level is considered a medical exam subject to the ADA requirements of job-relatedness and business necessity.

The 1988 Drug-Free Workplace Act requires most federal government contractors to take specific steps to keep illegal drugs out of the workplace, but does not require testing employees for illegal use of controlled substances. However, a number of federal government agencies require, either through interim or final rules, drug testing of "sensitive" (security or safety-related) employees, including the Departments of Defense, Transportation, and Energy; the Federal Highway Administration; the Federal Aviation Administration; the Federal Railroad Administration; the Urban Mass Transportation Administration; the U.S. Coast Guard; the Research and Special Programs Administration; the Nuclear Regulatory Commission; and the National Aeronautics and Space Administration.

The Supreme Court has upheld the federal government's right to require mandatory testing even in the absence of individualized suspicion, although the testing must provide guarantees of accuracy and reliability.

State Law. Generally, states with drug-testing provisions prohibit random testing of employees or job applicants, and in many cases require employers to develop a written substance abuse policy, to confirm positive test results, and to protect employee privacy and confidentiality. Most state laws, like the federal requirements, apply to "sensitive" public employees. Some state laws include private as well as public employees, and some distinguish between random and mandatory testing. Rhode Island's law prohibits mandatory drug testing of both public and private employees, and Michigan has issued a policy stressing its opposition to drug and alcohol testing.

Polygraph or Honesty Tests

Lie detector testing by most private employers is prohibited under the federal Employee Polygraph Protection Act of 1988. Employers providing security services or involved in the manufacture of controlled substances, and federal, state, and local employers are exempt.

Under this law, employers may not:

- Require, request, suggest, or cause any job applicant or current employee to take or submit to a lie detector test;
- Use, accept, refer to, or inquire about the results of any lie detector test of any job applicant or current employee;
- Discharge, discipline, discriminate against, or deny employment or promotion to any prospective or current employee who refuses to take the test;
- Use the results as the basis for an adverse employment action; or
- Retaliate against an individual for exercising rights under the law.

On the other hand, current employees can be tested if there is:

- An investigation of a workplace theft or other incident leading to an economic loss for employers;
- Reasonable suspicion the employee was involved and the employee had access to the property; and
- Notice given to the employee about the investigation and the reasons for testing.

Where polygraph tests are allowed, employers must protect the confidentiality of the results. Also, employees with a physician-verified medical or psychological condition that can affect the test results may refuse to take the test. Employers giving polygraph tests where allowed must notify the employee of the date, time, and location of the test and the test instruments to be used.

State Polygraph Laws

Most states regulate lie detectors through licensing of polygraphers. Some states limit the use of lie detector tests as a condition of employment or continued employment, limit the questions that can be asked, or require confidentiality of records and results. Criminal or civil penalties may be imposed for violations.

States that ban all use of polygraph tests in private employment include Delaware, Hawaii, Massachusetts, Michigan, Minnesota, Oregon, and Rhode Island. Still others, like Massachusetts, New Jersey, Oregon, and Pennsylvania, prohibit employers from demanding or requiring that employees take lie detector tests. Nine states, including Arkansas, California, Michigan, Minnesota, New York, Oregon, Pennsylvania, Utah, and Wisconsin, prohibit the use of psychological stress evaluation tests or voice stress analyzers. The use of honesty tests has been restricted in Massachusetts and Rhode Island.

Physical Agility Tests

Since specific physical abilities may be needed to perform certain types of jobs, some employers require job applicants to take an agility test. The federal Equal Employment Opportunity Commission distinguishes an agility test from a medical examination on the basis of whether a physician is involved. Agility tests, when given, must be given to all similarly situated applicants or employees, regardless of disability. If the test screens out an individual or a class of individuals in a protected class because of a disability, the employer must show that the test is job-related and consistent with business necessity and that the job cannot be performed with reasonable accommodation.

Genetic Screening

Genetic screening, a form of "predictive" screening to determine which applicants or employees are at increased risk of future illness, is not specifically covered by federal law, but like other employment selection criteria, may be questionable under equal opportunity laws if screening has an adverse impact on members of a protested class.

Some states prohibit certain kinds of tests or screening for specific genetic conditions. Florida, Louisiana, and North Carolina prohibit screening for sickle cell traits; New Jersey for atypical genetic traits; Florida for DNA testing; and Iowa, Oregon, Rhode Island, and Wisconsin prohibit the use of brain-wave tests although Iowa does permit the testing to be done on request of the employee so long as no adverse employment action is taken on the basis of the test.

Handwriting Analysis

Handwriting analysis or graphology tests, while not prohibited, like genetic screening, may be challenged if they result in screening out a disproportionate number of individuals in a protected class.

5

TERMINATING THE EMPLOYMENT RELATIONSHIP

Most employment relationships are entered into for an indefinite period of time and can be terminated by the worker at any time for any reason by simply quitting. An employer can likewise terminate an indefinite employment relationship by discharging the employee at any time, for any reason, or, for that matter, no reason at all, provided the employer does not violate any employment contract with the employee, any union contract, or any law restricting the circumstances in which the employee can be fired.

An employment relationship that can be terminated by either the employer or the employee at any time for any reason is known as an "employment at will."

Tenure

Some jobs, such as many teaching positions, provide for job tenure after a person serves a probationary period or reaches a certain job level. A probationary worker usually can be fired at any time, but a person with tenure is considered to have permanent employment status and cannot be terminated except according to procedures that have been spelled out in advance.

Employment Contracts

An employer and an employee can enter into a written employment contract stating the terms of their agreement, including the length of time the employment will last. When the contract states that the job is for a definite period of time, the employer cannot terminate the worker before that time is up unless it has valid grounds for firing the employee. But if there is no contract, or the contract is silent on the job's duration, the relationship is considered an employment at will.

An employee, on the other hand, can stop working for an employer at any time, even though he or she has signed a contract stating the length of time the job will last. Courts ordinarily will not force employees to continue in the service of an employer for whom they no longer want to work. However, an employee's right to work for another employer may be restricted if the employee has agreed in writing to perform services only for the employer he or she is quitting and not for a competitor. Courts will generally hold employees to that aspect of the contract by barring them from working for a competitor, provided the restriction is reasonable, is not for too long a period of time, and does not prevent them from earning a living in another line of work that is not in competition with the prior employer.

An employment contract between an employer and an employee, or a collective bargaining agreement between an employer and a union representing its workers, can state the circumstances in which an employee can be fired, although the length of the employment remains indefinite. Under a union contract, for example, a worker's job is not usually guaranteed for any set period of time even though the contract itself may run for two or three years, but the worker cannot be discharged unless the employer has good or just cause.

PERMANENT REPLACEMENTS

In some circumstances an employer cannot discharge an employee, but can "permanently replace" the employee with a new worker. Unlike a discharge, this action does not terminate the employment relationship between the employer and employee.

This situation occurs when employees strike to gain better pay or benefits (which is referred to as an "economic" strike). Despite a strike, an employer has the right to continue operating its business. The law, attempting to balance these respective rights of employers and employees, prohibits an employer from firing the striking workers, but allows it to hire new employees to replace those on strike. In the situation where employees strike to protest an unfair labor practice, the employer is required to reinstate the strikers to their former jobs even though it may be necessary to fire replacements to make room for them.

If the economic strike is settled or abandoned, the employer must allow striking employees to return to their jobs unless the employer has hired new employees as permanent replacements to fill the jobs held by the strikers. Although the replacements do not have to be discharged to make room for the returning strikers, the employer must place on a preferential hiring list any striker whose job was filled by a replacement and offer him or her a job when one opens up.

Many strike settlements, however, include a commitment by the employer to the union representing the striking workers to promptly restore the strikers to their jobs and, if necessary, discharge the replacements to make room for the returning strikers. But in doing so the employer may be liable to the terminated replacements for breach of its employment agreement with them if it had indicated to them that they were being given permanent employment.

Interference With an Employment Contract

An employer may offer an employee of another employer a job, but it cannot interfere with a lawful employment relationship by maliciously enticing an employee to quit a job, nor can it, or anyone else, maliciously cause the employee's discharge. Such conduct is called "tortious" interference with an employment contract. Injured employees or employers, as the case may be, can sue the wrongdoer for the injury it causes by such unlawful interference.

Termination Notice and Severance Pay

In the absence of a contract or coverage under the federal or state plant closing laws discussed below, neither an employer nor an employee has to give advance notice before terminating the employment relationship, and an employer in the absence of a contract does not have to provide severance pay to terminated workers. However, all states require that terminated workers be paid the wages they have earned at the time of discharge, by the next regular pay day, or by some specified number of days.

Several states, including California, Connecticut, Illinois, Louisiana, Maine, and Rhode Island, provide for payment upon termination for vested, accrued vacation pay and in some cases for other earned benefits. Mississippi provides for payment for accrued vacation pay to state employees.

Terminations Caused by Plant Closings

Under federal law, some employers must give their employees notice of a planned plant closing. The Worker Adjustment and Retraining Notification Act (WARN) provides that, with certain exceptions, an employer of 100 or more employees must give advance notification of a planned layoff or shutdown that results in loss of work, termination, or a certain reduction in work hours for at least 50 employees for more than six months. Mass layoffs involving at least 33 percent of the active work force and at least 50 workers are also covered. Written notice must be given 60 calendar days before the anticipated or scheduled date of closing or layoff to affected employees or, if applicable, to their union, to the state's dislocated worker unit providing training or assistance, and to the chief elected local government official.

Temporary facilities and projects, agricultural and construction work, contract-related work, strikes and lockouts (except for nonstrikers), "faltering businesses," "unforeseeable business circumstances," and natural disasters are exempted from many provisions of WARN.

Although regarded only as a requirement for notification of a plant closing, WARN provisions are complex with costly penalties for noncompliance. An employer failing to provide the required notice may have to give any employees who suffer a loss of employment back pay plus any benefits covered by the Employee Retirement Income Security Act

(ERISA), including medical benefits, that they would have received if the loss of employment had not occurred.

Employers covered under WARN are also subject to coverage under state laws requiring notification of plant closings and/or mass layoffs. Some states and a few municipalities, including Philadelphia and Pittsburgh, have adopted laws or ordinances or promulgated regulations relating to plant closings. Some but not all state laws specify when notice must be given. Hawaii requires 45 days advance notice, Maine, 60 days, New Jersey, 48 hours, and Wisconsin, 60 days.

Other states impose conditions for notification on plant closings. South Carolina, for example, provides that if employers require employees to give notice before quitting a job, they, in turn, must give employees notice of their intent to close a facility, whether temporarily or permanently. Some states, such as Connecticut, Hawaii, Maine, and Massachusetts, provide for continuation of health insurance or the payment of severance benefits. Other states—Hawaii, Illinois, Maine, Massachusetts, and Wisconsin—specify penalties for noncompliance. In Indiana, Pennsylvania, and Washington, employer or employer-related groups provide for voluntary guidelines for notification.

Some state laws, including those in Colorado, Georgia, Indiana, Montana, Nevada, New Hampshire, North Carolina, Oklahoma, Rhode Island, South Dakota, and Wyoming, affect only state workers.

Plant closing legislative measures adopted in Alabama, California, Hawaii, Illinois, Maryland, Massachusetts, Michigan, Minnesota, New York, Oregon, Pennsylvania, Washington, and Wisconsin provide for programs ranging from the encouragement of voluntary cooperation between the business being closed and the state labor department to alleviate the impact of the closing on the affected employees, to programs that provide technical and financial assistance to the affected workers to permit them to assume the ownership and operation of the business being closed.

BUSINESS CLOSURE BY GOVERNMENT ACTION

As noted in Chapter 3, Americans have a right to engage in a legitimate trade or business. This right is one of the rights to "liberty" and "property" protected against arbitrary action by the federal government by the Fifth Amendment to the Constitution, and against similar state action by the Fourteenth Amendment. These amendments provide that a person cannot be deprived of the constitutionally protected right to liberty or property (as well as life) without "due process of law." This constitutional protection extends to a person's business. The Supreme Court has held that if the government plans to close a person's business, or suspend or revoke an occupational or trade license, due process requires, usually at a hearing, that the government demonstrate, subject to court review, that its action is in the public's interest and is reasonable and necessary.

Terminations Resulting From Bankruptcy

Workers losing their jobs because their employer's business becomes bankrupt can file a claim with the bankruptcy court for unpaid wages. If they earn wages for work during the 90-day period prior to the time the employer files for bankruptcy or during the 90-day period prior to the termination of the business, the employees become priority creditors and are entitled to full payment, up to $2,000, for the wages they earned during these periods.

Continuation of Medical Insurance

Employers must offer to workers who are terminated (other than for gross misconduct) or laid off the option to continue their group health plan coverage under the federal Consolidated Omnibus Budget Reconciliation Act (COBRA). A terminated employee is covered for a period of up to 18 months. Additional requirements under COBRA are described in Chapter 7. More than 30 states have also passed COBRA-like laws requiring employers to provide laid-off or terminated employees any existing health insurance for a period ranging from 90 days to six months.

Legal Restrictions on "At Will" Terminations

Various federal and state laws, noted below, as well as union contracts restrict the circumstances under which an employer can terminate its workers. An increasing number of state courts have also held that there are circumstances, in addition to those spelled out in statutes, in which an employer's right to discharge employees "at will" may be restricted.

In some cases courts have ruled that an employee handbook or a verbal representation that could be construed as an implied contract are something like an employment contract and can be relied upon by a discharged worker as a basis for challenging the employer's grounds for firing the employee. Courts in other cases have held that an employee cannot be terminated for refusing to perform an unlawful act on the ground that a discharge in this circumstance would be against "public policy."

The public policy exception to an employer's right to fire an employee at will has been held to apply to employers that discharge workers for refusing to perform illegal acts. States where this has been held include Arizona, California, Colorado, Indiana, Kansas, Michigan, Minnesota, Missouri, New Hampshire, New Jersey, North Carolina, Ohio, South Carolina, Tennessee, and Texas. States where the public policy exception has been held to apply to employers that have discharged workers for asserting a right protected by statute or performing some act encouraged by public policy include Illinois, Michigan, New Jersey, Oregon, Virginia, West Virginia, and Wisconsin. It is also against public policy in most jurisdictions to discharge an employee for serving on jury duty or for attending a deposition.

In many of the early "at will" cases in which courts have held that an employer cannot fire a worker, the employer had attempted to discharge an employee for exercising the right to file a claim for workers' compensation. Most states protect both public and private employees from retaliatory discharge for filing workers' compensation claims.

An employee's discharge that can be challenged through direct court action is often referred to as a "wrongful" or "abusive" discharge to distinguish it from an "unlawful" discharge, which is one prohibited by a statute. A challenge to an alleged unlawful discharge is generally made to a government agency before going to court.

Whistleblower Protection

A whistleblower is someone who reports an employer's wrongdoing. Public policy considerations also come into play in cases involving retaliatory discharge of whistleblowers. Federal laws relating to whistleblowers include the Civil Service Reform Act, Occupational Safety and Health Act, Energy Reorganization Act, and the Whistleblower Protection Act, which protects whistleblowing federal employees from being fired or disciplined by their agencies.

More than half of the states have passed laws to protect whistleblowers. Some apply to either private or public sector employees and some apply to both. They generally prohibit discharge, threats, or other retaliatory actions, and provide reinstatement, back pay, damages, and fines for affected workers. Some limit protection to violations of specified laws, like workers' compensation, safety and health, and environmental laws. States with laws that apply only to public sector employees include Alaska, Arizona, California, Colorado, Florida, Georgia, Indiana, Kansas, Kentucky, Maryland, Mississippi, Missouri, Nevada, Oklahoma, Pennsylvania, South Carolina, Utah, Virginia, Washington, and West Virginia. State laws that apply to both private and public sector employees include Connecticut, Hawaii, Illinois, Iowa, Louisiana, Maine, Massachusetts, Michigan, Minnesota, Montana, Nebraska, New Hampshire, New Jersey, New Mexico, New York, North Carolina, North Dakota, Ohio, Rhode Island, South Dakota, Tennessee, and Wisconsin. Indiana's law applies to public contractors also.

State right-to-know laws also contain provisions that make it unlawful to dismiss, threaten, or otherwise discriminate against workers who report uncorrected workplace hazards resulting from use of toxic or other potentially dangerous substances.

Most states protect both public and private employees from retaliatory discharge for filing workers' compensation claims.

Federal Statutory Limitations on Terminating Workers

Federal laws, particularly legislation enacted in recent years, have placed far greater restrictions on an employer's right to terminate its workers than the courts have.

The two most well-known of the laws restricting an employer's right to discharge workers are the National Labor Relations Act (NLRA) and Title VII of the 1964 Civil Rights Act, both of which are discussed in more detail in later chapters. Briefly, the NLRA prohibits employers from discharging employees for union activity, lack of union activity, protected concerted activity, or for filing charges or giving testimony under the NLRA.

Title VII prohibits terminations based on a person's race, color, religion, sex, or national origin or in reprisal for exercising Title VII rights.

The NLRA and Title VII, however, are not the only federal laws restricting an employer's right to fire workers. Other federal laws containing prohibitions on discharges are:

- *Age Discrimination in Employment Act*—prohibits discharge of workers 40 years of age or older because of their age.
- *American With Disabilities Act*—prohibits discharge of workers because of a disability unless no reasonable accommodation can be made without imposing an undue hardship on business operations.
- *Rehabilitation Act*—prohibits federal contractors from discriminating against handicapped workers.
- *Fair Labor Standards Act*—prohibits discharge of workers for exercising rights guaranteed by the minimum wage and overtime provisions of the Act.

- *Occupational Safety and Health Act*—prohibits discharge of workers in reprisal for exercising rights under the Act.
- *Vietnam Era Veterans' Readjustment Assistance Act*—prohibits discharge of returning veterans for a limited period of time.
- *Employee Retirement Income Security Act*—prohibits discharge of workers to prevent employees from receiving vested pension benefits.
- *Energy Reorganization Act*—prohibits discharge of employees who participate in any proceeding under the Act.
- *Railroad Safety Act*—prohibits discharge of employees who institute or testify in any proceeding relating to the enforcement of railroad safety laws, or who refuse to work because of work conditions reasonably believed to be dangerous.
- *Federal Water Pollution Control Act*—prohibits discharge of employees who institute or participate in any proceeding under the Act.
- *Judiciary and Judicial Procedure Act*—prohibits discharge of workers for serving on a jury.
- *Consumer Credit Protection Act*—prohibits discharge of employees for wage garnishment for one indebtedness.
- *Bankruptcy Act*—prohibits discharge of employees who file for bankruptcy.
- *Immigration Reform and Control Act*—prohibits discharge of employees because of national origin or citizenship status.
- *Child Support Enforcement Act*—prohibits discharge of employees whose wages are withheld for child support.
- *Surface Transportation Assistance Act*—prohibits discharge of employees who file complaints relating to commercial vehicle safety.

State Laws Restricting the Discharge of Workers

Many states, as well as the federal government, have enacted laws restricting the circumstances in which workers can be terminated. Some states have adopted the same restrictions as the federal government, while others have extended the scope of the restrictions. Many states, for example, prohibit discharge for such matters as political activity, sexual preference, military duty, refusing to take a lie detector test, exercising a government-protected right, testifying at a court hearing, or having an arrest or conviction record. And, in 1987, Montana became the first state to enact an "at will" law that prohibits an employer from firing an employee without good cause.

The issue in most discharge cases, whether before a court or administrative agency, relates to whether a worker was fired because of race, sex, disability, or union activity. These matters are discussed in later chapters.

Service Letters and Letters of Reference

A number of states have passed laws either protecting the employer if he or she provides truthful letters of reference in good faith or protecting the former employees' right to a service letter.

Alaska, Florida, Georgia, Louisiana, North Carolina, and Virginia protect employers who provide letters setting forth the job performance of an employee or former employee to a prospective employer by presuming the former employers were truthful and acted in good faith, unless proven otherwise. Louisiana's provisions apply only to financial institutions.

Indiana, Kansas, Missouri, Montana, Nebraska, Oklahoma (only for public-service corporation employees), and Texas laws require former employers, upon request from a terminated employee (whether discharged or voluntary), to provide a service letter setting forth the nature and character of service. California requires that a request be made before a service letter is issued.

Four states—Montana, North Carolina, Texas, and Virginia—prohibit employers from engaging in any blacklisting of former employees.

6

PRIVACY IN THE WORKPLACE

The right to privacy is the right to be free from unwarranted intrusion by others. Some courts call it the "right to be left alone."

This right is significantly limited for both employers and employees, but in different ways. An employer's privacy is affected when, among other things, it must file various reports and forms with the government, both federal and state, relating to information about its business and employees. Under various federal and state statutes, employers are also required to keep certain records for specified periods. In addition, employers are subject to investigation by government agencies to determine their compliance with workplace laws and regulations and may have to produce those records in the course of the investigation.

An employee's privacy is largely affected by an employer's right to obtain information about the people it hires. This need for information is considered reasonable when it relates to the employer's interest in knowing about an employee's competence, reliability, and honesty as a worker, or when required by the government to obtain information about a worker.

A trucking company subject to regulation by the federal Interstate Commerce Commission, for example, is required by federal regulation to check the prior three-year employment history of a person it is considering hiring as a driver. A company holding a government defense contract must have a security check run on an employee who will have access to classified national defense information.

In some circumstances an employer's potential legal liability may require it to investigate a worker's background. This can arise when an employer hires a worker for a job allowing access to a person's living quarters, such as a job as a furniture mover or as a maintenance worker in an apartment building. The employer can be held liable if the worker criminally assaults or injures a person in his or her home or apartment when the employer failed to check the employee's background and a check would have revealed that the employee had a criminal record or showed other signs of a tendency toward violence.

Almost all the states have also enacted laws requiring background investigations to determine whether persons who operate or are employed by a child care facility have a criminal history of sex offenses or child abuse.

Government and Union Intrusions on Employee Privacy

There can also be intrusions on a worker's privacy by the government and, to a lesser extent, by unions.

If the worker is union "represented," for example, the union has the right to know such things as the worker's home address, job, and pay, and, pursuant to a union shop contract, can require the worker to pay union dues and fees as a condition of keeping his or her job. However, if the nonunion member worker objects, these fees cannot be spent on activities unrelated to collective bargaining activities.

The government for its part investigates and finger-prints persons applying for federal jobs and, as noted before, requires private employers to investigate their employees' background in some circumstances. It also requires, as discussed in later chapters, that employers report on the race, nationality, and sex of their workers, and that individual employees submit to the desire of the majority in deciding whether to have an agent represent them in negotiating their wages and working conditions with their employer. The government requires workers to pay income and Social Security taxes and has the right to investigate workers' compliance with the tax laws. Further, the government can request that workers undergo medical tests to determine the level of toxic substances where they work, or to determine whether they use unlawful substances.

Limitations on the Intrusions on an Employee's Privacy

Just as there are limitations on an employee's right to privacy, there are also limitations on the intrusion on that right by employers, unions, and government.

- *Reference and Information Checking.* Although an employer can contact a worker's previous employers for information about the individual's work history and can contact references that he or she provides, giving and checking references can expose employers to a host of legal problems, such as charges of discrimination, libel and slander, invasion of privacy, and negligent hiring claims. Many states already recognize negligent hiring claims, and in a number of instances have awarded substantial monetary damages.

   Under the Americans With Disabilities Act, before a conditional job offer has been made, an employer may not request any information about a job applicant from a former employer, family member, or other source that the employer itself may not request directly of the job applicant. Specifically, an employer may not ask about an applicant's disability.
- *Providing References.* An employer may provide information about a former employee to another employer who is considering hiring the former employee, as long as the information is not false or derogatory. If it is, the employer may be liable to the employee for defamation of character. An employer in some circumstances may be sued for intrusions on the employee's privacy if the employer makes public dis-

closure of embarrassing private information about the employee, such as revealing medical information or intelligence test scores found in the employee's personnel file.

- *Letters of Reference.* In many states, statutes bar employees from reviewing letters of reference. (See page 41 for discussion of service letters.)
- *Credit Checks.* If the employer intends to ask for a consumer or investigation report about the person from a consumer reporting agency, the federal Fair Credit Reporting Act requires the employer to notify the individual and provide a copy of the report if the individual requests one. If employment is denied, the employer must notify the applicant and supply the name and address of the consumer reporting agency that furnished the report. This law also prohibits a creditor from calling an employee at work or from contacting the employer about the debt without the worker's consent. Under some circumstances, employers may need to establish a business necessity for using credit checks and should inform applicants if hiring depends on such checks.

    Most states' fair credit reporting laws are modeled after the federal law, but vary on uses of reports for employment purposes, notice requirements, information available to applicants, and applicants' right to sue. States with such laws include Arizona, California, Louisiana, Maine, Maryland, Massachusetts, New Hampshire, New Mexico, New York, and Vermont. Other states that regulate the compilation, disclosure, dissemination, use, or correction of information in consumer reports are Arkansas, Connecticut, Florida, Kansas, Kentucky, Montana, Oklahoma, Texas, Utah, and Virginia, and the District of Columbia.

- *Surveillance and Monitoring.* Under the federal Crime Control and Safe Streets Act an employer cannot intercept an employee's confidential communication. In Virginia an employer cannot listen in on an employee's phone call with a customer without first informing the employee that such phone conversations may be monitored. Some states prohibit surveillance of union activities by employers, while Connecticut and Kansas have broader restrictions on surveillance of employees in general.

- *Medical Testing.* Under certain circumstances, an employer can require that employees or applicants take a medical examination or be tested for drugs to determine their fitness to perform the required work. This limitation on employees' privacy is treated in more detail in a separate chapter on testing.
- *Polygraph Testing.* Lie detector testing by most private employers is prohibited under the federal Employee Polygraph Protection Act of 1988. However, private employers in the security business or involved with the manufacture or distribution of controlled substances are exempt, as are government employers. Under certain circumstances, a current employee suspected of workplace theft can be tested. States also restrict use of polygraph tests. Further discussion of polygraph testing is found in Chapter 4.
- Use of psychological or voice stress evaluation tests is prohibited by California, Michigan, Minnesota, New York, Oregon, Pennsylvania, Utah, and Wisconsin.
- *Access to Personnel Records Under Federal Provisions.* A number of federal laws and regulations limit access to records or protect the confidentiality of certain kinds of information about public or private employees:
  —The federal Privacy Act provides that a federal government agency may collect personal information about an individual only if it is relevant and necessary to accomplish an agency purpose. Under the law federal workers have access to all records containing information about them, and are entitled to know how and by whom the information is used. Disclosure to third parties is restricted.

—The 1973 Rehabilitation Act and the Vietnam Era Veterans' Readjustment Assistance Act limit the disclosure by employers of employee medical information.

—The Freedom of Information Act regulates access to government records, including personnel files.

—The Family Educational Rights and Privacy Act permits release of postsecondary education records to verify employment applications information only with the students' written consent.

—The federal Hazard Communication Standard, like most state right-to-know laws, requires employers to disclose information to workers about, and grant employees access to records on, toxic or hazardous substances in the workplace.

—The Occupational Safety and Health Act (OSHA) Access Standard requires that workers be given access to employer-maintained records on past and current exposures to toxic workplace substances, related personal medical records, and analyses based on complaints. Access to employee exposure records is available to collective bargaining agents, but these agents can obtain access to individual employee's medical records only with the employee's written consent. OSHA has the right to obtain employee medical records, but public disclosure of this information is restricted and requires safeguards to protect confidentiality.

—The Americans With Disabilities Act imposes strict limitations on the acquisition and use of information obtained from medical examinations and inquiries, and also restricts employers' access to workers' compensation histories.

• *Access to Personnel Records Under State Laws.* A number of states have enacted laws that give private-sector employees the right to inspect their personnel records, although that right is seldom absolute. The states include Alaska, California, Connecticut, Delaware, Illinois, Iowa, Kentucky, Maine, Massachusetts, Michigan, Minnesota, Nevada, New Hampshire, North Carolina, Ohio, Oregon, Pennsylvania, Rhode Island, Tennessee, Utah, Washington, and Wisconsin, and the District of Columbia.

Generally, state laws provide workers with three procedural safeguards: the right to be informed about the existence of a personnel or a medical file used for employment purposes; the right to examine information in specified employment-related files; and the right to dispute or correct inaccuracies in an employment record. Some laws expressly exclude certain records from retention or access provisions; some stipulate to whom information may or may not be disclosed; some require employees' written consent for disclosure of information to third parties. Penalties for violations of statutory provisions are included in some laws but not others.

- *Medical Information.* The collection, use, and disclosure of medical information on employees, particularly in light of the Americans With Disabilities Act, is problematical for employers. Many states recognize a right to privacy in employee medical records and make it unlawful to reveal such information without an employee's written consent. Maintaining medical records in personnel files can expose an employer to possible invasion-of-privacy claims, and also to discrimination charges if employment decisions are affected by knowledge of the medical information.

- *Arrest and Criminal Records.* Almost all states have laws authorizing or requiring access to, restricting or prohibiting inquiries about, or defining use of arrest and conviction records for job applicants and/or employees. Most states impose greater restrictions on use of arrest records than conviction information. Within states, individual counties may have more or less restrictive provisions on access to and use of criminal history record information.

In Oregon and Washington an employer that examines a job applicant's criminal record must advise the applicant of such action. In Massachusetts an ex-offender receiving a pardon from the governor does not have to state on a job application that he or she had been convicted, and in Rhode Island an ex-offender whose criminal record has been expunged may state that he or she has never been convicted.

- *Searches.* An employer may search an employee's clothing or possessions for the theft of company property. However, if the circumstances of the employee's detention are unreasonable, the employer may be liable for false imprisonment.
- *Union Information.* Unions generally have the right to request information about the workers they represent for purposes of negotiating wages and working conditions. Some information, however, is restricted. An employer, for instance, is not required to turn over to a union a worker's test score without the worker's consent.
- *Union Membership.* The National Labor Relations Act allows a union, with the employer's agreement, to have a contract requiring that workers become union members as a condition of employment. Courts, however, have interpreted this provision to mean that employees are not actually required to join a union but must pay union dues and fees, or pay only that portion of the fees that covers a union's collective bargaining expenses. Workers who are union members have the right to resign their memberships at any time except for reasonable restrictions on the timing of a resignation contained in a union contract or constitution. However, under Section 14(b) of the Act, 21 states presently have right-to-work laws that prohibit employers and unions from entering into agreements requiring that workers join unions or pay dues as a condition of employment. These states are Alabama, Arizona, Arkansas, Florida, Georgia, Idaho, Iowa, Kansas, Louisiana, Mississippi, Nebraska, Nevada, North Carolina, North Dakota,

South Carolina, South Dakota, Tennessee, Texas, Utah, Virginia, and Wyoming.

- *Constitutional Safeguards.* The government's intrusions on an employer's or employee's right to privacy are generally restricted by the U.S. Constitution, which prohibits the government from engaging in an unreasonable search or seizure of a person or requiring a person to incriminate himself or herself. An employer in some circumstances can therefore require that a government agency wanting to inspect its facility obtain a search warrant. Federal privacy legislation allows workers to have access to information about them contained in the files of government agencies and restricts the disclosure of such information to unauthorized persons.

7

WAGES, BENEFITS, AND WORKING CONDITIONS

An employee can agree to work for an employer for the wages and under the working conditions the employer offers or according to those on which they mutually agree, provided the arrangement does not violate any law or any contract the employer has with a union that determines the employee's pay rate. If the employee's wage or salary is not specified, it is determined according to the wage paid in the area for the type of work the employee performs.

A worker's pay can be based on salary, work performed by the hour, or piecework. Most states require that, however the employee's pay is determined, it be paid at regular intervals, usually at least every two weeks, in cash or negotiable check. Less than half the states require that employers notify employees in writing of their wage rates, with 37 requiring that employees be given a statement containing an itemization of hours worked, wages paid, and deductions made. Alaska, Connecticut, Delaware, Hawaii, Illinois, Indiana, Iowa, Kansas (on request), Maryland, Massachusetts (at time of change), Missouri, New Hampshire, New Jersey, New York, Ohio, Pennsylvania, Utah, and West Virginia also require that workers be notified in advance of any change in their rate of pay. In most states a worker can request assistance from the state's labor department to collect unpaid wages.

Minimum Wage

The wage law with which most employers must comply is the federal Fair Labor Standards Act (FLSA), also referred to as the minimum wage or wage-hour law. The FLSA, covered in Chapter 8, sets the national minimum wage that employees covered by the law must receive whether paid by the hour or by salary. Most states also have their own minimum wage laws, and when an employer is covered by both federal and state laws, it must pay the higher of the two.

Payment on Termination

All states except Arkansas, Georgia, Mississippi, Ohio, and Tennessee specify a time limit for the payment of wages upon termination. Seven states—California, Connecticut, Illinois, Iowa, Louisiana (under the terms of a collective bargaining agreement), Maine, and Rhode Island—require that employers pay employees for any accrued fringe benefits, such as vacation time. More than 30 states have enacted laws providing for the right of terminated employees to continue their health insurance under laws similar to the federal COBRA law, discussed later in this chapter.

Hours of Work

The FLSA does not restrict the number of hours an employee over 18 years old can be required to work in a day or a week, but it does require that covered workers be paid at the rate of 1 1/2 times their regular hourly rate for hours worked in excess of 40 hours in a workweek. Some states require daily overtime pay.

Every state except Delaware, Hawaii, Louisiana, Maine, Mississippi, Oklahoma, South Carolina, Tennessee, Vermont, and Virginia, and the District of Columbia has laws containing some form of restriction on the maximum number of hours some employees can be required to work, such as placing a limit on the hours that can be worked in a week, requiring a 24-hour rest period each week, or prohibiting work on Sundays. For safety reasons, federal transportation laws and some state laws restrict the number of hours a truck driver, bus driver, or airline pilot subject to federal or state regulation can work in a day or week. Just under half the states require that employers allow workers time off for breaks or meals after working a specified number of hours.

Fringe Benefits

A fringe benefit is any benefit a worker receives in addition to pay, such as paid holidays, vacations, sick leave, medical insurance, and pensions. Although most employers provide some fringe benefits to their workers, federal and state laws do not require the payment of fringe benefits except for the payments that have to be made on the employees' behalf for Social Security, workers' compensation, and unemployment insurance, or when an employer is performing work under a government contract. However, all states require that if employers provide health insurance to their employees they provide minimum benefits, usually by requiring coverage for newborn children and for pregnancy.

Welfare and Retirement Benefits

Employers who engage in any activity affecting commerce and who provide a health and welfare or retirement plan for their employees are regulated under the federal Employee Retirement Income Security Act (ERISA). ERISA covers any welfare plan (fund or program) established or maintained by an employer or an employee organization, or both.

These include plans that provide medical, surgical, or hospital benefits; sickness, disability, death, unemployment, or vacation benefits; apprenticeship or other training programs; day care centers; scholarship funds; prepaid legal services; or health care, vacation, holiday, severance pay, and child care.

Under ERISA, all health and welfare plans must meet the following criteria:

- All plans must be in writing;

- Employees' rights must be legally enforceable;
- The employer must intend to continue the plan indefinitely;
- Employees must receive reasonable notice about the benefits; and
- The plan must be maintained for the exclusive benefit of employees and their eligible dependents and beneficiaries.

The Pregnancy Discrimination Act requires that women unable to work due to pregnancy, childbirth, or other related medical conditions be provided with the same benefits as disabled workers, under the same conditions. Additionally, no special conditions may be placed on the number of days or dollar amounts for maternity coverage unless those limitations apply to all other disabilities covered under an employer's plan.

ERISA's requirements for retirement plans are covered in Chapter 25.

Continuation of Medical Benefits

Employers that provide a health care program and that have more than 20 employees are required to offer employees the opportunity to temporarily continue their group health care coverage under the employer's plan if their coverage would otherwise cease due to a termination, layoff, or other change in employment status. Under the Consolidated Omnibus Budget Reconciliation Act of 1986 (COBRA), qualified employees (as well as covered spouses and dependents) are entitled to extend (at their own expense, up to 102 percent of the cost of the coverage to the plan) for a period of:

- Up to 18 months for covered employees, as well as their spouses and dependents, when workers would otherwise lose coverage because of a termination or reduction of hours;
- Up to 36 months for spouses and dependents facing a loss of employer-provided coverage due to an employee's death, a divorce or legal separation, or certain other "qualifying events."

Working Conditions

The law that directly affects the conditions under which workers are permitted to work is the federal Occupational Safety and Health Act (OSHA), which requires employers to provide working conditions that are free from recognizable hazards to the workers' safety and health. The requirements under OSHA, as well as other safety laws, are covered in Chapter 10.

The federal equal employment opportunity laws affect working conditions indirectly by requiring that, whatever the working conditions are, they be provided to workers on a nondiscriminatory basis. The federal National Labor Relations Act does not prescribe working conditions, but does allow workers to select a union to negotiate on their behalf concerning their working conditions as well as their pay and benefits.

The federal Americans With Disabilities Act (ADA) also affects working conditions by prohibiting employers from discriminating against qualified individuals with disabilities. Covered employers must make reasonable accommodation to known physical and mental limitations of an otherwise qualified applicant or employee with a disability unless the employer can demonstrate that the accommodation would impose an undue hardship on its business operations. Thus, employers may be required to make existing facilities readily accessible so that employees can perform essential functions of the job and enjoy employment-related privileges such as access to break rooms, lunch rooms, training facilities, gymnasiums, and transportation. As of July 26, 1994, employers with 15 or more workers are covered by the ADA. Other requirements under the ADA are covered in Chapter 15.

Smoking in the Workplace

In a trend that started in the 1970s and proliferated in the 1980s, a growing number of states have enacted laws to regulate smoking in public places, including places of employment. More than 40 states and the District of Columbia have enacted laws restricting smoking in at least one public place, and hundreds of municipalities have adopted no-smoking ordinances, many of which are more comprehensive and more stringent than the state laws.

The state laws generally require employers to adopt a smoking policy, post notices, establish separate smoking and no-smoking areas, or to control smoke with existing physical barriers or ventilation systems. States that have not enacted laws to restrict smoking in the workplace include Alabama, Delaware, Georgia, Kentucky, Louisiana, Mississippi, North Carolina, South Dakota, Texas, West Virginia, and Wyoming.

Smoking in federal government workplaces is restricted under General Services Administration regulations, which prohibit smoking except in certain designated areas.

At this time, OSHA regulates smoking only in work areas where there is occupational exposure to asbestos. The federal government, however, is considering further restrictions on smoking.

Abstention from use of tobacco products outside employment cannot be required as a condition of employment in a number of states, including Colorado, Connecticut, Illinois, Indiana, Kentucky, Louisiana, Maine, Minnesota, Mississippi, Montana, Nevada, New Hampshire, New Jersey, New Mexico, New York, North Carolina, North Dakota, Oklahoma, Oregon, Rhode Island, South Carolina, South Dakota, Tennessee, Virginia, West Virginia, Wisconsin, and Wyoming.

In a unionized workplace smoking restrictions in addition to those required by law are a mandatory subject for bargaining under the Labor Management Relations Act (LMRA).

Transportation Services

Employers located in highly congested areas that the federal Environmental Protection Agency has designated as not meeting acceptable levels of air pollution are required under the federal Clean Air Act to develop and implement worksite programs that reduce vehicle trips and vehicle miles. These programs, known as trip-reduction programs, transportation demand management programs, or employee commute options programs, must encourage employees to use public transit, share rides in car- or vanpools, or use other commuting alternatives.

States that to date have enacted laws in one form or another requiring employers to adopt programs dealing with air pollution include Arizona, California, Connecticut, Delaware, Georgia, Hawaii, Illinois, Indiana, Maryland, Michigan, Minnesota, Missouri, New Jersey, New York, Oklahoma, Pennsylvania, Texas, Washington, and Wisconsin.

Payroll Deductions

Employers by law must withhold income and Social Security taxes from an employee's pay. In the absence of a law, they also may make deductions from a worker's pay for cash shortages or other expenses caused or incurred by the employee, and, with the employee's consent, make deductions for union dues or insurance benefits. However, about two-thirds of the states have laws placing restrictions on other deductions an employer can make from an employee's pay without his or her consent. Also, both federal and state laws and regulations establish limits on amounts that may be deducted from an employee's pay. The FLSA, for instance, prohibits deductions if they reduce the worker's pay below the federal minimum wage.

Since 1989 employers have been required to automatically withhold child support payments from employees' wages. In 1994, all support orders must provide for immediate withholding. Employers failing to comply with an order may be liable for the entire amount required to be withheld. In addition, a late fee for tardy payments may be imposed by the state of up to 6 percent of the overdue payment.

Three federal laws, the Child Support Enforcement Act, the Family Support Act, and the Consumer Credit Protection Act, require states to adopt rules governing withholding of wages pursuant to child support orders. States do have latitude in setting their own standards concerning such matters as administrative fees employers may charge and the definition of wages subject to withholding for child support.

Tax Levies

Individuals owing federal back taxes may have their wages attached by the Internal Revenue Service (IRS) for the full amount plus penalties. In an attachment proceeding an employer notified by the IRS as to the amount of the employee's unpaid taxes must pay the IRS the requested portion of the employee's disposable earnings or be held liable for the full amount. An exemption from the tax attachment is permitted to the extent of the employee's standard deduction plus personal exemptions allowed for the taxable year, divided by 52. Child support orders also take precedence over tax levies.

Time Off From Work

Unless required by law or union contract or other binding contract, an employer does not have to pay employees for the time they take off from work. Federal and state requirements for leave, including military, family, medical, maternity, and jury duty, are discussed in more detail in Chapter 9.

Mechanic's Lien

A mechanic's lien is a means by which a worker can enforce a claim for payment for work that he or she performs for another person and usually arises when the worker has possession of the property on which the work was performed. The worker has the right to retain possession of the property until the work is paid for and, by following the legal procedures required by state law for enforcing a lien, can sell the property to satisfy the claim for payment. A contractor or laborer can also obtain a lien on a building on which work was performed.

Garnishments and Wage Assignments

A garnishment is a legal procedure that a creditor can use to make an employee pay off a debt. In a wage garnishment proceeding, the employer is directed by a court to pay the employee's wages to the creditor until the debt is paid.

A wage assignment differs from a garnishment in that it is a voluntary agreement by the employee to transfer (assign) part of his or her wages to another person or organization to pay off a debt or for any other purpose.

Both federal and state laws regulate the garnishment of wages. Federal standards supersede state law, unless the state law is more favorable to the employee (that is, it protects a greater portion of the employee's wages from garnishment or provides greater protection from discipline for garnishment).

All states regulate wage garnishments by limiting the amount of an employee's wages that can be garnished. Some states prohibit an employee's discharge for garnishments. These laws also provide that an employee's wages can be garnished for spousal or child support and that more of an employee's wages can be garnished for this purpose than for other forms of indebtedness.

A federal wage garnishment law, like the state laws, exempts a certain percentage of an employee's pay from a garnishment, depending on the basis for the debt. For example, there is no limit on garnishments for bankruptcies, while the limits for tax levies and child support orders are set forth above. For other types of garnishment, the federal exemption is 75 percent of the worker's disposable weekly earnings, or 30 times the federal minimum wage, whichever is less. Federal law also prohibits an employer from discharging an employee for a garnishment arising from one indebtedness. The Equal Employment Opportunity Commission, moreover, considers the discharge of a minority employee for more than one garnishment to be a form of racial discrimination and is therefore prohibited.

SELECTED STATE LAW PROVISIONS CONCERNING MINIMUM WAGE AND WORKING CONDITIONS

	Minimum wage	Garnishments restricted	Wage assignments restricted	Deductions from wages restricted	State assistance in collecting unpaid wages	Workers not required to pay cost of medical exam	Time off to vote	Jury duty employment protection	Meal and/or rest period required
Alabama			✓	✓	✓				
Alaska	4.75	✓	✓	✓	✓		✓	✓	
Arizona		✓	✓	✓	✓		✓	✓	
Arkansas	3.65	✓	✓	✓	✓	✓	✓		✓
California	4.25	✓	✓		✓	✓	✓		✓
Colorado	3.00	✓	✓	✓	✓	✓	✓		✓
Connecticut	4.27	✓	✓	✓	✓			✓	✓
Delaware	4.25	✓	✓	✓	✓			✓	
District of Columbia	3.35–5.45	✓	✓	✓	✓			✓	
Florida		✓	✓	✓[a]				✓	
Georgia	3.25	✓	✓	✓	✓		✓	✓	
Hawaii	3.85	✓	✓	✓	✓	✓	✓	✓	✓[c]
Idaho	4.25	✓	✓	✓	✓			✓	
Illinois	4.25	✓	✓	✓	✓	✓	✓	✓	✓
Indiana	3.35	✓	✓	✓	✓			✓	
Iowa	4.25	✓	✓	✓	✓		✓		
Kansas	2.65	✓	✓	✓	✓		✓		
Kentucky	4.25	✓	✓	✓	✓	✓	✓	✓	✓
Louisiana		✓	✓	✓	✓	✓		✓	
Maine	4.25	✓	✓	✓	✓	✓		✓	✓
Maryland	4.25	✓	✓	✓	✓	✓	✓	✓	
Massachusetts	4.25	✓	✓	✓	✓	✓	✓	✓	✓
Michigan	3.35	✓	✓	✓	✓	✓	✓	✓	
Minnesota	4.00–4.25	✓	✓	✓	✓	✓	✓	✓	✓

State	Wage							
Mississippi		✓					✓	
Missouri	4.25	✓	✓		✓	✓	✓	✓
Montana	4.25	✓	✓	✓	✓	✓		
Nebraska	4.25	✓	✓	✓	✓	✓	✓	✓
Nevada	4.25	✓	✓	✓	✓	✓	✓	✓
New Hampshire	3.85	✓	✓	✓	✓	✓		✓
New Jersey	4.25	✓	✓	✓	✓	✓[c]		
New Mexico	3.35	✓	✓	✓	✓	✓	✓	✓
New York	4.25	✓	✓	✓	✓	✓	✓	✓
North Carolina	3.35	✓	✓	✓	✓	✓		
North Dakota	4.25[a]		✓	✓	✓	✓		
Ohio	4.25	✓	✓	✓	✓	✓		
Oklahoma	4.25	✓	✓	✓	✓	✓		
Oregon	4.75	✓	✓	✓	✓	✓		✓
Pennsylvania	4.25	✓	✓	✓	✓	✓		✓[d]
Rhode Island	4.45	✓	✓	✓	✓	✓		✓
South Carolina		✓	✓	✓	✓	✓		
South Dakota	4.25	✓	✓	✓	✓	✓	✓	
Tennessee	4.25[b]	✓	✓	✓	✓	✓	✓	
Texas	3.35	✓	✓	✓	✓	✓		
Utah	4.25	✓	✓	✓	✓	✓		
Vermont	4.25	✓	✓	✓	✓	✓	✓	
Virginia	3.65	✓	✓	✓	✓	✓	✓	
Washington	4.25	✓	✓	✓	✓	✓		✓
West Virginia	3.80	✓	✓	✓	✓	✓	✓	✓
Wisconsin	3.70–4.25	✓	✓	✓	✓	✓	✓	✓
Wyoming	1.60	✓	✓	✓	✓	✓	✓	✓

[a] State employees only.
[b] Certain blind employees only.
[c] Government employees only.
[d] Certain industries only.

Most states also regulate wage assignments, with some declaring that a wage assignment is not valid if its purpose is to have a worker pay off a debt.

Summary of State Law Provisions

Pages 60 and 61 contain a summary of state law provisions on minimum wage and working conditions. More information about these and other state laws regulating working conditions can be obtained from a state labor department. Appendix A lists the addresses of these departments.

A more complete summary of state and federal employment laws is also included in *BNA's Policy and Practice Series* and BNA's *Payroll Administration Guide.* Address inquiries to:

The Bureau of National Affairs Inc.
Attn: Customer Relations
1231 25th Street, N.W.
Washington, D.C. 20037

8

MINIMUM WAGE AND MAXIMUM HOURS

Federal and state laws and regulations governing wages and hours have become more complex since the Fair Labor Standards Act (FLSA) was first enacted in 1938 to set certain minimum employment standards for covered employers and employees. FLSA continues to be the single most comprehensive and important of these laws. It establishes a federal minimum hourly wage rate of $4.25, requires overtime compensation for all hours worked in excess of 40 per week, and restricts the employment of minors.

Despite the broad range of employment practices that are governed by the FLSA, there are many practices that are not regulated by the FLSA, such as rest periods, vacations, holidays, or sick leave. In many cases, however, such employment practices may be subject to state law requirements, as well as other federal employment laws.

Two Basic Types of Coverage

There are two broad categories of coverage established by the FLSA. The "individual employee" test focuses on the job duties of individual employees. The enterprise coverage test provides that all employees of a business enterprise are covered if the firm meets certain sales-volume tests and has two or more employees who are engaged in interstate commerce or the production of goods for commerce.

Employees Covered by the FLSA

Unless specifically exempted, all employees engaged in interstate commerce, engaged in the production of goods for commerce, or employed in "an enterprise engaged in commerce or the production of goods for commerce," must be paid the minimum wage and overtime pay set by the FLSA.

Interstate commerce includes goods coming into and going out of a state. Production of goods includes not only the actual production operations but any closely related process as well. Workers are covered by the individual employee test even if only a small percentage of their work duties or hours is devoted to interstate activities.

The courts, in interpreting the coverage of the FLSA, have extended the Act's coverage to the "farthest reaches of the channels of interstate commerce." Thus, under these tests, employees covered include those engaged in interstate communications or transportation; warehousing and distributing industries such as wholesaling, who receive, order, or keep records of goods moving in commerce; banking and insurance companies; public utilities furnishing gas, electricity, or water to firms in interstate commerce; maintenance, repair, or construction of business in interstate commerce; and mining, producing, processing, or distributing goods for commerce, even though the goods may leave the state through another firm.

INTERSTATE COMMERCE

Congress can enact laws to the extent that it is given the authority to regulate an activity under the United States Constitution. Federal laws affecting workplace-related activity have been enacted for the most part under the authority of Article I of the Constitution which provides that Congress can "regulate commerce" among the states. The Supreme Court, over the years, has interpreted this commerce clause to mean that Congress can regulate not only activities engaged in interstate commerce, but also any activity that "affects" commerce. As a consequence, any local activity that can be shown to affect commerce in some way is potentially subject to federal legislation. As frequently indicated in this book, both federal and state government often regulate the same activity. If federal and state law conflict, federal law prevails unless the state law is more beneficial to the worker.

Independent contractors are not considered employees under the Act. On the other hand, undocumented aliens, even though the Immigration Reform and Control Act prohibits their employment, are covered. Domestic workers are generally covered by the FLSA as long as they are employed in one or more homes for an aggregate total of more than eight hours in any workweek, or if they earn wages of at least $50 in any calendar quarter. In other words, anyone employing a domestic worker for eight hours in a week is considered an employer under the FLSA and must pay that person the minimum wage.

Enterprise Coverage

The FLSA covers firms with an annual business volume of at least $500,000. The business also must have two or more employees engaged in interstate commerce or the production or handling of goods for commerce. In most cases, new businesses are covered if it reasonably can be assumed that the firm's yearly gross sales or business will exceed $500,000.

Certain businesses are automatically covered by the Act without regard to the business-volume test:
- Hospitals, nursing homes, and institutions for the sick, aged, or mentally ill or disabled;
- Preschools, elementary and secondary schools, and institutions of higher learning;
- Schools for the mentally or physically handicapped;
- Public agencies; and
- Large farms.

Minimum Wage and Working Hours

Workers covered by the FLSA must be paid at least $4.25 an hour and must be paid for all the hours they work in any given workweek. This is generally considered to be all the time they are required by their employer to be at their place of work or on duty and are subject to their employer's control, including such activities as learning their jobs, correcting the work of others, and setting up machines. It does not ordinarily include the commuting time getting to and from a place of work or certain preliminary or postliminary activities.

Mealtime is not considered work time unless the employee is required to tend a machine or do other work while eating or is not allowed enough time to eat. Thirty minutes is usually considered enough time for meals.

The FLSA also does not require an employer to pay an employee for hours not worked because of holidays, vacations, illness, lack of work, or other similar reasons. The employer can, of course, pay workers for such nonwork time, and a union contract can require an employer to pay more than is required by the FLSA.

On the other hand, hours worked does include the following:

- Rest time and coffee breaks;
- Unauthorized work if the employer "suffers or permits" the employee to work;
- Waiting time if it is controlled by the employer; and
- On-the-job training.

The FLSA does not require employers to grant meal or rest periods, but such breaks are required by 22 states. Further discussion can be found in Chapter 9.

Tip Credit

If an employee customarily and regularly receives more than $30 a month in tips, his or her employer may credit the tips toward the employee's wages. This tip credit, however, cannot exceed 50 percent of the minimum wage.

Payment of Wages

Minimum wages and overtime must be paid to employees in cash or with a negotiable instrument. Employers can deduct the reasonable cost of board, lodging, and certain facilities furnished to employees from the cash amount paid.

Overtime Pay

Employees covered by the FLSA must be paid a higher hourly rate for overtime work, which for purposes of the FLSA is work in excess of 40 hours in a workweek. A "workweek" under the FLSA is a fixed and regularly recurring period of seven consecutive 24-hour periods. It does not have to coincide with a calendar week. A "workweek," provided it is a fixed period, can begin any day of the week and any hour of the day.

Overtime must be paid at a rate of $1\frac{1}{2}$ times the worker's *regular* pay rate (which must be at least the minimum wage but for many workers is more) for each hour worked in excess of the 40 hours in that employee's workweek. A hospital or residential care establishment, however, may pay overtime on the basis of a 14-day work period instead of a workweek. Alternative overtime pay plans of this kind must be set out in a collective bargaining agreement or otherwise consented to by the employees in question.

An employee's regular rate includes, in addition to wages, salary, commissions or piece rates, certain supplemental payments such as production bonuses; meals, lodging and other facilities; commission payments; shift differentials; tip credit; prizes; and suggestion awards. Generally excluded are such payments as daily or weekly premiums; work on "days of rest"; employer gifts; expense reimbursement; and vacation pay. Because there are very technical requirements for the calculation of the regular rate, and what should or should not be included, a person should consult an expert on the FLSA.

The FLSA does not require an employer to pay overtime rates or other "premium" pay to an employee for work on a Saturday, Sunday, or holiday, unless the hours worked on those days are in excess of the 40 hours in that employee's workweek.

Employees covered by FLSA who are paid by salary, piecework, or commission must also receive the minimum wage and overtime pay. Their hourly rate is usually determined by dividing their weekly pay by the number of hours worked. Overtime is then based on $1\frac{1}{2}$ times this rate. For example, a salaried worker who is paid $170 a week for a 40-hour workweek earns a regular hourly rate of $4.25 ($170 ÷ 40). If the employee works more than 40 hours, he or she would be entitled to $6.38 for each overtime hour ($4.25 × $1\frac{1}{2}$).

Alternative Overtime Pay Agreements

Compensatory time-off policies are generally not permitted by the FLSA, unless the time off is given in the same workweek as the extra work. There is an exception to this general prohibition for public sector employers, who can grant their employees compensatory time off at time-and-a-half for each hour of overtime worked, up to a maximum number of hours.

Guaranteed wage plans, or "Belo" plans, are permitted under certain circumstances to provide a guaranteed weekly payment for employees whose hours regularly exceed the statutory overtime limit of 40 hours.

Time-off and prepayment plans also are permitted under certain circumstances, to allow employers to balance overtime in one week against "undertime" worked in another week. Consult an expert before adopting any of these alternative overtime arrangements.

FLSA Exemptions

Certain groups of employees are exempt from the minimum wage or overtime provision, or both. However, each exemption is narrowly defined under the law. An employer is therefore cautioned to carefully check the exact terms and conditions of the exemption before applying it. The following are examples of some of the exemptions.

Exemptions from both minimum wage and overtime:

- White-collar employees who qualify as either executive, administrative, professional, highly skilled in a computer-related occupation, or work in certain types of outside sales, depending on whether they meet minimum earnings requirements;

- Employees of certain individually owned and operated small retail and service establishments not part of a covered enterprise;
- Employees of certain seasonal amusement or recreational establishments;
- Employees of certain small newspapers or switchboard operators of small telephone companies;
- Farm workers employed by anyone who used no more than 500 man-days of farm labor in a calendar quarter;
- Family members of the owner;
- Certain administrative employees of educational establishments; and
- Volunteers of services to government agencies.

Exemptions from overtime provisions only:

- Sales persons, partsmen, and mechanics engaged primarily in selling or servicing automobiles, trucks, farm implements, or aircraft;
- Certain highly paid commission employees of retail or service establishments;
- Employees of motion picture theaters;
- Farm workers;
- Live-in domestics;
- Taxicab drivers;
- Several types of transportation-industry employees actually engaged in transportation-related activities; and
- Employees of small scale forestry and logging operations.

Exemptions from minimum wage provisions only:

- Full-time students;
- Learners, student-learners, and apprentices;
- Certain disabled employees; and
- Messengers.

Young Workers

Workers 18 years of age or older may work at any time in any job. The FLSA, however, restricts the types of work and hours of work for persons under 18 years old.

Workers 16 or 17 years old may work in any occupation except those declared hazardous by the Secretary of Labor. This hazardous work includes:

- Manufacturing or storing explosives;
- Driving a motor vehicle or being an outside helper;
- Mining;
- Logging and sawmilling;
- Being exposed to radioactive substances and ionizing radiations;
- Using power-driven hoisting apparatus;
- Using power-driven bakery machines;
- Manufacturing brick, tile, and related products; and
- Wrecking, demolition, and ship-wrecking operations.

The following are also hazardous, but exemptions under specified standards are provided for apprentices and student-learners:

- Power-driven metal forming, punching, and shearing machines;
- Power-driven woodworking machines;
- Meat packing or processing;
- Power-driven paper products machines;
- Power-driven circular saws, band saws, and guillotine shears;
- Roofing operations; and
- Excavation operations.

Workers 14 or 15 years old may work in office, clerical, and sales jobs, and in retail, food service, and gasoline service establishments performing such duties as:

- Cashiering, price marking, and tagging;
- Assembling orders, packing, shelving, bagging, and carrying out orders;
- Serving foods and beverages;
- Car washing and polishing and operating gas pumps; or
- Doing errand and delivery work by foot, bicycle, or public transportation.

However, 14- or 15-year-olds may *not* work:

- During school hours;

- Before 7 a.m. or after 7 p.m. (9 p.m. from June 1 through Labor Day);
- More than 18 hours during school weeks;
- More than three hours on school days; or
- More than 40 hours in nonschool weeks.

Workers *at any age* may:

- Deliver newspapers;
- Act or perform in motion pictures or in theatrical, radio, or television productions;
- Work for their parents, except in manufacturing, mining, or hazardous nonfarm jobs; or
- Work on any farm owned or operated by their parents.

Farm Work

- Workers 16 years old may work at any time in any farm job.
- Workers 14 or 15 years old may work outside school hours in any farm job except those declared hazardous by the Secretary of Labor.
- Workers 12 or 13 years old may work outside school hours in nonhazardous farm jobs with their parents' written consent, or may work on a farm where their parents are employed.
- Persons younger than 12 years old may work outside school hours in nonhazardous farm jobs with their parents' written consent on farms where the employees do not have to be paid the minimum wage.
- Minors 10 or 11 years old may work for no more than 8 weeks between June 1 and October 15 for employers who receive approval from the Secretary of Labor. This work must be confined to hand-harvested short season crops outside school hours under very limited and specified circumstances prescribed by the Secretary of Labor.

Young workers must be paid the minimum wage and overtime pay rates regardless of their age, unless the Wage-Hour Administrator has expressly certified that they may be paid a lower wage.

Public Sector Employees

Originally, the FLSA applied only to private employers. Now, it also covers most federal as well as most state and local government employees. Many FLSA exemptions set forth on page 68 carry over to employees in the public sector. The biggest difference in the coverage is that state and local governments may grant employees compensatory time off instead of paying overtime, if certain conditions are met.

Recordkeeping

The wage and hour records required to be kept by employers do not have to be in any particular form, but must be kept in an accurate and intelligible manner and should contain the following information about employees covered by the FLSA:

- Name, home address, and birth date if under 19 years old;
- Sex and occupation;
- Hour and day when the employee's workweek begins;
- Regular hourly pay for any week when overtime is worked;
- Regular rate exclusions;
- Total daily or weekly straight time earnings;
- Total daily and weekly hours;
- Total overtime pay for the workweek;
- Deductions from or additions to wages;
- Total wages paid each pay period;
- Date of payment and pay period covered; and
- Retroactive payments.

Records also should be maintained for full-time students, learners and apprentices, messengers, and handicapped employees.

Employers must be able to prove any claimed exemption. Therefore, it is important to keep records that would help to prove the exemption. For white-collar exemptions, the records kept should include the total weekly wages and total pay, including fringe benefits.

If an employer uses an alternate method for determining overtime or minimum wage, such as compensatory time or tip credits, that employer must keep records to show compliance with the special rule.

These records generally must be kept for three years, while certain supplementary records—time cards and work schedules—need only be retained for two years.

Subminimum Wages

Learners and apprentices under certain circumstances may be paid less than the minimum wage, as may full-time students in retail or service establishments, agriculture, or institutions of higher learning. Workers who are 65 or older or mentally or physically disabled and whose earning abilities are reduced may also be employed below the minimum wage. However, before employers can pay less than the minimum wage, they must obtain a special certificate from the U.S. Labor Department's Wage and Hour Administrator.

What the FLSA Does Not Require

Although other federal statutes or state laws or a union contract may require the following, the FLSA does not require an employer to:

- Give employees a discharge notice or a reason for discharge. (An employer, however, cannot fire or discriminate against an employee for filing a complaint involving the FLSA.)
- Provide rest periods, holidays, or vacations.
- Grant pay raises or fringe benefits.
- Set a limit on the hours of work for employees 16 years of age or older.
- Provide severance or sick pay.
- Pay premium or overtime wages for work on weekends or holidays.

FLSA Enforcement

The FLSA is enforced by compliance officers from the U.S. Department of Labor's Wage and Hour Division. These officers have the authority to conduct investigations and gather data on wages, hours of work, and other employment conditions or practices to determine whether an employer is complying with the law. Where violations are found, they may also recommend changes in employment practices to obtain compliance with the law. Employers may also be subject to civil or criminal sanctions with fines up to $10,000 for willful violations.

Recovering Back Wages

Employees may recover minimum wages and/or over-time pay, as well as liquidated damages and reasonable attorney's fees and costs, through one of the following procedures:

- The Wage and Hour Division may supervise the payment of back wages that the employer agrees to pay.
- The Secretary of Labor may bring a court suit for back wages.
- Employees may file a private suit for back pay. However, they may not sue if they have been paid back wages under the supervision of the Wage and Hour Division, or if the Secretary of Labor has already filed suit.

A two-year statute of limitations applies to the recovery of back pay, except that in the case of a willful violation, a three-year statute applies.

Other Federal Wage Laws

In addition to the FLSA, there are four other federal wage-hour laws that apply to employers that work under a contract with the federal government. These laws are:

- The *Walsh-Healey Act*, which requires employers furnishing materials, supplies, articles, or equipment to the government under contracts exceeding $10,000 to pay their employees the prevailing wage in the industry and to pay time-and-a-half for hours in excess of 40 in one week.
- The *Davis-Bacon Act*, which requires employers working under a government contract exceeding

$2,000 involving the construction, alteration, or repair of public buildings or public works, including painting or decorating, to pay their laborers and mechanics the prevailing wages in the locality where the work is to be performed.

- The *McNamara-O'Hara Service Contract Act*, which requires employers furnishing services (e.g., guards and watchmen) to the government under contracts exceeding $2,500 to pay their employees the prevailing wages and fringe benefits in the locality.
- The *Contract Work Hours Act*, which requires the payment of overtime pay for hours worked in excess of 8 per day and 40 per week to mechanics and laborers while actually employed on any covered public work.
- The *Copeland "Anti-Kickback" Act*, which prohibits all contractors on federally funded construction projects from forcing any employee to kickback or rebate any portion of his or her entitled compensation.
- The *Portal-to-Portal Act*, which excludes from the FLSA's minimum wage and overtime pay requirements traveling to and from work, unless such activities are covered by contract, custom, or practice, and excludes from compensable time worked both preliminary and postliminary activities.

Like the FLSA, these laws are also enforced by the Wage and Hour Division of the Labor Department.

There is one other wage hour law, the Equal Pay Act (EPA), which amended the FLSA and made it illegal for employers to discriminate on the basis of sex by paying different wages to employees of the opposite sex who perform substantially equal work. White-collar employees are not exempt from the provisions of the Equal Pay Act. One other difference is that the Equal Employment Opportunity Commission, rather than the Wage and Hour Division, enforces the EPA.

More information on the FLSA and other laws administered by the Wage and Hour Division, including the federal wage garnishment law, may be obtained from any of its local offices. They are listed in the telephone directory under the U.S. Government, Department of Labor, Employment Standards Administration, Wage and Hour Division. Its national office address is:

U.S. Department of Labor
Employment Standards Administration
Wage and Hour Division
Washington, D.C. 20210

State Minimum Wage Laws

All but four states have minimum wage laws either specifying a minimum wage or permitting wages to be fixed by a wage board. State laws generally set a minimum wage that is higher or lower than, or tied to, the federal minimum wage. Employers in those states with a higher minimum wage must pay that higher rate. Where lower, the federal minimum wage must be paid. In other cases, state laws cover groups of employees not covered by the federal law. These laws typically either extend rights to the federal minimum rate to the unprotected groups or set a lower minimum wage rate that employers must pay. Some states issue wage board orders that set wage rates for particular industries or occupational groups (see chart on page 60).

State Maximum Hours and Overtime Rules

Many states have maximum hours and overtime rules similar to those of the FLSA. Keep in mind that the FLSA does not cover all employees and that a state may provide additional protections on hours or overtime that go beyond the federal requirements or that apply to businesses with less than $500,000 annual volume. Generally, when federal and state laws overlap, employers should comply with the standard that provides employees with the most protection. State laws include provisions on maximum hours before overtime; overtime pay for hours worked in excess of a daily or weekly maximum; employees covered; limits on hours worked; restrictions covering work on Sunday or other days of religious observance, as well as requirements entitling employees to a specified number of hours off each week; and specified periods of time employers must give employees each day for purposes of eating or resting.

It is important to check specific states' laws as well as the federal laws when making minimum wage and overtime decisions.

9

LEAVE AND TIME OFF FROM WORK

An employer does not have to to give employees time off from work unless required by law or by union contract. Employers also do not have to give employees time off on government-declared "legal" holidays. Various laws, however, do require that employees be allowed time off, usually through unpaid leave, to vote, perform jury duty, bear children, serve on temporary military duty, or under other circumstances covered later in this chapter. In 1993, a federal statute, the Family and Medical Leave Act, was enacted requiring that employees be allowed to take time off for such reasons as the birth of a child or the serious illness of an employee's family member.

Family and Medical Leave Act

All employers, public or private, with 50 or more employees within a 75-mile radius, are covered by the Family and Medical Leave Act (FMLA).

Eligibility for leave under FMLA requires that an employee work for his or her employer for at least 12 months, perform 1,250 hours of work during that period, and make the request for leave at least 30 days in advance. An eligible employee, male or female, is entitled to 12 weeks of unpaid leave during any 12-month qualifying period, provided that the leave is sought for one of the following reasons:

- For birth or placement of a child for adoption or foster care;
- To care for an immediate family member (spouse, child, or parent) with a serious health condition; or
- When the employee is unable to work because of a serious health condition, that makes it impossible to perform a job.

If the employee is not able to give 30 days' notice (e.g., when there is a premature birth or an unexpected illness or injury), notice must be given as soon as possible.

If both spouses work for the same employer, the husband and wife may take a combined total of 12 weeks to care for a family member, except when one spouse is caring for the other.

The leave does not always have to be taken at one time. An employee may take intermittent leave, subject to the employer's approval, for the birth or adoption of a child. It may be taken for a serious illness when medically necessary. Intermittent leave must be scheduled, if possible, at least 30 days in advance.

Certification

Employees seeking FMLA leave may be required to provide:

- Advance notice of 30 days of the need to take FMLA leave when the need is foreseeable;
- Medical opinions or certifications of a "serious health condition";
- Second or third medical opinions and periodic recertifications at the employer's expense; or
- Periodic reports during FMLA leave regarding the employee's status and intent to return to work.

An adequate certification must include the following information, where applicable:

- When the serious health condition began and how long it is expected to last;
- Medical facts;
- Schedule and duration of treatment; and

- The medical necessity for the leave.

If leave is sought because of the employee's own serious medical condition, the certification must include a statement that the employee is unable to perform the "essential" instead of "routine" functions of the job.

Benefits

During the FMLA leave, employees must continue to be covered under preexisting health care insurance. They do not continue to accrue seniority and other benefits tied to length of service, unless the employer agrees. No unemployment or other government compensation is available to the employee during the leave.

If an employee does not return to work after the leave, he or she must reimburse the employer for health care payments extended during the leave. However, the employee may be entitled to COBRA benefits, discussed in Chapter 7.

Use of Paid Leave

Workers with accrued paid leave, such as sick, annual, or personal leave, may substitute that leave for unpaid FMLA leave. The employer can also require that employees take the paid leave in lieu of FMLA leave. The FMLA does not require employers to provide paid leave where they normally do not provide such leave.

Other Provisions

Covered employers must post notices informing their employees of their rights under the FMLA.

The FMLA does not affect any other antidiscrimination law, nor does it supersede any state law offering greater family or medical leave protection or affect employers' obligations under a collective bargaining agreement between an employer and a union.

Anti-Retaliatory Provisions

Federal and state laws, in addition to granting rights to workers to take time off for certain protected purposes, also prevent employers from retaliating against them. State workers' compensation laws make it illegal to discriminate against workers for exercising their rights under those laws.

The FMLA prohibits employers from interfering with protected employee rights under the law, and from discharging employees who exercise these rights, or disciplining whistleblowers who report violations of the FMLA.

Return to Work

On return from FMLA leave, the worker is entitled to return to the same or an equivalent position, with duties, pay, benefits, and working conditions corresponding to those the employee had before taking leave.

A key employee who is salaried and among the 10-percent highest paid can be permanently replaced by the employer if keeping the job open would cause the employer "substantial and grievous economic injury." The employer must notify key employees before they take leave that their jobs will not be guaranteed.

State Family Leave Laws

At least 40 states have adopted what are commonly referred to as family leave laws. These laws include parental leave for both natural and adoptive parents, child care leave, and leave to care for certain other family members or relatives, such as grandparents. However, these laws do not usually extend to pregnancy or maternity leave.

Generally these laws make it possible for both public and private sector employees to take unpaid leave of a specified number of workweeks to care for a newborn child, a newly adopted child, or a seriously ill dependent or family member, such as a spouse, parent, or in-law. In some states, employees can use accrued sick leave for care of a sick family member.

Most leaves provide for unpaid leaves of absence, continuation of health or other benefits during the leave period, or reinstatement to the same or a comparable job upon return to work. Others require workers to give their employer advance notice, or to provide certification of the need for the leave.

Currently, family and medical leave provisions of one form or another are in effect in Alabama, Arizona, Arkansas, California, Colorado, Connecticut, Delaware, Florida, Georgia, Hawaii, Illinois, Iowa, Kansas, Kentucky, Maine, Maryland, Minnesota, Missouri, Montana, Nebraska, Nevada, New Jersey, New York, North Carolina, North Dakota, Oklahoma, Oregon, Rhode Island, South Carolina, South Dakota, Tennessee, Texas, Utah, Washington, West Virginia, and Wisconsin, and the District of Columbia.

Leave banks or voluntary sharing of leave among public employees are provided for in 22 states, including Alabama, Arizona, Arkansas, California, Colorado, Illinois, Kansas, Kentucky, Louisiana, Maryland, Massachusetts, Montana, Nebraska, New Jersey, New York, North Dakota, Oklahoma, South Dakota, Tennessee, Texas, Utah, and Washington, and the District of Columbia. Most allow public employees to donate or transfer leave when another employee or a member of any employee's immediate family has a catastrophic illness or injury.

Pregnancy Leave

Although there was no specific federal law requiring employers to give pregnancy leave or time off for the care of a newborn infant before FMLA, the federal Pregnancy Discrimination Act amending Title VII of the Civil Rights Act of 1964 required that pregnant employees be treated the same as other employees on the basis of ability or inability to work. In other words, if an employer grants disability leave, it must extend the same leave for pregnancy.

The Pregnancy Discrimination Act also:

- Prohibits terminating or refusing to hire or promote qualified women solely because they are pregnant;
- Bars mandatory leave for pregnant women that arbitrarily sets a time in pregnancy not based on the employees' inability to work;
- Protects the reinstatement rights of women on leave for pregnancy-related medical conditions, including

entitlements to credit for previous service, accrued retirement benefits, and accumulated seniority; and

- Requires employers to treat pregnancy and childbirth the same as other causes of disability under fringe benefit plans, such as granting the same leave for pregnancy as granted for a disability.

Furthermore, under Title VII, male and female employees cannot be treated differently. So if leave is granted to female employees, it must be granted to male employees on the same terms.

A majority of states and many municipalities have passed laws that are broader than Title VII, providing a specific leave period following childbirth or a guarantee of reinstatement in the case of leave for childbirth. These include Alabama, Alaska, Arizona, California, Colorado, Connecticut, Hawaii, Idaho, Indiana, Iowa, Kansas, Kentucky, Louisiana, Maryland, Massachusetts, Minnesota, Missouri, Montana, Nevada, New Hampshire, New Jersey, New York, North Carolina, North Dakota, Ohio, Oklahoma, Oregon, Pennsylvania, Rhode Island, South Carolina, South Dakota, Tennessee, Texas, Utah, Vermont, Washington, West Virginia, and Wisconsin.

Paid maternity leave, but not job security, under mandatory short-term disability programs is guaranteed by law in California, Hawaii, New Jersey, New York, and Rhode Island. The number of weeks a new mother is entitled to under these laws averages 10.

Military Leave

Under the Veterans' Reemployment Rights Act and Vietnam Era Veterans' Readjustment Assistance Act (and other earlier federal laws), employers must grant leave to employees who volunteer for or are ordered to active military duty or reserve training duty. On return from leave, these veterans must be reinstated to the same or substantially similar jobs, with full seniority, matching pay, working conditions, and benefits. Unlike employees on FMLA leave, veterans continue to accrue the same seniority while on leave as they would if still on the job.

State Maternity, Parental, and Family Leave Laws/Rules

	Maternity	Parental	Family		Maternity	Parental	Family
Alabama	●[a]		●[a]	Nebraska			●[a]
Alaska	●[a]		●[a]	Nevada	●		●[a]
Arizona		●[a]		New Hampshire	●		●[a]
Arkansas				New Jersey	●[a]		●
California	●	●	●	New Mexico			●[a]
Colorado		●	●[a]	New York		●	
Connecticut		●		North Carolina	●[a]		●[a]
Delaware		●[a]		North Dakota	●[a]		●[a]
District of Columbia			●	Ohio			
Florida			●[a]	Oklahoma			●[a]
Georgia			●[a]	Oregon	●	●	●
Hawaii			●	Pennsylvania	●	●	
Idaho	●[a]		●[a]	Puerto Rico	●		
Illinois		●	●[a]	Rhode Island		●	●
Indiana	●[a]		●[a]	South Carolina	●	●[a]	●[a]
Iowa	●		●[a]	South Dakota			●[a]
Kansas	●[a]		●[a]	Tennessee	●	●[a]	
Kentucky	●[a]	●	●[a]	Texas	●[a]	●[a]	●[a]
Louisiana	●			Utah	●[a]		●[a]
Maine			●	Vermont		●	●
Maryland	●		●[a]	Virginia			
Massachusetts	●			Virgin Islands	●		
Michigan				Washington	●	●	●
Minnesota		●		West Virginia			●[a]
Mississippi				Wisconsin	●		●
Missouri		●[a]		Wyoming			
Montana	●	●[a]					

[a] Covers public employees only.

Under most circumstances, returning active duty veterans cannot be discharged, except for cause, for at least a year after reinstatement, or for six months in the case of a return from reserve duty.

A returning veteran is also eligible for any "higher" position the veteran would have attained had he or she stayed on the job, with the employer providing whatever training the veteran will need to acquire the skills needed for the advanced slot. The returning veteran also is entitled to any promotion, pay raise, or cost-of-living hike he or she would have been entitled to before leaving. The Act further provides that employees cannot be discharged or denied promotions or any other employment benefit or advantage because of military service.

Although employers do not have to pay employees on active military duty, some employers do pay the difference between military and civilian salaries. Military leave must be provided in addition to earned vacation time.

Reinstatement rights extend for at least four years, with a fifth year included if necessary for the convenience of the government. The returning veteran must apply for reinstatement within 30 days from release from active duty.

State Military Leave Laws

All states (except Tennessee) and the District of Columbia have passed laws providing for leave and reinstatement rights of public or private employees with compulsory or voluntary military service or training obligations. Twenty-five states and the District of Columbia have enacted special laws or adopted emergency or permanent regulations providing certain leave, compensation, or other benefits for National Guard members or reservists.

Some of these state laws cover only state and local government employees; others apply to private sector employees as well. Some apply only to service in the National Guard; others cover state and local government employees serving in any sector of the military.

Time Off for Voting

Many states have passed laws providing a specified number of hours off to vote, with some granting time off with pay, usually two hours. Others specify that advance notice must be given by the employee.

Leave Under the Americans With Disabilities Act (ADA)

Under the reasonable accommodation provision of Title I of ADA, which prohibits job discrimination against the disabled, an employer must allow workers time off to obtain necessary medical treatment, to repair a prosthesis or equipment, to avoid dangerous temporary changes in working conditions, or to receive necessary training. According to the Equal Employment Opportunity Commission (EEOC), employers do not have to provide additional paid leave as an accommodation, but should consider allowing use of accrued leave, advanced leave, or leave without pay, where such an accommodation will not cause undue hardship on the business operations.

Jury Duty

All states and the District of Columbia have laws prohibiting employers from discharging or otherwise disciplining employees for requesting or taking off time for jury duty or to serve as a witness. A few laws contain notice requirements, while some have pay provisions. For example, employers in Alabama, Nebraska, New Jersey, and Tennessee must pay employees on jury duty their regular wages less any jury pay. Employers in Colorado, Connecticut, Massachusetts, and New York must also pay a portion of the employees' pay for a limited number of days.

Other State Laws

A number of states, including California, Illinois, Louisiana, Massachusetts, Minnesota, and South Dakota, have laws granting leave to attend school-related conferences that cannot be scheduled during nonwork hours. North Carolina provides four hours of leave per year for parents to participate in school activities, and Virginia has provided for a statewide study of the need for leave time to promote parental involvement in schools. Minnesota provides for time off to participate in a child's school conference or class-room activities.

Most of these laws provide for unpaid leaves of absence, continuation of health or other benefits during the leave period, or reinstatement to the same or a comparable job upon return to work. A number also require that workers notify employers in advance of leave, and some provide for the voluntary sharing, donation, or transfer of leave when an employee or a member of an employee's immediate family is experiencing a catastrophic illness or injury.

Other reasons for leave provided for in state laws include voluntary firefighting activities, time off for bone marrow transplants (Colorado, Louisiana, Minnesota, and South Carolina), and time off for organ and tissue dona-tions (Colorado).

Illinois requires employers to grant leave time for elected local government or school board officials to attend official meetings. Rhode Island requires that employers of part-time elected officials provide flexible work schedules to allow these officials to serve. Wisconsin requires that employers grant leave for election officials to serve on elec-tion day.

Meal and Rest Periods

Workers are not entitled to paid rest periods or a speci-fied period of time off for meals under the federal Fair Labor Standards Act. This law specifies that if the employer does provide this time off these meal or rest periods may be counted as hours worked (see discussion in Chapter 8).

Some states, however, do require employers to give their workers a meal or rest break after a specified number of hours of work, with the break usually for 30 minutes: Cali-fornia, Colorado, Connecticut, Delaware, Hawaii (public), Illinois, Kentucky, Maine, Massachusetts. Minnesota,

Nebraska, Nevada, New Hampshire, New Mexico, New York, North Dakota, Oregon, Pennsylvania, Rhode Island, Tennessee, Washington, West Virginia, and Wisconsin. State laws differ as to whether these breaks can be taken away from the employer's premises, whether there is to be a rest period in addition to the meal period, and length of time of the break. They also vary depending on the industry.

10

JOB SAFETY

Employers are required by the federal Occupational Safety and Health Act and by many state laws to provide safe and healthful working conditions for their employees. The law also requires both employers and employees to comply with health and safety standards issued by the federal government. The federal law is enforced by the Labor Department's Occupational Safety and Health Administration (OSHA).

The federal safety and health act states that employers have a "general duty" to provide employees with a job and a workplace that are free from recognized hazards that are causing or are likely to cause death or serious harm. An employer is expected to take the initiative in identifying and eliminating recognized hazardous conditions.

Employer's Duties

Employers must be familiar with OSHA standards and provide copies of them to employees, inform employees of their rights and duties, examine the workplace and then eliminate or take steps to guard against hazards, establish operating procedures and make sure employees have and use safe tools and equipment, comply with posting rules and warn employees of potential hazards, train them to follow safe work rules, and provide required medical examinations. They also have recordkeeping and reporting responsibilities, and must cooperate during any OSHA inspections.

Employee Rights

Workers have a right to a place of employment free from recognized hazards that are causing or are likely to cause death or serious harm. The law also requires employees to comply with standards issued by OSHA, although no penalties are specified if employees do not comply.

Workers have the right to report unsafe or unhealthful working conditions to OSHA. A worker in imminent danger of a job safety or health hazard can ask an employer to correct the matter or the worker can contact the nearest OSHA area office and request an inspection. If OSHA determines that a hazard exists, it requests the employer to eliminate the hazard and it can seek an order from a court requiring the employer to take corrective action.

An employer cannot punish or discriminate against workers for exercising their job safety and health rights by complaining about hazards to their employer, union, OSHA, or other government agencies. Workers also have the right to participate in OSHA inspections, conferences, hearings, or other OSHA-related activities.

A worker punished for exercising these rights has 30 days to complain to an OSHA area office. If after an investigation OSHA finds that the worker has been unlawfully punished, it will ask the employer to reinstate the worker (if the employee was fired) and to restore any earnings or benefits the employee may have lost. If necessary, OSHA can ask a federal court to enforce its order.

Labor unions have the right to participate in hearings on proposed standards and can contest any permanent standards issued by OSHA. Any labor representative can bring suit against the Secretary of Labor on behalf of an injured employee if the imminent danger provisions of the law are not followed.

In some instances, the refusal of workers to perform dangerous work may be protected by the National Labor Relations Board, usually when the worker's action was with, or on behalf of, other workers.

Standards

Employers and employees must comply with specific OSHA-prescribed job safety and health standards. These standards cover such matters as fire protection, construction and maintenance of equipment, worker training, machine guarding, confined spaces, housekeeping, air contaminants, exits, material handling and storage space, ventilation, medical and first aid, noise exposure, and protective equipment to be worn by workers.

OSHA can issue either permanent or temporary standards. If permanent, interested persons have a chance to comment under a specific timetable before the standards become final. Emergency temporary standards may be made effective immediately if OSHA determines that employees are exposed to a grave danger and that an emergency standard is needed to protect employees from that danger.

Variances

An employer unable to comply with an OSHA safety standard may ask OSHA, or the state government if there is an OSHA-approved plan, for a permanent or temporary "variance" from that particular standard. A permanent variance may be granted if the employer can show that its safety practice or procedure, while not in literal compliance with OSHA's standard, is nevertheless as safe.

An employer seeking a temporary variance must establish (1) that it is unable to comply with the standard by its effective date because of the unavailability of the means to comply by that date; (2) that it is doing all it can to protect its workers against the hazard covered by the standard; (3) that it has a plan to come into compliance with the standard as soon as practicable; and (4) that it has notified its employees, affected employers, and appropriate state authorities for each facility of its application for the variance. Its notice to the employees must inform them that they have the right to a hearing on its application.

Recordkeeping, Reporting, and Posting

An employer with 10 or more workers must maintain records of occupational injuries (other than those involving only first aid) and illnesses. Records also must be kept of certain potentially toxic or harmful physical agents that must be monitored or measured. Workers or their representatives have the right to review these records, as does OSHA under prescribed procedures.

Employers must report within 48 hours to the nearest OSHA area director any incident or accident that results in a fatality or hospitalization of five or more employees.

OSHA posters notifying employees of their rights and obligations, and citations and variance notices, must be posted at all covered workplaces.

Inspections

As with many regulatory agencies, OSHA has compliance officers who have the authority to inspect business operations for violations of the law and OSHA standards. Inspections can be triggered by a report of imminent danger (these take priority), an employee complaint, or as a follow-up. Normally, no advance notice is given that an inspection will be conducted. Employers can voluntarily agree to an inspection or can require that the inspector obtain a search warrant.

When an inspection is made, it ordinarily begins with a meeting ("opening conference") to discuss procedures for the inspection. The inspector then conducts a "walkaround" inspection of the facility, accompanied by representatives of the employer and its employees. The employer, of course, selects its representative. It cannot, however, select one for the employees. Their representative must be selected by the workers or their union (if they have one), or by the inspector. The employees' representative must be paid for the time spent on the inspection.

Workers have the right to talk to the inspector concerning the facility's health and safety problems and may do so on a private and confidential basis, even away from work.

If health hazards are found, another inspector trained as an industrial hygienist may be called in to measure levels of dust, noise, fumes, or other hazards. Test results are given to the employer's and the employee's representatives.

When the inspection is completed, the inspector confers with the representatives in a closing conference concerning the conditions and practices, if any, which he or she believes constitute hazardous conditions that must be modified or eliminated ("abated") and the length of time it will take to correct them.

The inspector then files a report with OSHA's area director, who decides what citations for safety violations, if any, will be issued, the deadlines for correcting job hazards, and the penalties to be imposed.

Voluntary Protection Programs

Employers may choose to participate in voluntary programs to provide workplace-specific safety and health programs to prevent or control job hazards that go beyond the standards and provide the best feasible protection. Participation in these programs means the employer is removed from programmed inspection lists.

Citations

The director may, of course, find that there were no safety violations. Should he or she find that there were violations, a written citation describing the nature of each violation and the time allowed for correcting it will be sent to the employer within six months of violation. The employer must post a copy of the citation at or near the place where the violation occurred for a period of three days or until the condition is corrected, whichever is longer. A citation must specify a date when the employer will correct the violation, a period usually not to exceed 30 days.

The employer, employee, or employee representative can contest a citation. If the employer does not contest the citation, the penalties assessed by OSHA are final and cannot be reviewed.

Penalties

OSHA's penalty policy, designed to be an incentive and not a punishment, encourages employers to correct violations voluntarily. The penalty for a safety violation depends on its seriousness.

For both serious and nonserious violations, the amount of the proposed penalty the OSHA director decides to assess against the employer depends primarily on the gravity of the hazard, but also taken into account are the company's history of previous violations, its good-faith efforts to comply with the law, and the size of the business. Additional penalties may be assessed if an OSHA follow-up inspection shows a failure to take necessary corrective action, unless the employer can show a good-faith effort to comply.

Examples of civil penalties assessed are:

- For a serious or other than serious violation, the maximum penalty is $7,000.
- For willful or repeated violations, the maximum penalty is $70,000, but not less than $5,000.
- For failure to post, the maximum penalty is up to $7,000.

Criminal penalties result where there are willful violations that result in a worker's death, but they are imposed only after a court trial.

Appeals

A citation, proposed penalty, and/or abatement date can be appealed by the employer by notifying the area director in writing within 15 days. If notice is not given within this time, the director's determination becomes final and must be complied with.

If the employer appeals (called a "notice of contest"), it must post a notice in its facility where it can be seen by its employees and inform their union (if they have one). The workers or their representative may participate in the appeal process by notifying OSHA.

Whether or not the employer appeals, the workers or their representative can challenge the time allowed by OSHA for correcting a hazard by following the same appeal procedure allowed their employer.

Administrative Hearing

After the appeal is filed, the Labor Department, within 30 days, issues a "complaint" setting forth its position on the issues raised in the employer's appeal. The complaint must be answered by the employer within 30 days by admitting, denying, or offering to explain the allegations in the complaint.

A hearing is held sometime later before an OSHA administrative law judge. At the hearing the Labor Department has the burden of proving the issues being contested. Employers have the right to present opposing evidence and arguments in support of their position. Their employees or their representative also have the same right to participate in the hearing. Settlement is permitted at any stage of the proceedings.

After the judge issues a decision, any party objecting to it can ask the Occupational Safety and Health Review Commission to review the judge's decision. The Review Commission, however, does not have to agree to review the case. If it does not agree, the judge's decision becomes final in 30 days. Any party adversely affected by the result can appeal to a federal appeals court.

Simplified Proceedings

Employers who receive a citation can file a request for simplified proceedings that are faster, do not require an attorney, and reduce paperwork and the expense of litigation.

State Programs

OSHA encourages states to develop and operate their own workplace safety and health programs. These programs have to be at least as effective as the federal program. Once the state has operated a fully effective program for at least one year, a state can take over the enforcement of job safety in its state. Some of the areas of the state's proposed program that OSHA will check before giving its approval include:

- *Worker rights.* The state law must provide workers with the same rights that OSHA provides.
- *Standards.* The state's safety and health standards cannot provide workers with less protection than that provided by OSHA's standards.
- *Inspectors.* The state must have trained inspectors who will be effective in finding and correcting hazards.
- *Appeals.* Workers must be allowed to participate in cases involving employer appeals of penalties or deadlines for correcting hazards, and to appeal state actions relating to safety and health.

Once the state plan is approved, OSHA will continue to monitor the plan to be sure the state is meeting its commitments and maintaining an adequate plan. Fewer than half the states currently have approved state programs.

Hazard Communication: Right-to-Know Rules

Employers must alert workers about the hazardous chemicals they use or might encounter on the job under OSHA's hazard communication rule. In addition to evaluating the hazards of their chemicals, employers must label their products and provide a material safety data sheet (MSDS) for each hazardous substance shipped to firms that use their products. Employers also are required to establish training programs for workers handling these chemicals, to use in-house labels on chemicals, and develop hazard communication programs.

A majority of states and municipalities have enacted right-to-know laws that in many cases are broader and stronger than the federal standard by covering all workplaces; requiring employers to post notices of employees' right to obtain information about the chemicals without risk of discharge or other discrimination; requiring employers to give public safety and law enforcement officials access to hazard information; and affording less trade secret protection to chemical manufacturers. State laws established under OSHA-approved state plans are not preempted by the federal standard.

More information about OSHA can be obtained from one of its regional or area offices listed in the phone directory or by writing to:

U.S. Department of Labor
Occupational Safety and Health Administration
Washington, D.C. 20210

11

UNEMPLOYMENT BENEFITS

Unemployment insurance (also referred to as unemployment compensation) is a weekly benefit paid for a limited period of time to workers to tide them over when they are out of work through no fault of their own. Unlike workers' compensation and Social Security disability programs, which provide benefits to workers who are unable to work because of a disability, a worker applying for unemployment insurance must be able to work.

Unemployment insurance is a joint federal-state government program, with each state administering its own program or system under laws that must be approved by the federal government. A special payroll tax on employers, both federal and state, funds the system. Alaska and New Jersey also require employees to share a part of the cost, while Pennsylvania and West Virginia tax employees only when the fund reaches a certain level or when federal advances must be repaid. The amount of the employer's tax depends on the unemployment rate among its employees. An employer with a higher unemployment rate than other employers pays a higher tax. The tax is adjusted annually according to the employer's unemployment rate.

Employers are covered by unemployment compensation laws if they employ one or more workers on a regular basis and if they pay wages of $1,500 or more during a calendar quarter of the current or previous year. Because of the dual federal-state system, employers must be familiar with the federal law and the laws of the states where they operate. The state laws vary in terms of benefits, coverage, and taxation procedures.

Workers Covered by Unemployment Insurance

Almost all employees performing services for which they receive compensation are covered by unemployment insurance. This includes a company's officers and executives as well as its rank-and-file workers; household workers whose employers pay them at least $1,000 (in cash) in a calendar quarter; and farm workers of farm operators having payrolls of at least $20,000 in a calendar quarter or having 10 or more employees working at least part of a day each week for 20 weeks. Temporary and part-time workers are also covered, although their unemployment benefits may be less than those of full-time workers. Not covered are independent contractors, newspaper carriers under 18 years of age, certain newspaper and magazine vendors, children who work for their parents, and individuals employed by their spouses or children. Employees of federal, state, and local governments and of nonprofit organizations are covered under state laws, even though they are not under federal law.

Qualifying for Benefits

A worker applying for unemployment benefits must be out of work, not at fault in causing his or her unemployment, be available for and able to work, register at the employment office and report as directed, file valid claims, and serve any required waiting period.

Each state also requires applicants to satisfy certain work and earnings requirements to be eligible for unemployment pay. These requirements generally provide that during a "base period"—usually a recent 12-month period prior to the time the worker became unemployed—the worker must have been employed for a prescribed period of time, usually for at least two calendar quarters during the base period, or have earned a specified amount of wages during the base period, or have a combination of both.

Disqualification

Workers who cause their own unemployment may be disqualified from some or all unemployment benefits. The grounds for disqualification vary from state to state, with the most common grounds for disqualification in all states involving situations where the worker:

- Voluntarily quits a job without good cause.
- Gets fired for work-related misconduct.
- Refuses to accept suitable work without a good reason.
- Receives certain other benefits such as dismissal pay, Social Security benefits, workers' compensation, or retirement benefits.
- Knowingly makes false statements or misrepresentation of material facts to obtain benefits.

Most states also disqualify workers who are out of work because of a strike or other labor dispute. The laws of New York and Rhode Island, however, provide that benefits can be paid to workers who are unemployed because of a strike or lockout after 49 days.

There is a long list of states that disqualify workers for involvement in a labor dispute other than a lockout, including Arkansas, Connecticut, Delaware, Florida, Georgia, Illinois, Kentucky, Maine, Minnesota, Mississippi (only if it is an unjustified lockout), New Jersey, Ohio, Oklahoma, Pennsylvania, South Dakota, Tennessee, Vermont, and Wisconsin, as well as the District of Columbia.

Colorado provides for reduced benefits for unemployment due to a labor dispute. Maine covers unemployment during a strike caused by an employer's failure to observe health and safety standards, and Montana if the employer did not comply with state or federal laws. Utah makes an exception where the employer fomented the dispute.

California, Illinois, Minnesota, Rhode Island, and Wisconsin cover employees who leave their jobs because of sexual harassment. Kansas makes an exception for employees who leave their jobs because of harassment in general, while the District of Columbia and Massachusetts additionally make an exception for racial and sex discrimination.

When a worker is disqualified, it can mean that benefits will be postponed for one or more weeks (in addition to any waiting period), or that they will be denied for the duration of joblessness. The time period for disqualification depends on the reason for the disqualification and varies from state to state.

Amount of Benefits

If an unemployed worker meets his or her state's work and earnings requirements, a determination is then made of the weekly benefit amount and the duration of the payments. The amount is related to the wages earned while employed, usually 50 percent of the worker's weekly pay. Each state, however, provides for a minimum and maximum weekly payment. In 1993, for example, the minimum ranged from $5 in Hawaii to $73 in Washington, while the maximum ranged from $165 in Alabama to $335 in the District of Columbia. Some states also allow additional payments for dependents.

Benefits may also be available for partial unemployment. In this case the amount is generally the difference between what the worker actually earns through partial employment and the amount of benefit he or she would have received if totally unemployed.

Duration of Benefits

The maximum length of time payments are made is 26 weeks in most states. When this time period ends, the payments end. To again be entitled to benefits, the worker must reestablish eligibility under the requirements of the state's law. Partial benefits may be received for a longer period of time in some states.

Extended Benefits

During times of high unemployment, a worker whose regular unemployment compensation benefits are exhausted without finding new employment may receive emergency extended benefits for an extended period of time, usually for 20 to 26 weeks, depending on the state's employment condition.

There are two forms of extended benefits. Under federal-state extended benefits, the federal government supplies 50 percent and the state pays the rest. Under the emergency unemployment compensation system, the federal government supplies 100 percent of the extended benefits.

Able and Available

A jobless worker collecting unemployment benefits is expected to actively seek work, report at the local employment service office at regular intervals, and accept suitable job offers.

He or she must also be physically able to work and available for work. Workers are generally considered available for work if they are able to resume work in their customary occupation or in some other occupation reasonably consistent with their education, training, and experience. A worker may lose benefits for any week in which he or she does not look for work or is not available for work.

Disabled Workers

Workers who are unable to work because of sickness or other disability are considered in most states not to be able to work and therefore ineligible for unemployment benefits for the weeks they are unable to work. There are exceptions, however. In Colorado, Illinois, Indiana, Iowa, Kansas, Maine, New Hampshire, North Dakota, Tennessee, Texas, Vermont, Washington, West Virginia, Wisconsin, and Wyoming, employees terminated because they are deemed by a physician to be physically or mentally unable to work are eligible for unemployment pay. And in North Dakota, workers who become disabled during a period of unemployment do not lose their eligibility for benefits. Five states— California, Hawaii, New Jersey, New York, and Rhode Island—also provide special disability benefits under state temporary disability laws to jobless workers who are temporarily disabled because of illness or injury not related to their employment. In all states, disabled workers may be eligible for workers' compensation or Social Security disability benefits. Chapter 12 covers the eligibility requirements for these benefits.

Pregnancy

Benefits cannot be denied solely because of pregnancy. A pregnant woman, however, must still meet the general requirements of ability to work and availability for work despite her pregnancy.

Waiting Period

Most states require a one-week period before a person who is out of work becomes eligible for unemployment pay. There is, however, no waiting period in Alabama, Connecticut, Delaware, Iowa, Kentucky, Maryland, Michigan, Nevada, New Hampshire, or Wisconsin. In some states a worker may be compensated later for the waiting period if he or she is unemployed for a specified period of time.

Relocating

An unemployed worker moving from one locality to another—or from one state to another—continues to be entitled to unemployment benefits, provided the chances of finding a job are about the same in the new state as in the one that the worker left. If a worker moves to another state, his or her weekly benefit will be the amount that is paid in the state in which he or she became unemployed.

Aliens

Citizens of another country who are not lawfully admitted to the United States are not eligible for unemployment pay. However, aliens who have been lawfully admitted for permanent residence are eligible.

Claims Procedure

A claim for unemployment benefits is usually filed in person in the state employment office in the state in which the worker resides. A claims examiner determines whether the worker is eligible for benefits and, if eligible, the amount and duration of the benefits the worker will receive.

As the claim will affect the amount of unemployment tax employers will have to pay, employers are considered interested parties to the claim when one or more of their out-of-work employees files for benefits. The employer is therefore notified of the claim and allowed to state its reasons for the worker's unemployment.

If the worker disputes either the employer's reasons for his or her unemployment or the examiner's determination of eligibility, the worker has the right to a hearing and representation by an attorney or other representative. At the hearing, the worker has the right to testify and present evidence in support of the claim. Both the employee and the employer also have the right to appeal a decision by the unemployment agency to a state court.

Information about a state's unemployment program is available in a local employment security or Job Service office, which is listed in the telephone directory.

Job Loss Because of Foreign Imports

Workers who are totally or partially unemployed because of increased foreign import competition may be eligible for help under the federal government's Trade Adjustment Assistance (TAA) program. This assistance includes cash benefits, retraining, job search help, relocation allowance, and additional unemployment compensation when a worker's regular unemployment pay runs out.

Applications (petitions) are available at local employment security or Job Service offices and may be filed by three or more workers or their representative. The completed applications should be sent to:

Office of Trade Adjustment Assistance
Employment and Training Administration
U.S. Department of Labor
601 D Street, N.W.
Washington, D.C. 20213

Disaster-Caused Job Loss

A worker whose employment has been lost or interrupted as a direct result of a major disaster—e.g., hurricane, tornado, flood, or earthquake—which the President determines warrants federal assistance to communities and individuals may be eligible for special Disaster Unemployment Assistance (DUA).

An application for DUA is made at the local employment security or Job Service office. The amount of the DUA benefit is based on the amount of unemployment compensation the state pays, with the DUA benefit being reduced to the extent the worker receives regular unemployment pay or other forms of income protection.

12

DISABILITY BENEFITS

The two principal programs providing financial assistance to persons unable to work because of a disability caused by a physical or mental illness or injury are Social Security and workers' compensation. Social Security benefits are provided through a federal program to persons unable to work because of an injury or illness regardless of whether it is job-related. Workers' compensation programs, which are operated by the states, provide benefits to workers unable to work because of a job-related injury.

The two programs define disability differently. Workers' compensation programs generally define disability as a person's inability to perform his or her past regular or customary work, while the Social Security law defines disability as a person's inability to perform past work, and also an inability to perform any other substantial and gainful work.

There are also special disability programs for coal miners, military veterans, and law enforcement officials.

SOCIAL SECURITY DISABILITY BENEFITS

Insured Status

In order for workers to be eligible for Social Security disability benefits they must be under 65 years of age and provide proof from a doctor, hospital, or clinic providing treatment, establishing their inability to engage in any substantial gainful activity because of a physical or mental impairment that has lasted or is expected to last at least 12 months or to result in death. They must also be "insured."

A worker becomes insured by working long enough and recently enough under Social Security to earn sufficient credits for eligibility for disability benefits. These credits are earned when contributions—taxes—are deducted from the worker's pay by the employer and paid into a special Social Security fund. The employer contributes an equal amount. A worker who is self-employed pays directly into Social Security. (These payments are also used to fund Social Security's retirement system, which is covered in Chapter 25.)

The amount of credit a worker needs to become insured depends on the worker's age at the time disability begins:

- Workers becoming disabled before reaching age 24 are insured if they earned six credits under Social Security in the three-year period before the disability begins.
- Workers 24 through 30 years of age are insured if they have worked half the time under Social Security between age 21 and the time they become disabled.
- Workers 31 years old or older are insured if they have worked at least five years under Social Security in the 10-year period ending when they become disabled, and have also worked overall under Social Security for a minimum number of years, depending on their age at the time the disability begins. The following chart shows the years of credit that are needed.

Applying for Benefits

The time limit is very important in applying for benefits, since a delay of more than 12 months may result in loss of past benefits. Special conditions, however, may warrant an extension. Claims for disability benefits may be filed with any Social Security office.

An applicant cannot refuse referral to and assistance from the state vocational rehabilitation agency. Recipients of disability benefits who are participating in an approved vocational rehabilitation program may continue to receive

Persons born after 1929 and becoming disabled at age	Persons born before 1930 and becoming disabled before age 62 in	Years of work needed
42 or younger		5
44		5 1/2
46		6
48		6 1/2
50		7
52		7 1/2
53		7 3/4
54	1983	8
55	1984	8 1/4
56	1985	8 1/2
58	1987	9
60	1989	9 1/2
62 or older	1991 or later	10

benefits in some circumstances even after the disability ceases.

Disability Determination

If a worker applying for disability benefits—referred to by the Social Security Administration as a "claimant"—is insured, the next step is to determine whether the worker is disabled. This determination will be based on a review of the information from doctors, hospitals, clinics, or other institutions that have provided treatment for the worker's condition. The worker may also be asked to undergo additional examinations or tests at government expense in order to determine the severity of the condition. The worker, however, has the burden of showing that he or she is disabled and should therefore submit in support of the claim all the medical information relating to the alleged disabling condition.

Social Security's rules for determining whether a person is disabled are generally more stringent than those of other government and private disability programs. The Social Security Administration therefore does not necessarily find that a person is disabled because he or she was found to be disabled under workers' compensation or any other disability program. To be considered disabled under Social Security law a person must not only be unable to perform past work, but must also be unable to perform any other substantial and gainful work activity that exists in the national economy.

A doctor's opinion that a worker is "disabled" is also not binding on the Social Security Administration. The Social Security Administration will, however, look at the doctor's medical findings concerning the extent to which the person's condition limits the ability to engage in activities necessary for work. It will then determine, on the basis of all the evidence, whether the person is so limited by a severe physical or mental condition that he or she would be unable to engage in any work activity.

Should the medical condition prevent the worker from performing past work, the Social Security Administration will take into account the person's age, education, and work experience as well as the physical or mental limitations imposed by the condition in deciding whether there are any other jobs the person can perform. When insured workers are found to be unable to do their past work or any other work, and the severity of the condition has lasted or can be expected to last for at least 12 months, or result in death, they will be found to be disabled.

Payment of Benefits

Workers applying for disability benefits will receive a written notice from the Social Security Administration advising them whether or not the claim has been approved. If approved, the notice will show the amount of monthly benefits to be received. Benefits, however, do not begin until after the disability has lasted for five months. If the sixth month has passed by the time the claim is approved, the first check could include back payments for up to 12 months.

The amount of disability payments is generally the same as the retirement benefits the worker would receive at age 65—an amount based on the worker's lifetime earnings covered by Social Security.

Payments continue for as long as the person cannot work because of the disability. Most cases are periodically reviewed to verify that the person continues to be eligible for benefits. The worker must notify the Social Security Administration if the condition improves or if he or she returns to work activity.

Effect of Workers' Compensation Benefits

Social Security benefits are offset, but not reduced below zero, by workers' compensation benefits under federal, state, and local government programs. Disability benefits provided under the Veterans Administration and private insurance are not included in determining the offset.

Returning to Work

Workers returning to work in spite of their impairment, continue to receive benefits during a "trial work period" of up to nine months as an incentive for personal rehabilitation efforts. After the nine-month trial work period, benefits will continue for an adjustment period of three additional months for workers able to continue working. However, benefits may be discontinued during the trial work period if medical evidence shows that the disability has ceased. On the other hand, benefits continue for workers whose condition has not improved to the extent that they are able to continue working after a trial work period.

If a previously disabled employee returns to work and subsequently becomes disabled within five years, that employee can receive benefits for another period of disability without serving another five-month waiting period, provided the second disability is expected to last 12 months or more. Only one trial work period is allowed in any period of disability.

Dependent Benefits

Dependent children of a disabled worker are also eligible for benefits. Dependent children include unmarried children under the age of 18 and unmarried children 18 years of age or older who become disabled before age 22 and continue to be disabled. Also eligible for benefits is the worker's spouse who is 62 years old or older, or who cares for a child who is disabled or under age 16.

Survivor Benefits

If a worker dies, his or her dependents may also be entitled to monthly benefits. Additionally, a lump-sum payment of $255 can be made to an eligible surviving widow, widower, or dependent child.

Supplemental Security Income

Another program administered by the Social Security Administration is Supplemental Security Income (SSI). This program makes basic monthly payments to disabled or blind persons and to persons 65 years of age or older who, in either case, have little income and resources (assets). For individuals the resource limit for eligibility for SSI is $2,000 and the income limit is $454 a month. For a couple the resource limit is $3,000 and the income limit is $652 a month. Personal effects or household goods valued at less than $2,000 and a person's home are not counted toward the resource limitation.

SSI is supported by general tax money rather than by money paid into the Social Security fund by workers and employers. A person eligible for SSI, including a disabled child, is not required to have worked to receive SSI.

Disabled workers and persons over age 65 who receive regular Social Security disability or retirement benefits may also be eligible for SSI if their Social Security benefits (which are counted toward the income limitation), together with their other income and resources, do not exceed the limits for eligibility for SSI.

Appeal Procedure

A written notice is sent to a worker each time a determination is made on a Social Security claim. If the worker does not agree with the determination, he or she has the right to appeal. The worker has the right to be represented at any stage of the claim by an attorney or anyone the worker chooses as a representative.

Briefly, there are four steps in the appeal process:

1. Reconsideration of the initial determination;
2. Hearing before an administrative law judge;
3. Appeals Council review; and
4. Federal court action.

Claimants have 60 days from the date they receive a notice at each step of the appeal to proceed to the next stage.

1. *Reconsideration.* A reconsideration, the first step in an appeal, is a review of the claim to determine whether the original determination was correct. Workers have the right to review their files and to submit any additional information that they consider helpful to their claims.

2. *Hearing Before Administrative Law Judge.* If the worker disagrees with the reconsideration determination, he or she may request a hearing before an administrative law judge who is independent of the initial and reconsidered determinations. This hearing is usually held in the same city as the Social Security office that handled the claim. At the hearing the claimant or a representative may question any witnesses, present new evidence, and examine the evidence on which the judge's decision will be based. The judge has the authority to require that vocational or medical experts testify at the hearing concerning the severity of the worker's condition or whether there are any jobs the person can perform despite the physical or mental impairment.

   The worker may request that the judge make a decision without a hearing, in which case the judge will base the decision on the evidence in the file together with any additional evidence or statements that the worker may submit.

3. *Appeals Council Review.* If the worker disagrees with the judge's decision, he or she may request review of the decision by an Appeals Council, located in Washington, D.C. Should the Council decide to review the judge's decision, the worker has the right to file a written statement and to request an appearance to present oral argument. Most reviews, however, are decided on the basis of the written statement and the evidence in the file without oral argument.

4. *Federal Court Action.* If the worker believes that the Council's decision is not correct, or if the Council declines to review the case, the worker may bring suit in a federal district court within 60 days of the date the notice of the Council's decision or denial of review was mailed.

Requests for reconsideration, a hearing, or Appeals Council review must be in writing and filed with any Social Security office by the worker or by a representative. The necessary forms are available in these offices and the staff there will help a worker complete the forms.

Social Security offices, which are listed in the telephone directory, have a wide variety of publications available to workers and the public, explaining all aspects of the Social Security system and its disability and retirement programs.

WORKERS' COMPENSATION DISABILITY BENEFITS

All states have workers' compensation systems that provide replacement income to employees for earnings lost due to job-related accidents or occupational diseases and medical treatment. These programs do not ordinarily provide benefits for injuries that are not job-related. However, five states—California, Hawaii, New Jersey, New York, and Rhode Island—have separate disability programs providing benefits to temporarily disabled workers who do not qualify for workers' compensation (see section on State Temporary Disability Laws below).

No-Fault System

For employees with job-related injuries, and their employers, workers' compensation is a "no-fault" system: An employer pays benefits to the employee for job-connected injuries without regard to who was at fault in causing the injury, while the employee in return forgoes the right to sue the employer. Some states have elective laws that permit employers to reject coverage, but employers who do so may be sued by workers for their injuries. Some states have laws that are part compulsory and part elective. For example, Delaware's law is compulsory for private employers and elective for employees of the state and certain counties, cities, and towns. However, if the worker's injury was caused by a third party—for example, because of a defect in a product or machine made by another company—the employee can collect workers' compensation from the employer and sue the third party separately for causing the injury.

Workers Covered

Workers' compensation may apply to both private and public employment, but no law covers all employees or all types of diseases or disabilities. Practically all industrial employment is covered. In one state, coverage is compulsory only for "hazardous" employment, and some states exempt employers with fewer than a specified number of workers. Agricultural, domestic, and casual workers are also often excluded from compulsory coverage. In most states, exempt employees may be brought in voluntarily by the employer or by administrative order.

Depending on state law, employers required to provide disability compensation may obtain coverage by buying insurance from a private insurance company, by paying into a state-run compensation program, or, if financially able and legally permitted, through self-insurance. In states permitting self-insurance, there are specific requirements to be met. North Dakota and Wyoming do not permit self-insurance arrangements, and Texas permits only state and political subdivisions to self-insure. In New Mexico, Oregon, and Washington, both employers and employees are assessed for workers' compensation costs. Montana employers, whether self-insured or insured with a carrier, also pay an assessment based on their gross payroll. However, in three states—New Jersey, South Carolina, and Texas—employers can elect not to participate in the state's workers' compensation program. If they elect not to participate, they can be sued by their employees for job-related injuries.

Benefits

Workers' compensation benefits attempt to cover most of the workers' economic loss due to injury or occupational disease. They include payments to an injured worker for necessary medical expenses and, in the event of death, benefits, including burial expenses, to the worker's family. Many states also provide special payments, such as a lump sum for disfigurement, rehabilitation services to help the worker obtain new employment, or extra benefits for minors injured while illegally employed.

Types of Disabilities Covered

Medical benefits must be furnished by employers in all states. Many states have established fee schedules, and employers are not liable for charges greater than those scheduled.

The amount of benefits an injured worker receives because of lost work time depends on the type of disability. An employee unable to work at all while recovering from an injury, but expected to recover and return to work, is considered to have a *temporary total disability*. Monetary benefits for this type of disability are usually based on a percentage of the worker's predisability average wages, which in most states is two-thirds of the worker's average weekly wage, but with limits on the minimum and maximum amount that can be received.

An employee unable to work at all, or unable to work regularly in any stable branch of the labor market and not expected to be able to return to work, is considered to have a *permanent total disability*. In most states a worker who is totally disabled receives benefits for life or for the period of disability. However, some states limit the total amount that can be received.

A worker with a permanent impairment that is not totally disabling—one that limits the ability to work to some extent but does not prevent a worker from returning to his or her old job or to another type of employment after recovery—has what is referred to as a *permanent partial disability*. There are in turn two classes of permanent partial disabilities: "scheduled" and "nonscheduled" injuries. A scheduled injury is one that causes the loss of a part of the worker's body, such as an arm, an ear, or a leg. A predetermined schedule lists the payments to be made for a lost body part, with each state maintaining its own payment schedule. Generally, the payment is determined by a formula based on a percentage of average weekly earnings for a specified number of weeks.

Nonscheduled injuries are those of a more general nature, such as injuries to the back or head. In some states nonscheduled permanent partial disabilities are compensated as a percentage of the total disability cases, or scheduled injuries, or on the difference between the worker's wages before the injury and the wages he or she is able to earn afterwards.

Where there is a *total disability*, most states provide payments extending through an employee's lifetime.

Benefits are paid in all states following a *fatal injury*. Coverage includes a burial allowance as well as a proportion of the worker's former weekly wages for the spouse and surviving children. Some laws provide for a maximum total benefit expressed as a maximum period for the payment of benefits.

All states have extended coverage for *occupational diseases*, although the definition of what constitutes an occupational disease varies widely.

Waiting Period

Most state laws require a waiting period of three to seven days following a disabling injury before the payment of benefits for lost work time begins. In almost all states, benefits are retroactively paid to the date of injury if disability continues over an established period of time. There is no waiting period for necessary medical or hospital care.

Claims Procedure

When employees are injured they must notify their employer and file for benefits within a specified period of time. Employers in most states are required to post notices informing their employees of these reporting and filing requirements. The procedure for paying claims after an employer becomes aware of an injury varies from state to state, but generally it begins with the employer reporting the injury to its insurance carrier and to the state's workers' compensation agency. If there is no dispute that the injury was job-related, the carrier usually accepts the claim and begins paying benefits. In many cases this involves paying only for the medical expenses because the injury caused little or no loss of work. However, if the time lost from work exceeds the waiting period, payments for lost work begin and continue until the worker recovers, or, if the injury is permanent, until an assessment can be made of the extent to which the worker is permanently disabled.

Disputes sometimes arise between the employee and the carrier over the payment of claims. When they do, they usually relate to such issues as whether the injury was job-related, the extent of the permanency of the injury, or, if the injury was permanent, whether the worker will eventually be able to return to the old job or to some other employment.

The parties are often able to resolve their dispute through a settlement agreement whereby they compromise their differences, with the worker-claimant releasing the carrier from subsequent liability in return for a monetary award payable in a lump sum or over a period of time. If they are unable to resolve their differences, however, the case is referred to an impartial examiner, referee, or judge (depending on the state procedure) for a hearing and a resolution of the dispute. Medical experts may be called by either or both parties to testify on the extent of the worker's injury, and vocational experts may testify on whether there are jobs available that the worker is capable of performing. All parties are entitled to be represented by lawyers and, if the worker receives a monetary award, state law or regulation determines the fee the worker's lawyer can charge.

Rehabilitation

Most state workers' compensation laws provide for rehabilitation services for injured workers who, although unable to return to their former jobs because of an injury, can obtain other employment with medical care, counseling, guidance, schooling, or training. The federal Vocational Rehabilitation Act also provides funds for federal-state rehabilitation programs operated by a state's vocational rehabilitation department or agency.

Reopening an Award

All states allow awards to be reopened for modification to meet changes in the claimant's condition, such as an increase, decrease, or termination of disability. Some states allow awards to be reopened at any time, while most set a fixed period of time (from 1 to 10 years) for reopening following an award.

Discrimination Under ADA

The Americans With Disabilities Act (ADA) provides that employers may not discriminate against a "qualified individual with a disability." However, not all employees who have been injured on the job are covered by the ADA, since most job-related injuries do not result in impairments sufficiently severe to "substantially limit" a major life activity, a criterion for ADA coverage.

Employers should be aware that an individual considered disabled under a state workers' compensation statute may not be an individual with a disability under the ADA. State workers' compensation laws are designed to assist workers who are injured on the job, while ADA is designed to prevent workplace discrimination on the basis of disability whether work related or not. An employer cannot base an employment decision on the concern that a particular worker may cause increased future workers' compensation costs. The ADA does, however, allow employers to take reasonable steps to avoid increased workers' compensation costs while protecting persons with disabilities against exclusion from jobs they can safely perform.

For further information about the ADA, see Chapter 15.

Other Prohibited Discrimination

The laws of most states specifically provide that it is unlawful for an employer to discharge an employee for filing a workers' compensation claim.

Although employees cannot be discriminated against for filing a claim, they can lawfully be terminated if they are unable to work because of a disability. Hawaii's law, however, provides that an employer cannot suspend or discharge employees because of a work injury unless the employees are no longer capable of performing their work and there is no other suitable work that they are capable of performing.

Employers performing work under a contract with the federal government are required to hire handicapped workers, including persons who have recovered from a disability but who continue to have difficulty finding employment because of their prior disability.

Second Injuries

Some businesses do not hire workers who have been injured in prior employment because of the concern that if the worker is reinjured the employer will be required to compensate the worker for the total disability resulting from both the new and old injuries. To meet this problem, most states have adopted "second" or "subsequent" injury funds. Under these arrangements, if a subsequent injury does occur, the employer has to pay only for the last, or second, injury. The employee, however, is compensated for the disability from the combined injuries with the additional compensation being paid from the state-supported second injury fund.

More information on a state's workers' compensation system can be obtained from a state labor department listed in Appendix A. The U.S. Chamber of Commerce has prepared an "Analysis of Workers' Compensation Laws." Address inquiries about the publication to:

Chamber of Commerce of the United States
1615 H Street, N.W.
Washington, D.C. 20062

STATE TEMPORARY DISABILITY LAWS

California, Hawaii, New Jersey, New York, and Rhode Island have laws providing benefits for workers who are temporarily disabled by injuries or illness unrelated to their employment. Benefits may be paid by a state fund, by a private insurance company, or directly by a self-insured employer, and cover persons who are unable to work because of illness or injury but do not qualify for benefits under workers' compensation or unemployment compensation laws.

New York's temporary disability law is administered in conjunction with the state workers' compensation law; Hawaii's law stands alone; the other states administer their laws as adjuncts to their unemployment compensation laws.

These state laws also vary considerably with respect to financing provisions, level of benefits, types of plan, and amount of employee and employer contributions.

VETERANS' DISABILITY BENEFITS

Service-Connected Injuries

Veterans with a physical or mental disability caused by military service may be eligible for a service-connected pension. Payments are based on a percentage of the disability according to the Veterans Administration's schedule for rating disabilities and are paid to the veteran regardless of any other income the veteran may have.

Nonservice Injuries

Veterans with disabilities that are not service-connected may be eligible for pensions if they are 100-percent disabled regardless of whether their disabilities are related to military service.

Unlike a service-connected disability, however, compensation for a nonservice impairment is an aid payment and is reduced in accordance with a veteran's other income. The veteran must also have served in the military service during specified periods of time and received a discharge under other than dishonorable conditions after 90 or more days of military service.

The Veterans Administration and private organizations such as the Disabled American Veterans can provide more information to veterans applying for benefits.

OTHER DISABILITY BENEFITS

Short- and Long-Term Disability Plans

Many employers voluntarily provide short- and long-term disability insurance plans for their employees. Often such plans coordinate benefits with the disability benefits available under Social Security or worker's compensation benefits.

Black Lung Disability Benefits

The federal Black Lung Benefits Reform Act provides for the payment of monthly cash benefits to coal miners who are totally disabled because of pneumoconiosis ("black lung"). Benefits are payable to the miner's dependent spouse, divorced spouse, children, and to surviving dependents of a miner who dies while disabled because of pneumoconiosis.

To be entitled to black lung benefits, the coal miner must:

- Be totally disabled by pneumoconiosis;
- Have pneumoconiosis as a result of employment in a coal mine; and
- File a timely application for benefits.

A miner is considered disabled if, because of pneumoconiosis, he or she is unable to engage in comparable and gainful work. Comparable and gainful work is work in the miner's immediate area of residence requiring skills and abilities comparable to those of any work in a mine or mines in which the miner previously worked.

Applications for benefits can be made in any Social Security office, which will provide the information needed to establish a disability claim. An applicant whose claim is denied is entitled to a hearing before a U.S. Department of Labor administrative law judge.

Benefits for Law Enforcement Officers

State and local (nonfederal) law enforcement officers who are injured while trying to prevent the commission of a crime against the United States or while apprehending a person who has committed a crime against the United States are eligible for federal disability benefits. Benefits are also payable to the officer's survivors in the event of death.

The benefit amount is generally the difference between the disability compensation received by state and local law enforcement officers and that received by federal officers. The agency to contact for these benefits, or for more information, is:

Office of Workers' Compensation Programs
U.S. Department of Labor
Washington, D.C. 20211

13

EQUAL EMPLOYMENT OPPORTUNITY

Equal employment opportunity (EEO) laws are intended to protect certain classes of persons from discrimination in employment. The federal government, most states, and even many localities have adopted anti-discrimination measures. In some jurisdictions, these laws are referred to as "fair employment practices" or "human relations," but, regardless of what they are called, their purpose is to provide nondiscriminatory equal employment opportunity for the classes of persons identified in the law. For simplicity, they will be referred to here as EEO laws. Some laws protecting EEO rights are relatively new, while others date back more than 100 years. The courts have interpreted the U.S. Constitution's First, Fifth, and Fourteenth Amendments to include EEO protection.

The first state EEO law—in New York in 1945—prohibited discrimination on the basis of a person's race or color. Since then, however, the classes of protected persons have been greatly expanded by lawmakers. Federal EEO laws, for example, now cover, in addition to race and color, religion, sex, nationality, age (40 and older), disabilities, and certain veterans, while some states and localities have expanded the protected classes even further to prohibit discrimination on such grounds as a person's sexual preference or criminal record. The District of Columbia's EEO law identifies 16 classes of persons protected by its law. Under these laws, employers can be liable for discrimination in their job application procedures, for treatment on the job, or for coercive early retirement procedures.

A summary of the types of discrimination prohibited by the states and the District of Columbia appears on pages 128–129.

Federal Laws

A law enacted after the Civil War, the Civil Rights Act of 1866, has been interpreted to allow persons to sue employers in federal court for employment discrimination based on race, ancestry, or ethnic characteristics. But the principal federal employment discrimination law is the 1964 Civil Rights Act.

Title VII of this Act makes it illegal for employers, employment agencies, and unions to discriminate in employment on the basis of a person's race, color, religion, sex, or national origin. The Pregnancy Discrimination Act, which amended Title VII, added pregnancy and its related conditions.

The list of "persons" protected against job discrimination under Title VII is comprehensive—everyone from hourly paid workers to supervisors, managers, professionals, and executives. Coverage is extended to any employer having 15 or more employees in one or more locations.

Other titles of the Civil Rights Act include Title VI, which prohibits discrimination on the basis of race, color, or national origin in programs and activities receiving federal assistance, and Titles IX and XI, which extend procedural rights to victims.

Other Federal EEO Laws and Executive Orders

Other federal EEO law and executive order coverage, discussed in greater detail elsewhere, includes:

- The 1967 Age Discrimination in Employment Act—prohibits discrimination against employees or applicants for employment who are 40 and older.
- The 1972 Vietnam Era Veterans' Readjustment Assistance Act—requires government contractors to

employ disabled veterans and qualified veterans of the Vietnam era.

- The 1973 Vocational Rehabilitation Act—requires employers having contracts with the federal government to employ and promote qualified handicapped persons.
- The Rehabilitation Act of 1973—prohibits discrimination by federal contractors against applicants or employees because they are handicapped.
- The Equal Pay Act of 1963—amends the Fair Labor Standards Act and prohibits discrimination in the payment of wages on the basis of sex.
- The Older Workers Benefit Protection Act—prohibits age discrimination in employee benefits and protects workers who sign waivers of claims under the ADEA.
- Title IX of the Education Amendments of 1972—prohibits sex discrimination by educational institutions receiving federal funds.
- The Immigration Reform and Control Act of 1986—prohibits discrimination on the basis of citizenship or national origin.
- The Americans With Disabilities Act of 1990—prohibits discrimination against qualified persons with disabilities.
- The Civil Rights Act of 1991—provides for compensatory and punitive damages and jury trials in cases of sex, religious, and disability discrimination.
- Presidential Executive Orders, including E.O. 11246—prohibit discrimination on the basis of race, sex, religion, color, and national origin by federal contractors with contracts in excess of $10,000.

Equal Employment Opportunity Commission

Title VII created the Equal Employment Opportunity Commission (EEOC) to investigate complaints of discrimination and to correct violations through conciliation or, if necessary, through court action. It also authorizes private individuals to bring lawsuits if their complaints are not resolved to their satisfaction. Independent contractors, however, are not covered by Title VII.

The EEOC has jurisdiction over all employers with 15 or more workers, labor unions with 15 or more members, employment agencies, apprenticeship committees, and state and local governments. See Appendix C for a list of EEOC offices.

The Age Discrimination in Employment Act is enforced by the EEOC, as are the Americans With Disabilities Act, the Immigration Reform and Control Act (partially), and the Civil Rights Act of 1991. The Veterans' and Vocational Rehabilitation EEO laws are enforced by the Labor Department's Office of Federal Contract Compliance Programs. The procedures of the EEOC are covered in Chapter 16.

Prohibited Discrimination

Under Title VII and other laws there can be no discrimination in recruiting, hiring, firing, or promotions, or in pay or benefits, on the basis of a person's race, color, religion, sex, national origin, or age. This includes—but is not limited to—overtime pay, shift premium, job assignments, training opportunities, advancement, holiday pay, commissions, leaves of absence, and insurance, retirement, and welfare plans.

Benefits paid to an older worker under an insurance, retirement, or welfare plan need not be the same as that paid to a younger worker if the cost incurred on behalf of the older worker is equal to that incurred for the younger worker. However, retirement benefits for men and women must be the same regardless of the cost incurred by the employer.

Title VII does not require employers to hire, promote, or retain workers who are not qualified, and it does not prohibit employers from basing wage differentials for their workers on such objective factors as merit, incentive, or seniority, provided of course that there is no attempt to use these plans to discriminate.

Affirmative Action Program

An employer may voluntarily adopt an affirmative action employment program to increase the number of minorities and women in its work force when a conspicuous imbalance in the employer's work force is shown by the underrepresentation of minorities and women in traditionally segregated job categories.

Employment Selection Procedures

Title VII does not prohibit (as some states do) preemployment inquiries about a person's race, color, national origin, religion, sex, or age. The EEOC, however, frowns on such inquiries on the ground that they may be irrelevant to a person's job qualifications. They may be allowed if the information is really needed to judge an applicant's qualifications. The EEOC recommends that such information, which is necessary for filing EEO reports with the government, be obtained after a person is hired and that the information be kept separate from the individual's other personnel records.

When employers consider persons for employment or advancement, the EEOC requires them to avoid selection procedures that cause women, minorities, or other protected classes to be "screened out." An employer's procedure may be unlawful under Title VII even though the employer does not knowingly discriminate against an individual if its practices have the effect of excluding disproportionately more women or minorities from consideration for employment or advancement.

If an employer, for instance, requires that applicants take tests to determine their job aptitude and more women or minorities fail the test, the test is considered discriminatory. In this circumstance the employer must prove that the test is "job-related," that is, it accurately predicts successful performance in the job for which the test is used. Even then, it may still have to be discontinued if the EEOC or a complaining party can show that there are other procedures

DISCRIMINATION PROHIBITED BY STATE LAW

	Race	Sex	Religion	National Origin	Age[c]	Disability	Equal Pay	Marital Status
Alabama								
Alaska	✓	✓[b]	✓	✓	✓	✓[a]	✓	✓
Arizona	✓	✓	✓	✓	40 to 70	✓	✓	
Arkansas	✓	✓	✓	✓	40 and over[a]	✓	✓	
California	✓	✓	✓	✓	40 and over[a]	✓	✓	✓
Colorado	✓	✓	✓	✓	40 to 70	✓	✓	
Connecticut	✓	✓	✓	✓	✓	✓	✓	✓
Delaware	✓	✓	✓	✓	40 to 70	✓	✓	
District of Columbia	✓	✓[b]	✓	✓	18 to 65	✓		✓
Florida	✓	✓	✓	✓	✓	✓	✓	✓
Georgia	✓[a]	✓[a]	✓[a]	✓[a]	40 to 70	✓	✓	
Hawaii	✓	✓[b]	✓	✓	✓	✓	✓	✓
Idaho	✓	✓	✓	✓	40 and over	✓	✓	
Illinois	✓	✓	✓	✓	40 and over	✓	✓	✓
Indiana	✓	✓	✓	✓	40 to 70	✓	✓	
Iowa	✓	✓[b]	✓	✓	18 and over	✓	✓[a]	✓
Kansas	✓	✓	✓	✓	18 and over	✓	✓	✓
Kentucky	✓	✓[b]	✓	✓	40 to 70	✓	✓	
Louisiana	✓	✓[b]	✓	✓	40 to 70	✓		
Maine	✓	✓[b]	✓	✓	✓	✓	✓	✓[a]
Maryland	✓	✓[b]	✓	✓	✓	✓	✓	✓
Massachusetts	✓	✓[b]	✓	✓	over 40	✓	✓	✓
Michigan	✓	✓[b]	✓	✓	✓	✓	✓	✓
Minnesota	✓	✓[b]	✓	✓	18 and over	✓	✓	✓
Mississippi	✓[a]	✓[a]	✓[a]	✓[a]	✓[a]	✓[a]		
Missouri	✓	✓	✓	✓	40 to 70	✓	✓	
Montana	✓	✓[b]	✓	✓	✓	✓	✓	✓
Nebraska	✓	✓[b]	✓	✓	40 to 70	✓	✓	✓
Nevada	✓	✓[b]	✓	✓	40 and over	✓	✓	
New Hampshire	✓	✓[b]	✓	✓	✓	✓	✓	✓
New Jersey	✓	✓	✓	✓	✓	✓	✓	✓
New Mexico	✓	✓	✓	✓	✓	✓		
New York	✓	✓	✓	✓	18 and over	✓	✓	✓
North Carolina	✓	✓	✓	✓	40 to 70 40 and over[a]	✓		
North Dakota	✓	✓[b]	✓	✓	40 and over	✓	✓	✓
Ohio	✓	✓[b]	✓	✓	40 and over	✓	✓	

DISCRIMINATION PROHIBITED BY STATE LAW—*continued*

	Race	Sex	Religion	National Origin	Age[c]	Disability	Equal Pay	Marital Status
Oklahoma	√	√	√	√	40 and over	√	√	
Oregon	√	√[b]	√	√	18 and over	√	√	√
Pennsylvania	√	√[b]	√	√	40 and over	√	√	
Rhode Island	√	√	√	√	40 to 70	√	√	
South Carolina	√	√[b]	√	√	40 and over	√		
South Dakota	√	√	√	√	40 and over[a]	√	√	
Tennessee	√	√	√	√	40 and over	√	√	
Texas	√	√	√	√	40 and over	√	√[a]	
Utah	√	√[b]	√	√	40 and over	√		
Vermont	√	√	√	√	18 and over	√		
Virginia	√	√[a]	√	√	√[a]	√	√	
Washington	√	√	√	√	40 and over	√	√	√
West Virgina	√	√	√	√	40 and over	√	√	
Wisconsin	√	√[b]	√	√	40 and over	√		√
Wyoming	√	√	√	√	40 to 70	√	√	

[a]Covers public employees only.
[b]Contains provisions prohibiting pregnancy discrimination.
[c]In states where upper and lower age limits are specified, protection generally ends when the upper limit is reached.

that would accomplish the same goal with less discriminatory impact.

Similarly, because educational requirements may disqualify a substantially higher rate of minorities than whites or women than men, it is unlawful for an employer to specify a high school or college education as a job requirement unless it can show that such a requirement is significantly related to successful job performance.

Minimum weight and height requirements may also be unlawful if they screen out women or ethnic groups and the employer is unable to show that the requirement is necessary for the safe and efficient operation of the job in question.

In short, when employers have an employment practice that appears fair on its face but has a discriminatory effect, they must show that the practice is necessary for the safe and efficient operation of the business and that there are no alternative practices that would have a less discriminatory impact.

Bona Fide Occupational Qualification

Title VII provides that an employer can prefer hiring persons of a particular religion, sex, or nationality if the preference is based on a "bona fide occupational qualification" (BFOQ). Religion, for instance, might be a BFOQ for a religious organization; a particular nationality, a BFOQ for an organization promoting the interests of that group; or sex, a BFOQ for acting or modeling positions.

The EEOC and the courts, however, do not favor BFOQs. An employer claiming a BFOQ must therefore clearly prove that religion, sex, or nationality is a genuine basis for preferring certain classes of persons for employment. Race or color can never be a BFOQ.

Arrests and Convictions

A potentially unlawful practice under Title VII is to ask an applicant about any arrests or convictions. Because members of some minority groups are arrested and convicted more often than whites, a personnel decision on the basis of an arrest or conviction record has a disproportionate effect on a job applicant from these groups. Employers therefore cannot disqualify a member of a minority group because of an arrest or conviction unless they can show that there is a direct relationship between an applicant's arrest or conviction and his or her fitness for a particular job.

Twelve states and the District of Columbia have enacted laws prohibiting discrimination against persons with arrest or conviction records. These states include Connecticut, Hawaii, Illinois, Kansas, Michigan, Minnesota, New York, Ohio, South Dakota, Washington, West Virginia, and Wisconsin. Five states—California, Colorado, Illinois, Michigan, and New York—restrict employers from asking job applicants about arrests.

In some circumstances this prohibition can present a conflict under state law where an employer must check the background of persons applying for positions where they will have access to another person's dwelling (see Chapter 6). Conduct leading to a person's arrest, even though it did not result in a conviction, may still demonstrate that the person would not be a safe risk for a job where he or she would have access to another person's home or apartment. The EEOC, as noted, does permit an employer to consider arrests and convictions in determining a person's fitness for certain types of positions.

Race and Color Discrimination

Title VII and Section 1981 of the 1866 Civil Rights Act apply across-the-board to any form of discrimination by employers, including harassment, against an applicant for employment because of race or color. An applicant of a race or color other than white who is qualified must be given the same consideration for the job as any other qualified applicant.

Whites as well as nonwhites are protected by Title VII. Giving preferential treatment to nonwhites, referred to as "reverse discrimination," is unlawful. However, where minorities or women are underrepresented in a particular job classification, it is permissible for an employer voluntarily to take steps to see that more minorities or women are hired to increase their proportionate share of the jobs.

Sex Discrimination

Employer responsibilities under the federal and state laws prohibiting discrimination on the basis of sex are discussed in Chapter 14.

National Origin Discrimination

National origin discrimination is the denial of equal job opportunities to a person because of place of origin, or the origin of the person's ancestors, or because the person has a physical, cultural, or speech characteristic of a national origin group.

An example of national origin discrimination, mentioned before, occurs when a Hispanic or Asian American is denied employment because of a height or weight requirement that is not based on business necessity. Other examples include fluency-in-English requirements and training and education requirements.

National origin discrimination can also occur when an employer allows ethnic slurs to take place in the workplace, or requires that English be spoken at all times in the workplace. It is permissible, however, to require that English be spoken at certain times when such a rule is justified by business necessity.

Because of concerns that the Immigration Reform and Control Act might cause employers to discriminate against "foreign looking" or "foreign sounding" persons, discrimination on the basis of national origin or citizen status is prohibited under that law.

The EEOC requires employers to evaluate hiring criteria for adverse impact and disparate treatment on the basis of national origin.

Religious Discrimination

Denying or limiting job opportunities to individuals or basing leave policies or other employment decisions affecting workers because of their religious practices or beliefs or not making a reasonable effort to accommodate a person's religious beliefs is discrimination based on religion. An employer, however, is required to make reasonable accommodation only to the extent that it does not create an "undue hardship" on the business. A reasonable accommodation does not have to be the least restrictive or the one suggested by the employee.

A religious school or institution may legally require that the people it hires be members of its religion. It cannot, however, discriminate on the basis of race, color, sex, disability, nationality, or age.

Age Discrimination

Under the federal Age Discrimination in Employment Act and most state laws, it is unlawful for an employer to discriminate against persons 40 years of age or older in hiring, firing, pay, promotions, fringe benefits, and other aspects of employment. It does not prohibit discrimination against persons under age 40. (However, some state laws prohibit discrimination against persons in other age groups. See the chart on pages 128–129.) The federal law applies to all employers with 20 or more employees and unions with 25 or more members.

Several groups of employees are partially exempt, such as high-level managers, public safety personnel, uniformed military personnel, and tenured college professors.

Examples of age discrimination include:

- Indicating an age preference in help-wanted advertisements (such as using the term "under 40," or descriptive words such as "young," "boy," or "girl").
- Classifying workers in such a way that their employment opportunities would be adversely affected because of their age.
- Requiring a person to retire solely because of his or her age. Recent protections have been added so that workers may not waive any rights to protection under age discrimination laws when accepting early retirement offers unless the waiver is knowing, voluntary, and noncoercive.

An employer may base employment consideration on a person's age when age is a reasonably necessary requirement for the normal operation of the business (e.g., hiring an actor for a youthful role).

Employers must offer workers 65 years of age or older the same health insurance coverage offered to young workers. Although a person still becomes eligible for Medicare at age 65, anyone who continues to work at that age has the option of either accepting at no extra cost any health insurance coverage provided by the employer or electing to receive Medicare.

Disability Discrimination

There are three federal laws that prohibit discrimination against individuals with disabilities—the 1973 Rehabilitation Act, the Americans With Disabilities Act, and the Vietnam Era Veterans' Readjustment Assistance Act. They are discussed fully in Chapter 15.

Vietnam-Era Veteran Discrimination

The 1972 Vietnam Era Veterans' Readjustment Assistance Act requires employers with federal contracts of $10,000 or more to take affirmative action to hire disabled veterans and qualified veterans of the Vietnam era. They must also list their job openings with the Job Service, which gives Vietnam-era veterans referral priority to such jobs. This law is enforced by the Office of Federal Contract Compliance Programs.

Federal Contractors

Federal government contractors and subcontractors are also subject to EEO provisions under Title VII and two major executive orders, which specify that contractors doing more than $10,000 a year in business are prohibited from discrimination on the basis of race, color, religion, sex, national origin, or age. Contractors doing business of $50,000 or more must develop affirmative action plans and take positive steps to eliminate discrimination within their organization.

Under the Vietnam Era Veterans' Readjustment Assistance Act, veterans are entitled to the same affirmative action rights. These same affirmative action requirements were extended to include individuals with disabilities under the Rehabilitation Act of 1973. Federal contractors also must make reasonable accommodations to the disabilities of an employee or applicant as long as these accommodations do not create an undue business hardship.

14

SEX DISCRIMINATION

Although in the past more charges of racial discrimination have been filed than any other kind, a greater variety of issues arise in cases involving alleged sex discrimination. The types of problems the EEOC and the courts have had to resolve have related to job advertising, preemployment inquiries, stereotyping men and women as to the kinds of jobs they should or should not do, sexual harassment, equal pay, comparable worth pay, pension benefits, and maternity leave.

Job Advertising, Stereotyping, and Preemployment Inquiries

Preemployment inquiries or job advertisements that indicate a preference or limitation on the basis of a person's sex are unlawful unless the preference or limitation is a bona fide occupational qualification.

It is also unlawful to hire or promote men or women on the assumption that one sex is better than the other at performing certain types of work, or to label jobs as "men's jobs" or "women's jobs," unless, again, it can be demonstrated that sex is in fact a bona fide occupational qualification.

Unless the job in question is clearly one for which only one sex can qualify (e.g., an acting role calling for a man or woman), each applicant—man or woman—must be considered individually as to his or her ability to perform the work actually required. Neither men nor women are to be

135

arbitrarily stereotyped as to the types of jobs they can or should perform, regardless of whether one sex has traditionally performed certain types of work. In some situations a bona fide occupational qualification has been found to exist where employers have claimed that privacy, security, or health care concerns require hiring persons of a specific sex. The EEOC, moreover, does not consider state laws that prohibit or limit the employment of women in certain occupations to be a defense to an otherwise established discriminatory practice.

A job application may ask whether the applicant is a male or female or a "Mr., Mrs., Miss, or Ms.," provided that the inquiry is made in good faith for a nondiscriminatory reason.

A personnel policy that restricts the employment of married women but not married men is considered unlawful. For this reason the EEOC considers preemployment inquiries on marital status or the number or ages of an applicant's children to be an indication of discrimination against women. When such information is necessary, as it often is for insurance, reporting, or other business purposes, the EEOC suggests that it be obtained after the person is hired.

Under circumstances where nonpregnancy could be reasonably necessary to a job, it could be a bona fide occupational qualification. Similarly, workplace hazards as a basis for excluding or restricting pregnant or fertile employees from working in certain positions have been upheld by the courts. The EEOC requires that any policy be justified by objective, scientific evidence and that the employer prove that there are not less discriminatory means of protecting fertility or fetal health.

Sexual Harassment

Sexual harassment covers any "unwelcome" sexual advance, request for sexual favors, or other verbal, physical, or hostile conduct that is gender-based and directed at an employee by an employer or by its supervisors or agents. It also includes sexually charged workplace behavior that is offensive on the basis of gender to persons who are not necessarily the targets of the conduct.

Such conduct is unlawful if submission is a condition of employment and is used as a basis for making employment decisions affecting the employee. Such conduct is also unlawful if it has the effect of unreasonably interfering with the employee's work performance, or creates an abusive, intimidating, hostile, or offensive work atmosphere. Furthermore, unwelcome sexual behavior that creates a hostile working environment is unlawful even where there is no tangible or economic loss to the victim. The fact that the victim's participation was voluntary is not a defense.

An employer may be responsible for the sexual harassment of an employee by fellow workers, or even by nonemployees, if it knew or should have known about the conduct and failed to take appropriate corrective action. An employer is liable for the acts of its supervisors where submission is used as a basis for employment decisions. In cases where hostile environment has been found, the employer may be liable if it knew about the conduct, the victim had an opportunity to complain, and the employer did not take appropriate action after becoming aware of the unlawful conduct.

An employer can be held liable for the discharge by a manager or supervisor of a sexually harassed person and may also be held accountable for an employee's "constructive discharge," that is, the employee is effectively forced to quit because the sexual harassment was so severe that a reasonable person would quit rather than endure it.

Almost every state has a fair employment law similar to the federal Title VII in prohibiting sexual harassment. Unlike Title VII, however, many state laws cover employers with fewer than 15 employees. State laws may require employees to go to state agencies before they go to court, and some states provide for punitive as well as compensatory damages.

Sexual Orientation

In general, Title VII's ban on sex bias does not prohibit employment discrimination on the basis of sexual orientation. However, some state laws, such as that of the District of Columbia, do prohibit discrimination based on sexual orientation.

Dress Codes

An employer may establish a dress code that imposes different standards for the sexes, unless it reflects a demeaning sexual stereotype or it foreseeably encourages sexual harassment. Employment policies concerning gender-based differences in personal appearance that reflect social custom generally do not constitute sex discrimination.

Equal Pay and Fringe Benefits

Title VII prohibits discrimination between men and women with regard to their pay and fringe benefits, including pensions. In the past, many states adopted laws regarding working conditions and benefits intended to protect women from the hazards of industrial life. Such laws are now viewed as restricting job opportunities of women and have been found to conflict with Title VII. Employers providing retirement benefits to their workers must pay equal benefits to male and female retired workers even though the cost to the employer of funding the program may be greater for one sex than the other.

A separate law, the Equal Pay Act, which was enacted a year before Title VII as an amendment to the Fair Labor Standards Act, also makes it unlawful to pay wages to members of one sex at a lower rate than that paid to members of the other sex for equal work in jobs that require equal skills, effort, and responsibilities under similar working conditions. Exceptions for differentials are allowed for wages paid under a seniority or merit system, an incentive system based on quantity or quality of production, or any factor other than sex. The Act extends to the same employees as covered by the Fair Labor Standards Act. It also covers executive, administrative, and professional employees, and all state and local government employees. The EEOC now enforces the Equal Pay Act. Almost all of the states have adopted equal pay laws, modeled after the federal law.

Comparable Worth

Although some men and women perform the same work for which they receive the same pay, for various reasons men and women also continue to be employed in different jobs, with the jobs held mainly by women tending to pay less than the jobs held primarily by men. When the difference in pay for these jobs is based on the different work being performed (i.e., different skills, effort, and responsibility), there is no unlawful discrimination.

Under a theory called "comparable worth," employees of one sex performing one type of job would be allowed to establish a Title VII sex discrimination violation by comparing their wages to wages paid other workers of a different sex performing dissimilar jobs and by showing that their work has the same value or worth to the employer as that performed by the other group. In other words, under the comparable worth theory, jobs that are equal in value ought to be equally compensated.

There is, however, no universal standard at present for measuring the relative worth of jobs. The comparable worth theory therefore has not been generally adopted yet as a basis for establishing a Title VII violation.

Pregnancy and Maternity Leave

A woman cannot be discriminated against in employment-related matters on the basis of pregnancy, childbirth, or related medical conditions.

- A worker cannot be denied a job, or promotion, solely because she is pregnant. She must be judged on the basis of her ability or inability to work.
- A pregnant worker cannot be required to go on leave if she is able to do her job.
- Health insurance to cover expenses for pregnancy-related conditions must be provided to a pregnant employee if the employer provides health insurance

to cover expenses for other medical conditions. Employers must also provide insurance for the non-working wives of their male employees if they provide it for their female workers. However, they do not have to provide health insurance for an abortion except when the life of the mother would be endangered if the child were carried to full term. Health insurance must cover medical complications that arise from an abortion.

- If a pregnant worker requests maternity leave, she is entitled to it on the same basis that leave is granted to employees for other temporary disabilities. Her job must be held open on the same basis as jobs are held open for employees on leave for other disabilities, unless she has stated that she does not intend to return to work.

- After the child's birth, the employee has the right to return to her job when she is able to perform it if other employees who have been absent because of a temporary disability are also allowed to return to work. She cannot be prohibited from returning for any arbitrary predetermined period following childbirth. On her return she is entitled to fringe benefits and seniority on the same basis as other employees returning from leave for other disabilities.

For a fuller discussion of family and medical leave, see Chapter 9.

15

DISABILITY DISCRIMINATION

Until 1990, the federal laws prohibiting discrimination against individuals with disabilities were the 1973 Rehabilitation Act, which applies to federal contractors and programs and activities receiving federal funds, and the Vietnam Era Veterans' Readjustment Assistance Act of 1974, which applies to Vietnam-era veterans with disabilities. The federal coverage of employers was greatly broadened in 1990 with the enactment of the Americans With Disabilities Act (ADA).

As of July 26, 1994, ADA applies to all employers with 15 or more employees, including state and local government agencies. In addition, the majority of states prohibit disability discrimination as part of their broad fair employment practice laws or by separate disability laws. Under both federal laws, employers are prohibited from discriminating against qualified applicants and employees with disabilities, and are required to provide reasonable accommodation for such individuals unless doing so would cause an undue hardship.

What Is a Disability

The ADA defines a person with a disability as someone who has "a physical or mental impairment which substantially limits one or more of such person's major life activities, a record of such impairment, or who is regarded as having such an impairment." This has been interpreted to mean an individual who is likely to experience difficulty in securing, retaining, or advancing in employment because of a disability. A person may be considered disabled, even though recovered from a previous physically or mentally disabling impairment (such as a heart attack or cancer), if he or she has difficulty in getting a job because of the prior disability.

It is not the name of the condition that determines whether it is a covered disability, but the effect the condition has on a person's life activities. The ADA does not define "impairment," but the EEOC, which enforces the ADA, uses the same definition it uses under the Rehabilitation Act: A disability that substantially limits one or more of such person's major life activities. Certain conditions are specifically excluded, such as kleptomania, homosexuality, bisexuality, and pyromania. Also, the law protects workers who have a relationship with a person with a disability. The EEOC therefore holds that an employer, for instance, cannot refuse to hire the spouse or companion of an individual with AIDS.

Hiring Process and Testing

Employers may not ask job applicants health or disability questions or require preemployment medical examinations. The law also prohibits preemployment questions about the nature and extent of the person's disability, even for an obvious impairment. However, applicants can be asked about their ability to perform job-related functions, and a job offer can be made conditional on the results of a subsequent physical exam.

Once a tentative offer of employment is made, the employer may then ask health questions and require a medical examination, as long as all tentatively hired employees are treated the same and the resulting information is kept confidential. A more complete discussion of testing under ADA is found in Chapter 4.

Physical or medical exams, medical questions, and medical history questions may be given to current employees only as part of a wellness program or other employee health program.

Who Is a Qualified Individual

A qualified person is someone who can, with or without reasonable accommodation, perform the essential functions of a job. A job description, though not required under the law, can be considered in determining what constitutes an essential job function.

A person who poses a direct threat to the health or safety of others is not considered qualified. For example, a person with an infectious disease that can be transmitted through food would not be considered qualified to be a food handler, even if able to perform the essential functions of the job.

Reasonable Accommodation

An accommodation in a work setting is the adjustment needed for a person to perform the essential functions of a job. In the absence of the ADA, an employer does not ordinarily have to accommodate applicants unable to perform the functions of the job the applicant seeks. However, when the person has a physical or mental impairment that limits that person's ability to perform the job's functions, but who could do the job if given some accommodation, the ADA requires employers to accommodate such person to the extent the accommodation is "reasonable." The test in determining whether an accommodation is reasonable—and therefore one that an employer would be required to provide—is whether it would impose an "undue hardship" on the employer, with cost being a major part of this test. What might be considered a reasonable accommodation for a large employer, might be found to be an undue hardship on a smaller employer just because of the cost involved. However, a disabled person denied a job because of the cost of the accommodation may provide the needed accommodation.

Disabled job applicants requiring accommodation must inform the employer either during the job interview or after being offered employment. If an employer provides an accommodation, it does not necessarily have to be the one the applicant prefers.

Factors that determine whether a proposed accommodation creates an undue hardship include:

- Nature and cost of accommodation;
- Size, type, and financial resources of the covered employer;
- Size, type, and financial resources of the specific facility where the accommodation would have to be made; and
- Type of operation, including the composition, structure, and functions of the business and the geographic separateness and administrative or fiscal relationship between the specific facility and the covered employer.

Reasonable accommodation might include changing work schedules, redesigning training programs, reassigning an employee to another job, or making facilities accessible. If the accommodation would change the nature of the goods or services offered, however, it would not be reasonable.

Because of the law's lack of clear guidelines, making a reasonable accommodation may require guessing on the part of an employer. Changing work schedules or making them more flexible or reassigning job duties may be a reasonable accommodation for a disabled worker, but may conflict with the legitimate concerns of other employees. These conflicts, for instance, may impinge on the seniority rights of other workers for purposes of work scheduling, shift preference, and work assignments.

Employee Rights Under the Act

Employees with disabilities must be allowed the same workplace opportunities as other workers, such as attending training sessions and having access to break rooms and cafeterias. They are not, however, entitled to any special treatment, apart from any special accommodation required to allow them to perform their jobs or any reasonable physical modifications to the facility that may be needed to provide them with such things as access to buildings, rest rooms, or machinery.

Drug Addicts and Alcoholics

The ADA does not affect the rights employers have to test for illegal drugs or to prohibit use of drugs and alcohol in the workplace. Current illegal drug users are not protected by the ADA, but rehabilitated former drug users, those participating in a supervised rehabilitation program, or those erroneously regarded as drug users, are covered by the ADA.

Alcoholics are also covered under the ADA, provided they are qualified, meet the same performance standards as other employees, and can safely perform the job.

AIDS

Persons with AIDS are likewise covered under the ADA, as are persons who associate or live with someone with AIDS. Employers therefore have the same legal duty to provide a reasonable accommodation to persons with AIDS as they do to other disabled workers covered by the ADA.

Employees with AIDS are also protected under the Rehabilitation Act of 1973, even if they do not manifest symptoms of the disease, so long as they are not a direct threat to the health and safety of others.

Employee Benefit Plans

Employers must provide disabled workers with the same fringe benefits as other employees. A company pension plan, health insurance, disability benefits, life insurance, sick leave, and other benefits must apply equally to disabled and nondisabled employees. Employers are also prohibited from changing the availability or type of fringe benefits because of a disability of a member of an employee's family.

The ADA does not require an employer to extend a full range of benefits to all employees. The ADA requires only that any fringe benefits the employer provides must be offered equally to all employees, disabled or not. For example, the ADA permits employee health insurance coverage that excludes preexisting conditions (medical conditions that arise before the employee is hired), as well as policies that exclude certain types of claims, such as psychological counseling or alcoholism.

Employees with disabilities do not have to be provided with extra medical coverage. However, a person with a disability that does not pose increased risks cannot be denied coverage or be subjected to different terms or conditions of coverage based on the disability alone, unless the employer provides an actuarial basis for the differential treatment.

Workers' Compensation

An employer cannot make a preemployment inquiry about an applicant's workers' compensation history. It also cannot deny an applicant with a prior workers' compensation claim a job on the grounds that another injury may put it at an increased risk for a large workers' compensation claim. Increased costs of workers' compensation, health insurance, or other types of disability insurance cannot be used to discriminate against a disabled applicant or employee.

Physical Facilities

Current work sites do not have to be modified to make them accessible to disabled employees unless it is a reasonable accommodation for a specific disabled employee or group of employees and then only if it does not create an undue hardship for the employer. However, all "commercial facilities" that are renovated or newly built are subject to stricter physical accessibility requirements than existed in the past.

Affirmative Action

There are no affirmative action requirements under the ADA. The Rehabilitation Act, on the other hand, requires federal contractors with contracts of more than $10,000 to take affirmative action to hire persons with disabilities. Federal departments and agencies, and federal contractors with 50 or more employees and contracts of $50,000 or more, are required to prepare written affirmative action plans. No goals or quotas are required under the Rehabilitation Act.

The Vietnam Era Veterans' Readjustment Assistance Act also has affirmative action requirements for federal contractors with contracts of more than $10,000 to employ and advance qualified special disabled veterans and veterans of the Vietnam era.

Religious Organizations

Religious organizations may give preference to individuals of their particular religion, even if this results in denying a job to a disabled person.

State Laws

All states protect disabled employees or applicants from discrimination under their fair employment laws, and give them the same protection as other protected groups. Some states have included AIDS specifically as a protected disability.

States declaring AIDS to be a protected disability include Arizona, Connecticut, Florida, Illinois, Iowa, Maine, Massachusetts, Michigan, Minnesota, Missouri, New Jersey, New Mexico, New York, Oregon, Washington, and Wisconsin. It is considered a covered handicap by state fair employment practice agencies under existing antidiscrimination laws in Delaware, Maryland, New Hampshire, and Pennsylvania. In Rhode Island, discrimination in employment against HIV-infected individuals and those perceived to be infected is prohibited by law. In Idaho, workplace discrimination against the handicapped is barred, although AIDS is not mentioned by name. Virginia and North Carolina protect state workers, and Vermont prohibits employment discrimination on the basis of a positive HIV test result.

Alabama and Mississippi extend this protected disability status to public employees only.

Affirmative action toward individuals with disabilities generally is required only of state contractors and/or state agencies. These programs usually provide for accommodation for the disabled in job placement, rehabilitation, training, and promotion.

16

EEOC PROCEDURE

The procedure for a person claiming to be aggrieved by an alleged discriminatory act, called an "unfair employment practice," is to file a charge first with a state or local EEO agency (if there is one) before filing with the EEOC. Sixty days later he or she can file a charge with the EEOC. (A sample of the EEOC charge form appears later in this chapter.) As a practical matter, the EEOC will often refer such a charge to the state or local agency and then, after 60 days, if the charge is not resolved, proceed with its own investigation. The addresses of state EEO agencies are listed in Appendix C.

An individual filing a charge with a state or local agency has 300 days from the date of the occurrence of the alleged discriminatory act to file the charge with the EEOC, or must file within 30 days after receiving notice from the state or local agency that it is terminating the proceeding. If there is no state or local agency, the charge must be filed with the EEOC within 180 days of the occurrence of the alleged discriminatory act.

After a charge is filed with the EEOC, the EEOC must serve a notice of the charge on the employer within 10 days. The employer is asked to come to the EEOC office for a "fact-finding" conference to discuss the allegations in the charge. At the conference, conducted by an EEOC agent, both the individual and the employer are given the opportunity to state their views, with the EEOC agent exploring with both parties the possibilities of a settlement. Many charges are settled at this stage of the proceeding.

If no settlement is forthcoming, the EEOC proceeds with its investigation to determine whether there is reasonable cause to believe that discrimination has occurred and must make its determination as promptly as possible, and if practicable within 120 days.

If it finds no reasonable cause, the EEOC must dismiss the charge; if it finds reasonable cause, it will attempt to conciliate.

If the EEOC is unable to secure an acceptable conciliation agreement within 30 days, it may bring a civil action in federal court. If the EEOC does not bring an action within 180 days, it will give the complaining party a "right-to-sue" letter, giving that person 90 days to file suit in federal court.

Court Action

The right-to-sue letter gives the individual the right to take his or her case to court. If the individual decides to sue, a complaint must be filed in federal court within 90 days after receipt of the letter. The EEOC may also bring court action, but actually does so in relatively few cases.

When a suit is filed the burden is on the individual, as the plaintiff, to prove that he or she was discriminated against. In most cases this burden is referred to as establishing a "prima facie" case. When the issue concerns a rejection for a job, for example, the individual's prima facie case would be established by presenting evidence showing that he or she:

- Was a member of a class of persons protected by Title VII;
- Applied for a vacant job for which he or she was qualified; and
- Was rejected for the position.

In addition the applicant must show that after he or she was rejected, the employer continued to seek other applicants for the job.

The burden then shifts to the employer to present evidence showing that the individual was rejected for a legitimate nondiscriminatory reason. The individual is then given the opportunity to present evidence showing that the reason given by the employer was "pretextual," and that the underlying reason was discriminatory.

Remedies

Should the individual win, the court will usually order that the individual be given the job in question with back pay for any wages, bonuses, vacation pay, and benefits that would have been earned but for the discrimination. Reasonable attorney's fees are also usually awarded in the court's discretion to the prevailing party. Courts do not ordinarily require complainants to pay attorney's fees if they lose. However, there have been occasions where courts have required such individuals and their attorneys to pay attorney's fees to the employer when the basis for the complaint was frivolous. Reinstatement, hiring preferences, or promotion, where appropriate, may be awarded.

Individuals also may be entitled to "front" or future pay, a remedy designed to compensate a person when it is not immediately possible to hire, reinstate, or promote the person to the position he or she would have had if the discrimination had not occurred.

Retaliation

Under Title VII employers are prohibited from retaliating against any employee, union member, or applicant for employment or union membership who has opposed an unlawful employment practice, filed a charge, or participated in an EEOC investigation.

Affirmative Action, Quotas, and Reverse Discrimination

Title VII is intended to prohibit discrimination against members of a protected group; it is not intended to establish a preference for those persons. It is, therefore, ordinarily as unlawful to discriminate against, say, a white male (commonly referred to as "reverse discrimination") as it is to

EEOC-5, CHARGE OF DISCRIMINATION

CHARGE OF DISCRIMINATION	AGENCY	CHARGE NUMBER
This form is affected by the Privacy Act of 1974; See Privacy Act Statement before completing this form.	☐ FEPA ☐ EEOC	

_____ and EEOC
State or local Agency, if any

NAME *(Indicate Mr., Ms., Mrs.)*	HOME TELEPHONE *(Include Area Code)*

STREET ADDRESS	CITY, STATE AND ZIP CODE	DATE OF BIRTH

NAMED IS THE EMPLOYER, LABOR ORGANIZATION, EMPLOYMENT AGENCY APPRENTICESHIP COMMITTEE, STATE OR LOCAL GOVERNMENT AGENCY WHO DISCRIMINATED AGAINST ME *(If more than one list below.)*

NAME	NUMBER OF EMPLOYEES, MEMBERS	TELEPHONE *(Include Area Code)*

STREET ADDRESS	CITY, STATE AND ZIP CODE	COUNTY

NAME	TELEPHONE NUMBER *(Include Area Code)*

STREET ADDRESS	CITY, STATE AND ZIP CODE	COUNTY

CAUSE OF DISCRIMINATION BASED ON *(Check appropriate box(es))*

☐ RACE ☐ COLOR ☐ SEX ☐ RELIGION ☐ NATIONAL ORIGIN
☐ RETALIATION ☐ AGE ☐ DISABILITY ☐ OTHER *(Specify)*

DATE DISCRIMINATION TOOK PLACE
EARLIEST   LATEST

☐ CONTINUING ACTION

THE PARTICULARS ARE *(If additional space is needed, attach extra sheet(s)):*

☐ I want this charge filed with both the EEOC and the State or local Agency, if any. I will advise the agencies if I change my address or telephone number and cooperate fully with them in the processing of my charge in accordance with their procedures.

I declare under penalty of perjury that the foregoing is true and correct.

NOTARY - *(When necessary for State and Local Requirements)*

I swear or affirm that I have read the above charge and that it is true to the best of my knowledge, information and belief.

SIGNATURE OF COMPLAINANT

SUBSCRIBED AND SWORN TO BEFORE ME THIS DATE
(Day, month, and year)

Date   Charging Party *(Signature)*

EEOC FORM 5 (Rev. 06/82)

discriminate against a woman or a black. However, when there is a past history of discrimination against women or blacks, an employer may be ordered to establish an "affirmative action" program which gives preference to the recruitment, hiring, and promotion of blacks or women. In some circumstances, courts have also ordered employers to establish job quotas that are reasonable and necessary to correct past discriminatory practices.

An employer doing business with the federal government is required under Executive Order 11246, as a condition of obtaining a government contract, to develop an affirmative action program to employ women and blacks when they have been "underutilized" in the past.

Reports, Recordkeeping, and Notices

The EEOC requires covered employers to keep and preserve records, to file reports, and to post notices to make employees aware of their rights. These records are used to determine whether the employer has discriminated in employment on the basis of race, sex, age, disability, or other prohibited factor. Charts describing these requirements appear in Appendix D.

More information about Title VII is available from local EEOC offices listed in Appendix C. The address for the EEOC's national offices is:

Equal Employment Opportunity Commission
2401 E Street, N.W.
Washington, D.C. 20506

For information about the EEO requirements for federal government contractors, contact:

Office of Federal Contract Compliance Programs
Employment Standards Administration
U.S. Department of Labor
Washington, D.C. 20210

17

UNIONS

A labor union is an organization that serves as a bargaining agent for workers by representing them in negotiations with their employer concerning their wages, benefits, hours of work, and other terms and conditions of employment.

Unions are based on the concept that employees as individuals often lack the power to negotiate effectively with their employer on a one-to-one basis but can strengthen their bargaining position by working together through collective action. The right of employees to have a union represent them in collective bargaining with their employer is protected by the National Labor Relations Act.

Workers who want a bargaining agent to represent them can select an already established union, form one themselves, or even designate an individual instead of a union as their representative.

An organization can become a union and act as a bargaining agent even though it lacks a formal structure. An employee committee, for example, can be considered a union and serve as a bargaining representative if it exists, at least in part, for purposes of representing workers in negotiations and is not organized or dominated by the employer.

The area of employment law that involves unions and collective bargaining is called labor relations, a subject covered in later chapters. This chapter and the one following it deal with a union as an organization and the rights of employees as members of a union.

Local Unions

The basic union organization is the local union or lodge that represents workers in a particular area, plant, office, or other business facility. A local union, of which there are about 41,000 in the nation, can be completely independent of other unions or can be one of a number of other local unions that make up a national or international union. An international union is a national union with members in another country, usually Canada. Overall, unions represent approximately 17 percent of American workers who collectively are sometimes referred to as "organized labor."

Local union officials, such as the president and secretary-treasurer, are elected by the union's members and, except for the larger locals, usually continue working at their regular employment while holding office, performing their official union duties on a part-time basis. Collective bargaining agreements frequently permit workers to take leave to attend to necessary union matters. Generally, two factors are considered: the nature of the business and the anticipated duration of the leave. Some locals employ full-time business agents to handle the union's day-to-day activities and assist with contract negotiations. Virtually all local unions have stewards, who are workers elected or appointed to act as the union's unpaid agents in helping other workers represented by the union with any grievance they may have with their employer. A grievance in a union setting is a complaint by the employee that the employer is failing to follow some provision in the contract it has with the union.

Unions generally require new members to pay an initiation fee and sometimes may impose special assessments on their members, but their principal means of financial support are the dues paid by union members.

Reporting Requirements

As noted before, a union can be created to represent workers in collective bargaining without having any formal

structure. However, once it becomes a bargaining representative it must adopt a constitution and bylaws that must
be filed with the U.S. Department of Labor, together with
annual reports covering such matters as the names and
titles of its officers, their salaries and expense reimburse-
ments; any loans it makes to union officers, members,
employees, or business enterprises; its dues, fees, fines,
and assessments; assets, liabilities, disbursements, and
receipts; and its policies regarding qualification for membership, electing officers, calling meetings, disciplining
members, ratifying contracts, and authorizing strikes. It
also must comply with the requirements covered in the next
chapter regarding the rights of its members.

International Unions

A local union becomes affiliated with a national or international union by receiving a charter from the international
union. Delegates elected by members of the local unions
affiliated with the international select the international's
officers.

The international's constitution spells out the duties
and powers of its officials, the rights and duties of its members, the procedures for the conduct of union business,
and, generally, what local unions can and cannot do. It may,
for example, require that the local obtain the international's
consent before signing a contract with an employer or before
calling a strike. If the local fails to comply with the international's policies, the international may place the local under
a "trusteeship" and temporarily take over the local's operations.

The international, in turn, provides various services to
its locals, which often include the payment of benefits to
local union members during an authorized strike. The international also employs field representatives who assist local
unions in such matters as bargaining, arbitration of grievances, and organizing nonunion workers through efforts to
persuade them to select the union as their bargaining agent.
The international's activities are financed by per capita dues
paid by its local unions.

Some international unions engage in direct negotiations with employers, usually for national or industrywide agreements. Such contracts may cover multiplant operations of one or more employers.

AFL-CIO

Most national and international unions in the United States—but not all—are members of the American Federation of Labor-Congress of Industrial Organizations (AFL-CIO), which was formed in 1955 by the merger of the then separate AFL and CIO. Prior to that time unions affiliated with the AFL were historically those that represented workers with specialized skills or crafts, such as electricians, carpenters, and plumbers, while unions affiliated with the CIO, such as the Steelworkers and Auto Workers unions, organized and represented all workers in a plant or industry regardless of whether they were skilled or unskilled. AFL unions today are still often referred to as "craft" unions, while CIO unions are referred to as "industrial" unions.

The AFL-CIO's activities, like that of many business associations, include promoting laws that it favors and providing various services for its members. Its leaders are selected by delegates from its affiliated national and international unions, which also pay per capita dues to the AFL-CIO to support its activities.

In all states and in the larger cities, unions affiliated with the AFL-CIO belong to central labor councils that coordinate their efforts on legislative issues and other matters that concern them on the state and local level.

Union Jurisdiction

A union's constitution also defines its "jurisdiction," that is, the types of workers it principally organizes and represents. This does not, however, restrict either an AFL or CIO union—or any other union—on the types of workers it can actually represent in most circumstances. A union has the right to organize and represent almost any appropriate grouping of workers, whether in a manufacturing plant or an office, and may lawfully attempt to displace another union as the employees' bargaining agent. An attempt by an "outside" union to take over a group of employees represented by another union is referred to as "raiding," a practice many unions oppose. The AFL-CIO has encouraged its members to participate in no-raid agreements.

Appropriate Unit

One of the functions of the National Labor Relations Board (NLRB) is to determine whether a grouping of workers is appropriate for collective bargaining. For purposes of allowing a union to serve as a bargaining agent, the NLRB requires not only that the union be willing to represent the employees in the appropriate group, but also that it demonstrate, usually through an NLRB-conducted secret election, that a majority of the workers want it as their representative.

Although unions generally have the right to represent any appropriate group of workers, there are a few circumstances in which a union's representation rights are limited. These include:

- *Plant guards.* The NLRB will not permit a union to represent plant guards if it represents other types of workers.
- *Supervisors.* Because supervisors are considered part of management, they do not have the protection of other workers if they form or join unions.
- *Confidential employees.* Confidential employees, who are workers having access to an employer's labor relations information, can join a rank-and-file union, but cannot be included in a bargaining unit with other employees.
- *Craft severance.* Among other NLRB requirements, a union wanting to represent a group of skilled craft workers who are already represented by another union in a larger industrial group must have had experience representing that type of worker before being allowed to carve out the craft workers from the larger group.

- *Jurisdictional work disputes.* When two or more unions at a construction project where a number of craft unions are working become involved in a dispute as to which union or group of workers is to perform a certain type of work, the NLRB will consider (among other factors) which of the contending unions has traditionally performed such work in determining which union-represented group of workers should do the disputed work.

18

RIGHTS OF UNION MEMBERS

A union's affairs are extensively regulated by federal law. A union is prohibited by civil rights legislation from discriminating against its members or the employees it represents because of their race, color, religion, sex, national origin, disability, or age. A union's workplace activities in organizing and representing workers are subject to the NLRB's scrutiny. And as an organization its internal affairs regarding its relations with its members must conform to the requirements of the federal Labor Management Reporting and Disclosure Act (LMRDA), also referred to as the Landrum-Griffin Act.

One provision of the LMRDA, mentioned briefly in the last chapter, requires unions to file copies of their constitutions, bylaws, and annual reports with the Labor Department. Anyone can examine these documents, which are maintained by the Labor Department's Labor Management Services Administration (LMSA). Furthermore, a union must make these reports available to its members for examination and, for just cause, allow them to examine any books, records, or accounts that may be necessary to verify the union's reports. Under the LMRDA, a union member is anyone who has fulfilled the requirements prescribed by the union for membership.

Every employee, whether a union member or not, is also entitled on request to receive from a local union a copy of a collective bargaining agreement the local made that directly affects that person's rights as an employee. The

160

employee is also entitled to examine at the local union's office any contract that the international has entered into that affects the employee.

Union members, however, do not have the right to ratify or reject agreements negotiated by their union unless given that right by the union's constitution or bylaws.

Other provisions of the LMRDA cover:

- Procedures for electing union officers;
- Responsibilities of union officers;
- Procedures for removing officials from office;
- Safeguards for the rights of union members; and
- Limitations on trusteeships.

Responsibilities of Union Officials

All union members in good standing are eligible to hold union office, subject to reasonable qualifications that the union uniformly applies to all its members. However, the LMRDA prohibits any person convicted of specified crimes from serving as a union officer or a labor relations consultant for a period of 3 to 13 years after conviction or imprisonment. Every officer or agent of a union that has property and annual receipts exceeding $5,000 must be bonded.

Officers are required to:

- Use the union's money and property solely for the benefit of the union and its members;
- Manage, invest, and disburse union funds only as authorized by the union; and
- Refrain from any financial or personal activities that conflict with their positions as union officers.

A union member who believes that an officer is violating his or her duties can request that the union take action against the official. If the union refuses, the member can bring suit if, in the court's opinion, the individual has shown a reasonable basis for the suit.

FINANCIAL SUPPORT FOR POLITICAL CANDIDATES

The federal Corrupt Practices Act prohibits unions from using the dues money paid by their members to support the election of a person for political office. They may, however, ask their members to voluntarily contribute to an individual's election campaign, provided they advise their members that they do not have to make a contribution. The money that unions receive as a contribution must be kept separate from the dues money paid by their members.

Employers are also prohibited from requiring their employees to contribute to the support of a political candidate.

Electing Union Officials

Officers of a national or international union must be elected at least once every five years; officers of a local union must be elected at least once every three years. Unions may also hold elections at more frequent intervals.

The LMRDA requires that elections be conducted according to the procedures provided by the union's constitution. These procedures must in turn conform to the following federal standards:

- Secret ballots must be used in local union elections and to elect delegates who will nominate or elect officers of the parent national or international union.
- All union members have the right to nominate candidates for union office, vote for officers, and express their views on the candidates.
- Every member in good standing has the right to be a candidate and to hold office, subject to uniform and reasonable qualifications established by the union.
- Members must be given at least a 15-day notice by mail of the election.
- All candidates must be allowed to have an observer at each location where ballots are counted.
- Candidates must be allowed reasonable opportunities to distribute campaign material.
- Candidates must be allowed to examine the union's list of its members and their addresses.
- Union funds received from dues or assessments, or employer contributions, cannot be used to support any candidate.

- Election records must be preserved for at least one year after the election.

A union member who believes that any of these election procedures has been violated and that his or her complaint to the union about the matter has not been resolved can file a complaint with the Labor Department, which will investigate to determine whether or not a violation has occurred. If it believes that there has been a violation, it will file suit to have the election set aside and a new election held.

Removing Union Officials

Most union constitutions and bylaws of the local union provide for the removal of an official who engages in serious misconduct. Any member who believes that the union's procedure for removing an officer is inadequate can complain to the Labor Department, which will determine whether or not the procedure is adequate. Should the Labor Department determine after a hearing that the officer is removable, a secret ballot will be held to allow the members to decide whether the officer should be removed.

Other Rights of Union Members

Other protections for union members provided by the LMRDA include:

Equal Rights. All members in good standing have the right to attend and participate in membership meetings, nominate candidates for union office, and vote in elections or referenda, subject to reasonable rules and regulations set forth in the union's constitution and bylaws.

Freedom of Speech and Assembly. Union members have the right to meet with other members to exchange views, arguments, and opinions, and to express at union meetings their views on candidates for union office. A union, however, has the right to adopt and enforce reasonable rules defining the responsibilities of union members, including rules relating to conduct that would interfere with the union's right to carry out its proper duties.

Dues, Fees, and Assessments. A local union may increase its dues and fees and impose assessments only by:

- A majority vote by secret ballot of the members in good standing at a special or regular meeting, after reasonable notice of the proposal has been given; or
- A majority of the members in good standing voting for the raise in a secret ballot membership referendum.

A national or international union may raise dues or fees or impose assessments only by:

- A majority of the delegates voting at a regular convention, or at a special convention for which affiliated local unions have received a 30-day advance notice; or
- A majority vote of the members voting in a secret ballot membership referendum; or
- A majority of the members of the organization's executive board voting for the raise if the board has such authority under the union's constitution and bylaws. This action, however, is effective only until the union's next regular convention.

Right to Sue. A union member has the general right to bring a suit or an administrative action against the union or its officers. A member, however, is first required to pursue reasonable hearing procedures provided by the union to try to resolve the matter before taking legal action.

Discipline. A union has the right to fine, discipline, suspend, or expel members for violation of its rules, but, except for the nonpayment of dues, it must first serve the members with a written list of the specific charges against them, allow a reasonable time for them to prepare a defense, and provide a fair hearing on the charges.

A union, however, cannot fine, suspend, expel, or otherwise discipline members for exercising their rights under the LMRDA. A member whose rights have been violated can file suit in a federal district court. It is also a criminal offense for any person to use force or violence against, or threaten, a member for purposes of interfering with the exercise of his or her rights.

Trusteeships

A trusteeship is any method of supervision or control of a local labor union by its parent national or international union that causes the local to lose the autonomy that it ordinarily is entitled to under its constitution and bylaws.

A parent union may place one of its locals under a trusteeship, but only in accordance with its constitution and bylaws, and only for the following purposes:

- To correct corruption or financial malpractice;
- To assure the performance of a collective bargaining agreement;
- To restore democratic procedures; or
- To otherwise carry out the legitimate objectives of the union.

The parent union is prohibited from transferring to itself the funds of the trusteed local union, except for the per capita fees and assessments the local normally pays to the parent. It also is prohibited from counting the votes of delegates of a trusteed union in a convention of the parent body unless the delegates have been selected by secret ballot in an election in which all members in good standing of the trusteed union were eligible to vote. The parent must also file periodic reports on its trusteeship with the Labor Department. A trusteeship is presumed valid for not more than 18 months.

A union member believing that any of these trusteeship provisions are being violated by the parent union may file a complaint with the Labor Department. If, after an investigation, the Labor Department believes there is a violation, it may bring suit against the parent.

A member of the trusteed local union also has the right to sue the parent union unless the Labor Department has already done so.

For more information about the rights of union members under the Labor Management Reporting and Disclosure Act, write to:

Office of Labor Management Standards
U.S. Department of Labor
Washington, D.C. 20210

19

UNIONS AND PROTECTED EMPLOYEE ACTIVITY

The Labor Department has the general responsibility under the LMRDA for protecting the rights of workers as members of a union. The National Labor Relations Board (NLRB), an agency independent of the Labor Department, has the responsibility under the National Labor Relations Act (NLRA) for protecting the rights of union members in the workplace. It also has the responsibility for protecting certain rights of nonunion employees.

Under the NLRA workers have the right to engage in union and other lawful activity for purposes of seeking changes or improvements in their wages, benefits, hours of work, or working conditions. Action by one or more employees seeking such changes through a union is usually protected by the NLRB. But for such action by nonunion employees to be protected, the activity must be "concerted"—that is, it must involve two or more workers.

The activity in which employees can and cannot engage, and what an employer can and cannot do in response, depends on the level and type of employee activity.

First Level: Action by One Employee

An employee in a nonunion facility may act on his or her own behalf, as many do, to seek a pay raise, better benefits, or an adjustment in working conditions. As a general rule, action by an individual worker relating only to his or her pay or working conditions, although lawful, is not protected by the NLRB. Employers may consider an employee's request and make a change or improvement, or they may lawfully refuse to consider the request and, indeed, since the action is not ordinarily protected, may even penalize the employee for the action.

Second Level: Concerted Activity by Two or More Employees

When two or more workers act together in a nonunion facility through a complaint, proposal, suggestion, request, or demand that the employer make a change or improvement in pay, benefits, or working conditions, or for their mutual aid and protection, their activity is considered concerted. When the concerted activity of two or more employees is for a lawful purpose (that is, an activity protected by the NLRA), the workers are protected against retaliation from their employer. The activity of one employee also may be considered concerted if the employee acts on the authority of other workers and not solely on his or her own behalf.

Two or more employees also have the right, even in the absence of a union, to engage in a strike—which is a form of protected concerted activity—to back up their lawful request or demand. Workers engaging in a lawful peaceful strike cannot be fired. Their employer, on the other hand, is not required to consider the employees' request or demand (unless they represent a majority of the workers, as discussed below) and it can temporarily replace any employees who strike with other workers or hire permanent replacements for them.

As an alternative, the employer lawfully may discuss the matter with the employees or negotiate with them, or respond by making a change or improvement. The employer also may do nothing, and, in the following situation, it is in effect required by law to do nothing: If a union is currently engaged in trying to organize the workers, an employer cannot make any improvement in pay, benefits, or working conditions that it would not have made in the absence of union activity. Such action in the face of union activity is considered unlawful interference with the employees' protected right to decide whether they want a union to represent them.

Third Level: Activity by a Majority of the Employees

When a majority of the employees in a grouping of employees that the NLRB would find appropriate for bargaining participates in lawful concerted activity, they have the protection outlined above. In addition, if they select a union as their representative to do the bargaining for them, or form their own independent organization for this purpose, their employer is required to engage in formal negotiations with the bargaining agent they select. The usual procedure for selecting a bargaining agent is a secret ballot election conducted by the NLRB. See Chapter 21 for an explanation of appropriate bargaining units and the procedure for a secret ballot election.

When a union or an employee organization, or even an individual, becomes the employees' lawful bargaining agent as a result of a free choice of a majority of the workers in an appropriate bargaining group, it becomes the *exclusive* representative for all workers in the group it represents. The employer must thereafter deal *only* with the bargaining agent and no one else concerning any matter relating to the pay, benefits, hours of work, or working conditions of all the employees in the group. It cannot deal separately with any of the represented employees concerning any of these matters. The representative is the exclusive spokesperson for all the employees in the group for these purposes for as long as it remains their bargaining agent.

The represented employees are likewise required to channel their concerted activity on pay, benefits, and working conditions through their designated representative, but they retain the right to decide whether they want to continue to have a bargaining representative or to change representatives. There are, however, limitations on the times and ways in which this right can be exercised, as covered in Chapter 24.

LABOR RELATIONS LAWS

The National Labor Relations Act, enacted into law in 1935, gave workers the right to join unions and engage in collective bargaining. Also called the Wagner Act, it created the NLRB. Section 7 of the Act spelled out the rights of workers to join and participate in union activities, and Section 8 prohibited employers from engaging in unfair labor practices that interfered with the workers' Section 7 rights.

Twelve years later the Act was amended by the Labor Management Relations Act, which was referred to at the time as the Taft-Hartley Act. Section 7 was amended to provide that workers had the right to refrain from union activities as well as to engage in them, and Section 8 was amended to prohibit unions from engaging in unfair labor practices.

In 1959 Congress enacted another significant amendment to the Act with the Labor Management Reporting and Disclosure Act. This amendment, called the Landrum-Griffin Act, prohibited unions from engaging in certain forms of picketing and established a code of conduct for unions for the protection of their members.

The National Labor Relations Act applies to most private businesses, but not to railroads and airlines. The labor relations activities of these industries are governed by the Railway Labor Act, which became law in 1926. This Act created a National Mediation Board to conduct elections to determine whether or not workers want union representation and to mediate disputes that arise during contract negotiations. The National Railroad Adjustment Board provides procedures for settling disputes in the railroad industry arising out of grievances or the application of contracts.

In 1974, Congress passed an amendment extending NLRA coverage to private nonprofit hospitals and nursing homes. The NLRB already had asserted jurisdiction over proprietary hospitals and nursing homes by decision.

Unprotected Activities

Not all concerted activity is protected. Employees, whether union represented or not, lose the law's protection and may be disciplined, including being discharged, when the object of their activity is unlawful, or when they are insubordinate or disloyal, engage in violence or destruction of company property, or participate in an unlawful strike.

20

UNFAIR LABOR PRACTICES

The NLRB, as indicated in Chapter 19, protects the right of employees to engage in concerted activities for their mutual aid or protection and to form, join, or assist unions. It also protects the right of workers to refrain from any of these activities.

A violation of any of these rights by an employer or a union is called an "unfair labor practice." There are many ways in which employers and unions can commit an unfair labor practice. The following are just a few examples of each type.

Employer Unfair Labor Practices

- Discharging an employee for engaging in lawful concerted activities;
- Threatening workers with loss of jobs or benefits if they engage in concerted activities or join or vote for a union;
- Threatening to close the plant if the employees join a union;
- Questioning workers about their union activities;
- Spying on union meetings or even pretending to spy;
- Granting deliberate wage increases to discourage employees from joining or voting for a union;
- Taking an active part in organizing a union;
- Refusing to reinstate a qualified worker because the worker took part in a lawful strike;

- Refusing to reinstate an employee because the employee testified at an NLRB hearing;
- Refusing to bargain, or bargaining in bad faith, with an organization or union lawfully selected by a majority of the employees as their bargaining agent; or
- Announcing a wage increase without consulting the union lawfully selected by the employees.

Union Unfair Labor Practices

- Threatening employees that they will lose their jobs unless they support the union;
- Mass picketing that physically prevents nonstriking workers from entering the plant;
- Acts of violence committed either on the picket line or in connection with a strike;
- Entering into a contract with an employer to be the employees' bargaining agent when the union has not been selected by a majority of the workers;
- Entering into a contract with an employer that requires it to hire only members of the union or employees "satisfactory" to the union;
- Insisting on illegal provisions in a contract, such as a closed shop or a hiring hall that discriminates against nonunion workers;
- Picketing an employer to force it to stop doing business with another employer that has refused to recognize the union; or
- Asking workers not to work on equipment manufactured either by a nonunion company or by a company that has employees represented by another union.

NLRB Procedure

The process for determining whether or not an unfair labor practice has been committed starts with the filing of a charge with the appropriate regional office of the NLRB by a person believing that an employer or a union engaged in unlawful activity. (Samples of NLRB forms appear on pages 173–174.) The charge, which must be filed within

FORM NLRB-501
(11-88)

FORM EXEMPT UNDER 44 U S C 3512

UNITED STATES OF AMERICA
NATIONAL LABOR RELATIONS BOARD
CHARGE AGAINST EMPLOYER

DO NOT WRITE IN THIS SPACE	
Case	Date Filed

INSTRUCTIONS:
File an original and 4 copies of this charge with NLRB Regional Director for the region in which the alleged unfair labor practice occurred or is occurring.

1. EMPLOYER AGAINST WHOM CHARGE IS BROUGHT

a. Name of Employer		b. Number of workers employed
c. Address *(street, city, state, ZIP code)*	d. Employer Representative	e. Telephone No.
f. Type of Establishment *(factory, mine, wholesaler, etc.)*	g. Identify principal product or service	

h. The above-named employer has engaged in and is engaging in unfair labor practices within the meaning of section 8(a), subsections (1) and *(list subsections)* _____ of the National Labor Relations Act, and these unfair labor practices are unfair practices affecting commerce within the meaning of the Act

2. Basis of the Charge *(set forth a clear and concise statement of the facts constituting the alleged unfair labor practices)*

By the above and other acts, the above-named employer has interfered with, restrained, and coerced employees in the exercise of the rights guaranteed in Section 7 of the Act

3. Full name of party filing charge *(if labor organization, give full name, including local name and number)*

4a. Address *(street and number, city, state, and ZIP code)*	4b. Telephone No.

5. Full name of national or international labor organization of which it is an affiliate or constituent unit *(to be filled in when charge is filed by a labor organization)*

6. DECLARATION

I declare that I have read the above charge and that the statements are true to the best of my knowledge and belief.

By _____   _____
    (signature of representative or person making charge)   *(title if any)*

Address _____   _____
                    (Telephone No.)   *(date)*

WILLFUL FALSE STATEMENTS ON THIS CHARGE CAN BE PUNISHED BY FINE AND IMPRISONMENT (U. S. CODE, TITLE 18, SECTION 1001)

FORM NLRB 508
(6-90)

FORM EXEMPT UNDER 44 U S C 3512

UNITED STATES OF AMERICA

NATIONAL LABOR RELATIONS BOARD

CHARGE AGAINST LABOR ORGANIZATION
OR ITS AGENTS

DO NOT WRITE IN THIS SPACE	
Case	Date Filed

INSTRUCTIONS: File an original and 4 copies of this charge and an additional copy for each organization, each local, and each individual named in item 1 with the NLRB Regional Director of the region in which the alleged unfair labor practice occurred or is occurring.

1. LABOR ORGANIZATION OR ITS AGENTS AGAINST WHICH CHARGE IS BROUGHT

a. Name

b Union Representative to contact

c. Telephone No

d Address *(street, city, state and ZIP code)*

e. The above-named organization(s) or its agents has (have) engaged in and is (are) engaging in unfair labor practices within the meaning of section 8(b). subsection(s) *(list subsections)* _____ of the National Labor Relations Act, and these unfair labor practices are unfair practices affecting commerce within the meaning of the Act.

2. Basis of the Charge *(set forth a clear and concise statement of the facts constituting the alleged unfair labor practices)*

3. Name of Employer

4. Telephone No.

5. Location of plant involved *(street, city, state and ZIP code)*

6. Employer representative to contact

7. Type of establishment *(factory, mine, wholesaler, etc.)*

8. Identify principal product or service

9 Number of workers employed

10. Full name of party filing charge

11 Address of party filing charge *(street, city, state and ZIP code)*

12. Telephone No.

13. DECLARATION

I declare that I have read the above charge and that the statements therein are true to the best of my knowledge and belief.

By _____

(signature of representative or person making charge)

(title or office, if any)

Address _____

(Telephone No.)   *(date)*

WILLFUL FALSE STATEMENTS ON THIS CHARGE CAN BE PUNISHED BY FINE AND IMPRISONMENT (U. S. CODE, TITLE 18, SECTION 1001)

six months of the occurrence of the alleged unfair labor practice, can be filed by an employee, an employer, a union, or any other person. The NLRB, unlike some agencies that have the power to initiate action on their own motion, cannot file an unfair labor practice charge.

After a charge is filed, an NLRB representative will investigate the basis for the alleged unlawful activity, interview witnesses, and collect other relevant information. If the NLRB determines that the charge lacks merit, the charge will be dismissed. If, on the other hand, it finds merit, it will try to work out a settlement with the company or the union. Many charges are settled, but when the parties cannot settle the matter, the NLRB's general counsel issues a formal complaint against the alleged offending party—the company or the union as the case may be—and schedules a formal hearing on the complaint before an administrative law judge. The NLRB presents the case for the charging party at the hearing. The company or the union has the right to defend itself by presenting evidence in support of its side of the matter.

After the hearing, the judge issues a written decision stating whether or not an unfair labor practice was committed. Should the judge find a violation, he or she will order the company or the union to take appropriate corrective action, such as posting a notice where it can be seen by all employees advising them that the offending party will not engage in such unlawful activity in the future. In addition, if an employee was unlawfully discharged, the judge will order that the worker be reinstated to his or her job.

A party objecting to the judge's decision can appeal to the NLRB in Washington, D.C., which then issues its own decision in the matter after reviewing the record and the judge's decision. Any party to the proceeding objecting to the NLRB's ruling can appeal to a federal appeals court.

Although unfair labor practices occur most often in the context of a union organizing campaign—covered in Chapter 21—they can, and do, occur on occasion even where a union has long been established as a bargaining representative.

The locations of the NLRB offices where charges can be filed are contained in Appendix B. The NLRB's address in Washington, D.C., is:

National Labor Relations Board
1099 14th St., N.W.
Washington, D.C. 20570

21

SELECTING A BARGAINING AGENT

Union Organizing Campaigns

Although employees have the right to form their own union, workers who elect to have a bargaining representative usually select a local union affiliated with an established national or international union. This comes about in most instances as a result of an organizing campaign conducted by the union in which it persuades a majority of the workers in an appropriate group to vote for it as their representative in an NLRB-conducted election.

An employer, however, whose employees are the target of a union's organizing effort has the right prior to the election to try to persuade workers to vote for "no union," which is one of the choices presented to them on the NLRB election ballot. Both the employer and union, for that matter, have the right to resort to various forms of communications—speeches, letters, posters, pamphlets, handouts, meetings, and so on—to get their respective messages across to the workers. The ground rules for employer and union campaigning are set by the NLRB. Threats, bribes, and unlawful promises are not only clearly off limits, but also are unfair labor practices. Even conduct that is less than an unfair labor practice may be serious enough to interfere with the employees' free choice and may cause the NLRB to void the election and conduct a new one.

177

The list of what employers, employees, and unions can and cannot do during the campaign is extensive. To cite a few examples:

- A union can visit workers at their homes; employers generally cannot.
- An employer can call workers together on company time for a speech on its views on the union; the employer does not generally have to allow a union access to company property.
- Employees can campaign for or against a union during nonwork time (e.g., during breaks) and can distribute campaign material in nonwork areas.
- Either an employer or a union can throw a party to have an opportunity to present its views to the workers, provided the refreshments are not conditioned on how the employees vote.

Authorization Cards

An essential part of the union's organizing activities is to persuade employees to demonstrate their interest in the union by signing a petition or a membership or "checkoff" card authorizing the union to ask for an election. (See the example on the following page.) The NLRB will not conduct an election unless the union can show that at least 30 percent of the workers in the group want an election or support the union. A petition signed by the workers can be used for this purpose, but a union will generally ask employees to sign and date individual preprinted "authorization cards."

Petition for an Election

After the union obtains the required worker support, it can file a formal petition with the NLRB asking it to conduct an election. (See the following page for a sample petition.) A petition can also be filed by the employees or even by the employer if the union asks it for recognition as the employees' bargaining representative. Unlike a union- or employee-filed petition, an employer petition does not have to be supported by employee signatures.

EXAMPLE OF A UNION AUTHORIZATION CARD

```
                                    City _____

                                    Date _____

    I, the undersigned, presently employed by _____

    _____, do hereby designate Local Union No. _____,

    _____, of the International Union of Bricklayers &
    Allied Craftsmen, affiliated with the AFL-CIO, as my collective
    bargaining representative in all matters pertaining to labor conditions,
    wages and hours of employment, and

        (If not yet a member), I do hereby apply for membership in B.A.C.
    Local Union No. _____, _____, affiliated with the above
    International Union and agree to abide by all the provisions of the
    Constitution and By-Laws of said Local and the International Union.

                        Signature _____

    Social Security No. _____    Date of Birth _____

    Address _____    City _____    State ____

    Telephone:_____                  Zipcode _____
```

An employer may also lawfully recognize a union without an election if the union proves that it is supported by a majority of the workers. An employer may even be ordered by the NLRB to bargain with the union without an election if the employer engages in serious and widespread unfair practices that prevent the employees from making a free choice in deciding whether they want a union. In the absence of such unlawful conduct, however, an employer can insist that the union win an NLRB election before accepting it as the employees' representative.

NLRB Jurisdiction

When the NLRB receives a petition, it first determines whether it has the authority (jurisdiction) to handle the matter. It cannot conduct an election—or handle an unfair labor practice charge—unless the employer's business affects or can affect interstate commerce. There are, however, few businesses that do not affect commerce in some way. A radio station with listeners in another state, for example, is considered to affect commerce. Similarly, an

NLRB-502, PETITION

FORM NLRB 502 (5-85)			FORM LAFAR EUNDTH 11/7/11, 1/21
UNITED STATES GOVERNMENT		**DO NOT WRITE IN THIS SPACE**	
NATIONAL LABOR RELATIONS BOARD		Case No	Date Filed
PETITION			

INSTRUCTIONS: Submit an original and 4 copies of this Petition to the NLRB Regional Office in the Region in which the employer concerned is located. If more space is required for any one item, attach additional sheets, numbering item accordingly.

The Petitioner alleges that the following circumstances exist and requests that the National Labor Relations Board proceed under its proper authority pursuant to Section 9 of the National Labor Relations Act.

1. PURPOSE OF THIS PETITION *(If box RC, RM, or RD is checked and a charge under Section 8(b)(7) of the Act has been filed involving the Employer named herein, the statement following the description of the type of petition shall not be deemed made.)* **(Check One)**

☐ **RC-CERTIFICATION OF REPRESENTATIVE** - A substantial number of employees wish to be represented for purposes of collective bargaining by Petitioner and Petitioner desires to be certified as representative of the employees

☐ **RM-REPRESENTATION (EMPLOYER PETITION)** - One or more individuals or labor organizations have presented a claim to Petitioner to be recognized as the representative of employees of Petitioner

☐ **RD-DECERTIFICATION** - A substantial number of employees assert that the certified or currently recognized bargaining representative is no longer their representative.

☐ **UD-WITHDRAWAL OF UNION SHOP AUTHORITY** - Thirty percent (30%) or more of employees in a bargaining unit covered by an agreement between their employer and a labor organization desire that such authority be rescinded

☐ **UC-UNIT CLARIFICATION** - A labor organization is currently recognized by Employer, but Petitioner seeks clarification of placement of certain employees *(Check one)* ☐ In unit not previously certified ☐ In unit previously certified in Case No

☐ **AC-AMENDMENT OF CERTIFICATION** - Petitioner seeks amendment of certification issued in Case No.
Attach statement describing the specific amendment sought.

2. Name of Employer	Employer Representative to contact	Telephone Number

3. Address(es) of Establishment(s) involved *(Street and number, city, State, ZIP code)*

4a. Type of Establishment *(Factory, mine, wholesaler, etc.)*	4b. Identify principal product or service

5. Unit Involved *(In UC petition, describe **present** bargaining unit and attach description of proposed clarification.)*	6a. Number of Employees in Unit
Included	Present
	Proposed *(By UC/AC)*
Excluded	6b. Is this petition supported by 30% or more of the employees in the unit?* ___ Yes ___ No *Not applicable in RM, UC, and AC

(If you have checked box RC in 1 above, check and complete EITHER item 7a or 7b, whichever is applicable)

7a. ☐ Request for recognition as Bargaining Representative was made on *(Date)* _____ and Employer declined recognition on or about *(Date)* _____ *(If no reply received, so state)*.

7b. ☐ Petitioner is currently recognized as Bargaining Representative and desires certification under the Act

8. Name of Recognized or Certified Bargaining Agent *(If none, so state)*	Affiliation
Address and Telephone Number	Date of Recognition or Certification

9. Expiration Date of Current Contract, if any *(Month, Day, Year)*	10. If you have checked box UD in 1 above, show here the date of execution of agreement granting union shop *(Month, Day, and Year)*

11a. Is there now a strike or picketing at the Employer's establishment(s) Involved? Yes ___ No ___	11b. If so, approximately how many employees are participating?

11c. The Employer has been picketed by or on behalf of *(Insert Name)* _____ a labor organization, of *(Insert Address)* _____ Since *(Month, Day, Year)*

12. Organizations or individuals other than Petitioner *(and other than those named in items 8 and 11c)*, which have claimed recognition as representatives and other organizations and individuals known to have a representative interest in any employees in unit described in item 5 above *(if none, so state)*

Name	Affiliation	Address	Date of Claim *(Required only if Petition is filed by Employer)*

I declare that I have read the above petition and that the statements are true to the best of my knowledge and belief.

_____
(Name of Petitioner and Affiliation, if any)

By _____
(Signature of Representative or person filing petition)   *(Title, if any)*

Address _____
(Street and number, city, State, and ZIP Code)   *(Telephone Number)*

WILLFUL FALSE STATEMENTS ON THIS PETITION CAN BE PUNISHED BY FINE AND IMPRISONMENT (U. S. CODE, TITLE 18, SECTION 1001)

employer affects commerce if it sells goods to another company in the same state that sells outside the state.

The NLRB's legal jurisdiction is therefore extensive and potentially covers most businesses. It has, however, limited the cases it handles by adopting monetary jurisdictional standards. Under these standards a company must do at least the following amount of business each year for its type of operation before the NLRB will conduct an election or handle an unfair labor practice involving that company:

Nonretail operation. Sells $50,000 each year to consumers in other states; or purchases $50,000 each year from suppliers in other states.

Office building. Has an annual income of $100,000, of which at least $25,000 is paid by other organizations that meet any of the nonretail standards.

Retail. Has an annual volume of business of $500,000.

Public utility. Has an annual volume of business of $250,000.

Newspaper. Has an annual volume of business of $200,000.

Hotel or motel. Has an annual volume of business of $500,000.

Radio, telegraph, television, or telephone. Has a total annual volume of business of $100,000.

Taxicab. Has an annual volume of business of $500,000.

Transit. Has an annual volume of business of $250,000.

Transportation enterprise. Has an annual volume of business of $500,000 from furnishing interstate transportation services.

Private health care institutions. $250,000 annual volume of business for hospitals; $100,000 for nursing homes, visiting nurses' associations, and related facilities; and $250,000 for all other types of private health care institutions.

College, university, or secondary school. Has a total annual revenue of $1 million.

Day care center. Has a total annual revenue of $250,000.

Entertainment or amusement. Same as retail.

Law firm. Has a total annual revenue of $250,000.

Printing, publishing, or newspaper. Has an annual volume of business of $200,000.

Interstate commerce. Has an annual volume of business of $50,000.

Nonprofit organization. Same standard as for-profit.

The NLRB will also assert plenary jurisdiction over employers located in the District of Columbia, and employers who have a substantial impact on the national defense. Other types of businesses may also fall under the NLRB's jurisdiction even though they do not fall into one of the above categories. The NLRB has no jurisdiction over federal, state, or local governments.

Appropriate Bargaining Unit

The employee group in which an election is requested must be "appropriate" for collective bargaining before the NLRB will conduct an election. In labor law terminology, an appropriate group is called a "bargaining unit." Generally speaking, an appropriate unit for bargaining is a group of two or more employees having the same or substantially the same interests in wages, hours of work, supervision, and working conditions, such as a grouping of production and maintenance workers, office employees, or craft workers. All employees sharing a "community of interest" must be included in the unit. Unless it conforms to this requirement, it is not "appropriate" for bargaining, and the NLRB, which determines whether a unit is appropriate or not, will not conduct an election.

Certain individuals are not considered "employees" for purposes of determining an appropriate unit and are therefore excluded from bargaining units. These individuals include agricultural workers, independent contractors, managerial employees, and supervisors. A supervisor is an individual having the authority to hire, fire, or responsibly direct the work of other employees, or having the power to make effective recommendations on hiring, firing, transfers, discipline, or promotions. Confidential employees, who are employees having access to an employer's labor relations information, are also excluded. Plant guards are excluded from units with other workers but may form their own bargaining unit. Professional employees can be in the same unit with nonprofessional employees only if a majority votes for inclusion.

Election Agreement

When the employer and the union can agree on the time and place for the election and the employees eligible to vote, they usually sign an NLRB consent election agreement. If they cannot agree, the NLRB will conduct a hearing and, in a written decision resolving the disputed issues, will either dismiss the petition, if it finds there are reasons why an election cannot be held, or direct that an election be held at a time and place it sets.

Voter Eligibility

Only employees employed in the bargaining unit during the payroll period preceding the date on which the election was directed or on which an election agreement was signed are eligible to vote. But the following are also eligible if they show up to vote:

- Employees in the military service;
- Employees who are ill, on vacation, or temporarily laid off;
- Economic strikers (those striking over wages or working conditions) who are engaged in a strike that began within the past 12 months;
- Employees hired as permanent replacements for economic strikers;
- Regular part-time employees; and

- Temporary and seasonal employees, who have no firm termination date, and if employed at the time of voting.

Election Notice

Employers must post in conspicuous places in their operation NLRB-provided posters that notify the employees of the election, show them a sample ballot, and inform them of their rights. They must also turn over to the NLRB a list of the names and addresses of the eligible voters, which the NLRB in turn gives to the union.

The Election

The election, conducted under the NLRB's strict supervision, is ordinarily held in the employer's operation. As each employee enters the voting area, he or she is given a ballot by the NLRB agent, which the employee marks in the privacy of an NLRB-provided voting booth and deposits in a sealed ballot box. An employee does not have to tell anyone how he or she voted.

Both the employer and the union are entitled to have nonsupervisory workers present as observers at the election to see that only eligible employees vote. An individual whose right to vote is challenged by an observer may still vote, but his or her ballot will not be counted unless it can affect the election outcome. The NLRB determines whether the challenged individual's vote should be counted.

Neither the employer nor the union is allowed to do any election campaigning in the voting area.

After the balloting is completed, the NLRB agent and the observers open the ballot box, count the ballots, and note the results on a tally sheet.

Objections to the Election

Either the employer or the union—depending on which one loses—can object to the preelection conduct of the other party by filing objections within five days of the election alleging that the conduct of the other party unfairly interfered with the employees' free choice. The NLRB will investigate. If it finds merit in the objections, it will order a new election, but if it finds no merit it will do one of two things:

1. Certify the results of the election, if the union received 50 percent or less of the votes (which means the union lost); or
2. Certify the union as the employees' bargaining agent, if it received a majority of the votes.

Whether the union wins or loses, another election cannot be held involving the same unit of employees for at least 12 months. If the union wins, the next step is for the parties to enter into collective bargaining.

The NLRB will, on request, provide information on its election procedures. Union organizing and election campaigns are covered more comprehensively in *Organizing and the Law* and NLRB rules and procedures in *How To Take a Case Before the NLRB.* Both are available from:

BNA Books
Customer Relations
P.O. Box 6036
Rockville, MD 20850-9914

22

COLLECTIVE BARGAINING

Under the NLRA, an employer has a duty to negotiate in good faith with a union lawfully selected by the employees as their bargaining agent. It is expected to meet with the union at reasonable times, enter into negotiations with an open mind, and be willing to reach an agreement. It is an unfair labor practice for either an employer or a union to refuse to bargain or to bargain in bad faith.

Negotiations usually begin with representatives from the union and the employer sitting down together for the purpose of having the union present its formal proposals or demands for a contract. The subjects that a union can put on the bargaining table for the employer's consideration and for mutual discussion are any matters relating to the workers' wages, benefits, hours of work, or other terms and conditions of employment. These are considered mandatory subjects of bargaining. They may include, but are not limited to:

- Pay rates
- Holidays
- Insurance plans
- Safety practices
- Layoff procedure
- Recall rights
- Effect of plant closing
- Seniority
- Termination
- Promotions
- Drug and alcohol testing

186

- Union security
- Union dues checkoff
- Work hours
- Overtime pay
- Merit pay
- Profit sharing
- Shift pay
- Grievance procedure
- Arbitration
- Pensions
- Vacations

The duty to bargain does not require the employer to agree to any union demand, but it does require the employer to at least consider and respond to any lawful proposal presented by the union. The employer also may make proposals which the union must consider, but which, like the employer, it does not necessarily have to accept. Refusal to consider or discuss a mandatory bargaining subject, refusal to meet reasonable requests for information needed to discuss these subjects, or insistence that a nonmandatory subject of bargaining be included in a contract indicates bad faith and may be an unfair labor practice, discussed in Chapter 20.

Negotiations for the first agreement may be lengthy because, in addition to agreement on wages and benefits, the basic contract relating to terms and conditions of employment has to be negotiated. The employer and the union may each propose "form" contracts, but neither party has to accept any contract provision because it happens to be in another contract somewhere else. The parties have the right to hammer out every clause and provision that they agree should be in their contract. Everything to be included in the contract is negotiable. Because there sometimes has been a lengthy delay in achieving agreement on a first contract, there have been legislative proposals to require mandatory arbitration for first pact disputes.

The basic purpose of an agreement is, of course, to codify the parties' agreement on the employees' pay, benefits, and working conditions. The employer and the union, however, also usually want specific provisions in the agreement relating to their interests. An employer, for example, usually wants a "management rights" clause that specifically recognizes the employer's right to run the operation, make business decisions, and direct the work force. A union generally wants a union security clause that requires that employees join the union and pay dues as a condition of employment and a provision for the automatic deduction— "checkoff"—of dues from an employee's pay. As with all other provisions, management rights and union security clauses are negotiable.

A union, as a service as well as an employee organization, incurs expenses as a bargaining agent. Its principal means of meeting these expenses is through the dues paid by its members and by the employees it represents.

As indicated in Chapter 6, 21 states have right-to-work laws that do not allow compulsory union membership contracts, but voluntary checkoffs are permitted in all states. Moreover, even in states where compulsory union membership is lawful, workers do not actually have to join the union, although in some states under union security arrangements they can be required to pay the equivalent of union dues and fees (but not fees to be used for political expenses) as a condition of keeping their jobs. Union-represented employees do not have to pay these equivalent fees if they belong to a religious organization that prohibits them from joining or supporting labor organizations. They may, however, be required to pay the equivalent of union dues and fees to one of three nonreligious charitable funds listed in the agreement.

Employees may voluntarily join a union even in a right-to-work state and, in all states, may resign from a union, although a union's constitution may impose reasonable restrictions on the timing of a resignation.

A checkoff clause—a form of wage assignment—allows, but does not require, an employee to have union dues automatically deducted from his or her pay. The clause must allow an employee the right once a year to revoke the checkoff.

Grievances and Arbitration

A clause found in most collective bargaining agreements is one providing for a grievance-arbitration system. Under this system workers who have a complaint that the employer has not followed the provisions of the agreement, including such matters as pay, promotions, or layoffs, or that they were fired without just cause or disciplined too strictly for an offense they committed, may file a grievance with their supervisor. If the grievance is not resolved at that level, the employees, with the union's assistance, are allowed to appeal to a higher level of management. Most systems provide for a three- or four-step grievance procedure, with the last step being arbitration.

If a grievance is taken to arbitration, the company and the union select an impartial person to serve as an arbitrator or a board of arbitrators to hear and decide the grievance. The arbitrator's fees generally are paid equally by both parties. The arbitrator's decision, called an award, is generally binding on both the employer and the union. An arbitration award can be enforced by the courts. A few nonunion companies also have arbitration systems for their workers' complaints.

Arbitrators are usually lawyers, law school professors, or other persons experienced in labor relations and arbitration. An arbitrator, however, can be anyone the parties mutually accept to hear and decide the dispute. The Federal Mediation and Conciliation Service and the American Arbitration Association will, on request, provide the parties with the names of persons who regularly serve as arbitrators.

Although a union is not required to take every grievance to arbitration, it must treat all the employees it represents fairly in deciding whether to submit a matter to arbitration. A union failing to provide fair representation to all the employees it represents, whether union members or not, commits an unfair labor practice.

Many employers, in agreeing to an arbitration system as a means of resolving disputes, ask for a no-strike clause from the union, which is a provision stating that the union will not engage in a strike during the life of the contract.

Stalemated Negotiations and the Federal Mediation and Conciliation Service (FMCS)

If, after good-faith bargaining, negotiations for an agreement come to a standstill—become stalemated—the parties are considered to be at an impasse. The parties are not required to continue meeting until one or the other changes its position on one of the stalemated issues.

When little or no progress is being made, either party may request the assistance of a mediator either independently or through the FMCS, whose function is to help the parties with their negotiations. FMCS mediators, many of whom have had prior labor relations experience, are often able to get stalled negotiations moving again. Unlike arbitrators, mediators have no authority to decide disputes or to require either party to make any proposals or concessions. Nevertheless, through narrowing and defining issues and practical suggestions, they can often help the parties reach an agreement.

Interest Arbitration

A proceeding used at times by some public employers and unions to assist them in reaching an agreement is called interest arbitration. Each side presents its contract proposals to the arbitrator who, depending on the authority he or she is given by the parties, determines the contract terms. Interest arbitration has seen only limited use by private employers.

Strikes and Lockouts

A union can call a strike to back up its contract demands, while an employer can take equivalent action by locking out its employees. These matters are covered in Chapter 23.

Final Agreement

After a final agreement is reached and any necessary employee ratification is received, the contract is signed by the parties and copies are made for employees in the bargaining unit.

The contract's duration, a negotiable matter, is generally for two or three years, but can be for as long as the parties want it to last. Recent contracts have been for as long as nine years, but such agreements generally have reopening clauses that permit either party to reopen negotiation on a provision, usually wages, during the term of the contract. Sixty days prior to the termination of the agreement a party wanting to modify the agreement, or negotiate a new one, must notify the other party in writing and, 30 days later, if there is no agreement on a new contract, it must notify the FMCS and any state mediation agency.

As long as the union remains the employees' bargaining agent, whether it has a contract or not, the employer must continue to recognize the union as the bargaining agent and cannot make any changes in the employees' pay, benefits, or working conditions without notifying the union and negotiating with it. See the discussion in Chapter 24 on changing or decertifying bargaining representatives.

Bankruptcy

An employer filing for bankruptcy can ask the Bankruptcy Court to cancel its contract with a union. However, before taking this action, it must first negotiate with the union in a good-faith effort to arrive at a mutually agreeable modification of the contract to improve the employer's financial condition. If the parties are not successful in reaching an agreement, the employer can then apply to the court to cancel the contract. If the Bankruptcy Court does not act within 30 days of a hearing on the employer's application, the employer may cancel the contract unilaterally, pending further court action. The employer, however, must continue to recognize the union as the employees' representative.

Plant Closing or Relocation

Employers usually have the right to close a business, provided there is no specific contract language restricting this right. However, under the terms of the Worker Readjustment and Retraining Notification Act (WARN), employers with 100 or more workers, whether union represented or not, must provide them with 60 days' advance notice of shutdowns that will last more than six months and will affect at least 50 employees. If the business is being relocated, the employer must negotiate with any union representing its employees over the effects of the relocation.

Successor Employers

If a new employer takes over a plant and the business continues without interruption or substantial change, the new employer must recognize and bargain with any union representing the workers.

23

STRIKES, LOCKOUTS, AND LABOR DISPUTES

A strike or lockout results from a dispute or controversy between an employer and a union. Although disputes frequently arise when an employer and a union are unable to agree on the terms of an agreement, they can also arise in situations such as the following:

- The employer refuses to recognize and bargain with a union.
- The employer contracts out work performed by its employees to another company, or discharges or lays off its workers.
- Workers protest alleged employer unfair labor practices.
- The union objects to a company with whom the employer does business.

Every dispute, however, does not necessarily result in a strike or a lockout. Most disputes are in fact resolved peacefully, including most contract negotiations. But in every dispute or controversy there is always the possibility that one or both parties will escalate the dispute by resorting to pressure, rather than persuasion, to force the other party to accept its demands.

When this happens, pressure can be applied not only through strikes and lockouts, but also through picketing and boycotts. Picketing, which is usually accompanied by handbills, signs, or posters, in its simplest form is an attempt by workers, or a union, to enlist public support for their position by advertising their side of the dispute to other workers and to the public. Employees can engage in picketing without going out on strike.

As for boycotts, there are two kinds: primary and secondary. "Primary boycott," a seldom used term, is another word for a strike or work stoppage, which is in effect a refusal by workers to handle their own employer's goods. A secondary boycott, on the other hand, occurs when the workers apply pressure on the employer's customers or suppliers to have them stop handling the employer's goods or stop doing business with it. For example, when Company A is involved in a dispute with its workers, it becomes the "primary" employer. If Company A's employees or their union should cause Company B's employees to stop handling Company A's goods or cause Company B to stop doing business with Company A, Company B becomes the "secondary" employer and the union's action in relation to Company B is a secondary boycott.

Lawful and Unlawful Pressure

Strikes. Pressure in itself is not unlawful. A strike for a lawful purpose is protected concerted activity. This includes strikes by employees, whether union represented or not, to obtain better pay or working conditions (e.g., a strike in support of their contract demands) or to protest an employer's alleged unfair labor practices.

Workers applying pressure on an employer by engaging in a lawful strike cannot be punished or fired. An employer, however, can apply counterpressure by replacing strikers with other workers. If the strike is over pay or working conditions—which is called an "economic" strike—the employer can hire permanent replacements for the striking workers. When the strikers ask for reinstatement the employer must reinstate only those who were not permanently replaced, although unreinstated strikers are entitled to be placed on a preferential hiring list. A worker refusing to cross another union's picket line cannot be disciplined, but he or she can also be permanently replaced. As noted earlier in Chapter 5, there have been legislative proposals to prohibit employers from permanently replacing economic strikers.

Workers who strike to protest their employer's unfair labor practices cannot be permanently replaced, however. They are entitled to be reinstated to their jobs, even if their replacements have to be discharged to make room for them.

Workers also have the right to continue working even though their union has called a strike. A union member, however, who works during a lawful union-authorized strike can be fined by the union, but it cannot fine a worker who effectively resigns from the union before crossing a picket line and returning to work.

Lockouts. An employer can apply lawful pressure in a labor dispute by temporarily closing its plant and laying off—"locking out"—its workers. But it is unlawful for an employer to engage in a lockout to defeat the employees' efforts to form or join a union or to engage in other protected concerted activity.

Picketing and Boycotts. The law does not prohibit pressure through purely informational picketing at a primary or secondary employer. It is unlawful, however, for a union to engage in mass picketing that physically prevents non-strikers from working, or to engage in picketing that is intended to be a "signal" for workers to stop work. It is unlawful for a union to engage in picketing to force or require an employer to recognize the union as the employees' bargaining agent when:

- Another union has been lawfully recognized as the bargaining agent.
- A valid election has been conducted in the preceding 12 months.
- The picketing has been conducted for a reasonable period of time (not to exceed 30 days) and no election petition has been filed.

Another unlawful form of pressure occurs when a union engages in or encourages a strike for any of the following purposes:

- Forcing any person to cease doing business with any other person;
- Forcing an employer other than the one employing the union's members to recognize any union not certified by the NLRB as a bargaining agent;
- Forcing an employer to transfer work from one group of employees to another.

Timing of a Strike

Generally, a union can call a lawful strike at any time, with these five exceptions:

1. A union cannot ordinarily strike during the term of its contract with the employer if the contract contains a no-strike clause. Its members may also lose their protection as strikers if they engage in a work stoppage, whether initiated by their union or not, in "sympathy" with a strike by other union-represented workers.
2. A union cannot call a strike during the 60-day period immediately preceding the expiration of an agreement.
3. When negotiations involve a hospital or a nursing home, the union must give the employer at least 10 days' notice of its intent to strike.
4. If the strike would cause a national emergency, the President can require that the strike be postponed 80 days while efforts are made to resolve the dispute.
5. Unions are generally prohibited from engaging in strikes against the government.

Unprotected Strike Activity

Employees who participate in an unlawful or unprotected strike may be discharged by their employer. Even workers who participate in a lawful strike may be denied reinstatement to their jobs when they engage in serious and unprovoked conduct such as:

- Physically blocking persons from entering or leaving a struck facility;
- Threatening violence against nonstrikers;
- Attacking management representatives.

24

CHANGING OR DECERTIFYING BARGAINING REPRESENTATIVES

Once a union becomes the employees' bargaining agent, the employer must recognize and bargain with it until some lawful event occurs clearly showing that a majority of the employees no longer support the union as their representative. This event is usually an NLRB election. Another type of election, covered later in this chapter, is one to rescind a union's power to enter into a union security agreement.

An election challenging an incumbent union's representative status results from a petition filed either by the employees seeking to "decertify" the union, or by a rival union or an employee organization seeking to replace the incumbent as the employees' representative.

The procedure for getting an election in these circumstances is the same as that discussed in Chapter 21, including the requirement that the petition be supported by at least 30 percent of the workers in order to have the NLRB agree to conduct an election.

If the incumbent union receives a majority of the votes cast in the election, it is again certified as the employees' bargaining agent. But should a rival union or an employee organization receive a majority of the votes, it is certified as the bargaining agent, thus replacing the incumbent.

If, however, the "no union" choice on this ballot receives 50 percent or more of the votes, the incumbent is, in labor terminology, "decertified," which means that it loses its right to serve as the employees' bargaining representative, and should a rival union or an employee organization also be on the ballot, it too would lose in its bid to become their representative.

Timing of the Petition

When a union is currently serving as a bargaining agent, the NLRB places the following limitations on the times during which an election can be held or a petition filed:

- An election cannot be held during the year following the union's certification by the NLRB as the employees' bargaining agent. If an employer fails to bargain in good faith with a newly certified union, the certification year may be extended by the NLRB.
- If the union has a contract with the employer, a petition cannot be filed during the life of the contract, except during its "open period." For contracts of three years or less, the open period is between 90 and 60 days prior to contract expiration. If the contract exceeds three years, the open period is the 90-60 day period prior to the third anniversary of the contract's execution. In the health care industry the open period is between 120 to 90 days prior to contract termination.
- A petition cannot be filed during a "reasonable time" specified by a valid voluntary agreement entered into by a union and an employer.
- A petition can be filed after the contract has terminated, or after the end of the first three years of the contract, if a new contract is not negotiated before the petition is filed, or if the contract is not renewed automatically.
- A petition can be filed anytime when:
  —The contract does not have a specific termination date.
  —The contract has an illegal union shop clause.
  —The contract has not been ratified by the employees when ratification is required.

—The contract is unsigned or incomplete.

—The contract does not contain substantial terms and conditions of employment.

—The contract can be terminated by either party at any time for any reason.

—The bargaining unit covered by the contract is not appropriate.

—The union is no longer in existence or is unwilling to represent the employees.

—The contract discriminates among employees on racial grounds.

—The union is involved in a basic internal conflict that creates confusion as to which union properly represents the employees.

—The employer's operations have changed substantially since the contract was executed.

Employer Petitions

Employers or supervisors cannot file a decertification petition (called an RD petition). However, they may file a petition (known as an RM petition) where there is an incumbent certified or recognized union, under circumstances where the employer can show by "objective considerations" that it has some reasonable grounds for believing that the union has lost its majority status since certification and that an election is needed to resolve this doubt.

Before it will conduct an election, however, the NLRB must be satisfied that there is sufficient basis for the employer's doubt about the union's majority status. If the NLRB is not satisfied, it will dismiss the petition.

Union Security Deauthorization Election

A union shop deauthorization election determines whether a majority of employees wish to take away a union's power to enter into a union security agreement with the employer requiring the employees to join the union as a condition of employment. A petition for a union shop deauthorization, like other petitions filed by the employees, must be supported by signatures from at least 30 percent of the employees in the bargaining unit.

A deauthorization election can be held even though an existing contract would bar other types of elections. However, unlike the other elections in which the results are determined by the number of employees who actually vote, a union shop can be deauthorized only if a majority of the employees in the bargaining unit actually vote for the deauthorization.

Employer Conduct

Decertification and deauthorization petitions cannot be instigated by employers or their supervisors. Issues of employer instigation will not be considered in the decertification or deauthorization case, but will be considered as unfair labor practices.

25

RETIREMENT, PENSIONS, AND SOCIAL SECURITY

A pension is a system for putting money aside to provide workers with an income after they retire. The basic retirement program for most workers is Social Security, and for some it is their only pension system since employers are not required by law to provide pensions to their employees. Many businesses, of course, do provide some form of retirement income for their workers in addition to that provided by Social Security.

Although a retirement program, Social Security is not intended to replace all earnings a wage earner loses at retirement, and, indeed, may not provide sufficient income for many retired persons. As of January 1995, the average monthly Social Security check is $698. The highest monthly benefit a retired worker could receive, if he or she retires in 1995, is $1,199. Workers therefore often supplement their Social Security payments with savings or investments. They are allowed to continue to earn a limited amount of income from employment while also receiving Social Security, although if they earn beyond the maximum allowable, their Social Security benefits will be reduced.

SOCIAL SECURITY

The Social Security retirement system, a federal program, established under the Federal Insurance Contributions Act (FICA), provides benefits to retired workers, to certain dependents of workers who have retired or died and, as covered in Chapter 12, to disabled workers. FICA, under Medicare, also provides hospital insurance for retirees and the disabled eligible to receive Social Security benefits.

Social Security covers most workers, but exempts most federal employees hired before 1984, railroad employees with more than 10 years of service, employees of some state and local governments who chose not to participate in Social Security, and children under 21 who work for a parent.

The system is financed through mandatory employee contributions, based on earnings, which are withheld from workers' wages. Employers pay an equal amount. In 1995 a worker and the employer will each pay a Social Security tax of 6.2 percent of the first $61,200 of earnings plus a Medicare tax of 1.45 percent of all earnings. A self-employed worker will pay 12.4 percent of the first $61,200 plus 2.9 percent of all earnings. Self-employed persons make their payments when they file their federal income tax returns.

To qualify for benefits, a worker must have earned credits for a certain amount of work under Social Security. A credit is based on earning a certain level of income per year, adjusted for inflation. In 1995 one credit is earned for each $630 in earnings. Employees can earn a maximum of four credits per year. The number of credits a retiring worker needs to be eligible for Social Security depends on the worker's age (see table on page 209). The amount of retirement benefits a worker receives is based on his or her level of earnings.

Applying for Social Security Benefits

Social Security benefits do not start automatically. A person who is ready to retire must apply for them by filing a claim by mail, telephone, or in person with a Social Security office. To receive full benefits a worker has to wait until age 65 to apply (or later as shown in the schedule below). He or she can start collecting as early as age 62, but the monthly benefits will be permanently reduced.

Payments to a worker retiring before age 65 begin with the month the person applies. A worker retiring after age 65 can generally receive retroactive payments for up to six months before the month he or she applies. Because there is a lag in processing a claim from the time application is made until payments begin, workers should apply three months before they want benefits to start.

The full retirement age for individuals born in 1937 or earlier is 65. Those born in 1938 or after will reach full retirement age according to the following schedule:

FULL RETIREMENT AGE BY YEAR OF BIRTH

Year of Birth	Full Retirement Age
1937 and earlier	65 yrs
1938	65 yrs, 2 mos
1939	65 yrs, 4 mos
1940	65 yrs, 6 mos
1941	65 yrs, 8 mos
1942	65 yrs, 10 mos
1943–1954	66 yrs
1955	66 yrs, 2 mos
1956	66 yrs, 4 mos
1957	66 yrs, 6 mos
1958	66 yrs, 8 mos
1959	66 yrs, 10 mos
1960 and later	67 yrs

Information Needed When Applying

When applying for benefits—which can be done at any of Social Security's regional offices—the worker should bring to the office:

- His or her Social Security card or number;
- Proof of age;
- Form W-2 for the last two years or, if self-employed, a copy of the last two federal income tax returns. This information is important because earnings for this period will likely not yet be on Social Security's records and therefore will not be included when the amount of retirement benefits to which the worker is entitled are computed. Without this current infor-

mation, it could take at least two years before these earnings are reported to Social Security and the benefits are recomputed and reflected in the worker's monthly check.

Amount of Benefits

Initial retirement benefits primarily depend on the worker's level of earnings.

The benefits workers initially receive are determined by the Social Security Administration based on workers' lifetime earnings records, the age they become eligible for benefits, and their family situation (i.e., whether the claimant has dependents eligible for benefits). The Social Security Administration will on request estimate a covered worker's benefits.

Benefits are adjusted each year based on changes in the cost of living. In January 1995, benefits increased by 2.8%.

Individuals who return to work after they begin receiving retirement checks may, because of added earnings, become entitled to higher benefits. This is because Social Security automatically refigures benefits after additional earnings are credited to a worker's record. (But as noted below, a return to work can cause a reduction in the worker's current check.) A worker delaying retirement after reaching full retirement age also receives a 3 percent credit for each year's delay up to age 70, when full benefits are payable without regard to earnings from employment.

Continuing Work

A retired person, as noted, can return to work after starting to collect Social Security benefits. For that matter, he or she can collect benefits without stopping work altogether. However, the earnings of a person who both works and collects benefits can affect the amount of that person's Social Security check, depending on whether the earnings exceed an annual "exempt amount." A worker's earnings in retirement may affect his or her dependent's benefits as well, but not a divorced spouse's benefits. If the earnings go over the exempt amount and the individual is

65, $1 is deducted from the monthly check for each $3 earned *above* this exempt amount. Only earnings from work affect an individual's benefits. Benefits are not affected by income from savings, investments, or insurance.

The annual exempt amount for 1995 is $11,280 for persons age 65 or older and $8,160 for persons under age 65. A person retiring in 1995 will receive full monthly benefits for the month he or she does not earn more than $940, if aged 65–70 ($680 if under 65), or, if self-employed, does not perform "substantial services" regardless of the person's total earnings for the year. When a person reaches age 70, there is no limit on the amount he or she can earn.

An individual collecting Social Security who expects to earn more than the annual exempt amount should notify the local Social Security office so that it can determine whether some or all of the person's benefits should be withheld to avoid the payment of benefits that the individual may later have to repay. An annual report of earnings must be filed by April 15.

Medicare

Workers who are eligible for Social Security retirement benefits at age 65 are also automatically eligible to participate in the two-part Medicare program. One part, hospital insurance (Part A)—to which all workers contribute when Social Security taxes are deducted from their pay—helps pay for hospital care. The second part, medical insurance (Part B), helps pay for physician services. A monthly premium ($41.10 in 1994 and $46.10 in 1995) is charged for medical insurance. A person applying for hospital insurance (Part A), which is available at age 65 whether or not the person retires, is automatically enrolled for medical insurance (Part B), unless he or she decides to reject it by filing a notice that he or she does not wish to be enrolled.

A worker who continues to work after reaching age 65 has the right to remain covered by any health insurance provided by his or her employer, with Medicare being a secondary source of coverage.

Dependent Benefits

Monthly Social Security checks are paid to certain dependents of a retired worker, but benefit amounts are subject to family maximum benefit levels. These dependents include:

- Unmarried children under 18 years of age or under age 19 if full-time high school students;
- Unmarried children 18 years of age or older who were disabled before age 22 and continue to be disabled;
- Spouse age 62 or older unless he or she can collect a higher Social Security benefit on his or her own work record;
- Spouse at any age if he or she is caring for a child under age 16 who is receiving a benefit based on the retired worker's earnings record;
- Grandchildren living with worker, if their parents are dead or disabled;
- Divorced spouse at age 62 who was married to worker for 10 years, and has not remarried, and who is not eligible for an equal or higher benefit on his or her own record or on someone else's.

Death Benefits

If a worker dies, monthly Social Security benefits can be made to:

- Unmarried children under age 18, or under 19 years old if full-time high school students;
- Unmarried son or daughter 18 years old or over who was disabled before age 22 and continues to be disabled;
- Widow or widower age 60 or older;
- Widow, widower, or surviving divorced spouse of any age caring for the worker's child under 16 years of age who is receiving a benefit based on the earnings record of the dead worker;
- Widow or widower age 50 or older who becomes disabled not later than seven years after the worker died;
- Dependent parents age 62 or older;

- Surviving divorced spouse at age 60 or over (50 if disabled) who was married to deceased worker for 10 years and is not entitled to equal or higher personal benefit.

Each surviving dependent is entitled to a percentage of the worker's benefit, subject to the family maximum benefit.

In addition to monthly benefits survivors receive, the deceased worker's eligible spouse or minor children are entitled to a one-time $255 lump-sum death benefit.

Generally, a marriage must have lasted at least one year before dependents of a retired or disabled worker can receive monthly benefits, and a marriage must have lasted at least nine months for survivors to receive death benefits.

How Social Security Credit Is Earned

A worker becomes entitled to retirement benefits by earning sufficient credit through work, including part-time and temporary work, that is covered by Social Security. First, though, to receive credit, a worker (including a child who intends to work) has to obtain a Social Security number, which is a simple process of applying for a card at a Social Security office and showing evidence of age and citizenship, or immigration status. The number on the card is used by the government to keep a record of the individual's earnings from work. It is also used for federal income tax purposes. Only one number is issued to a person during his or her lifetime.

Employers are required to give their employees a statement of their earnings and the Social Security taxes deducted from their pay at the end of the year. In most cases deductions are shown on a W-2 form, which also shows the deductions for income taxes. The Social Security deductions are listed on the W-2 under "FICA taxes withheld." FICA stands for Federal Insurance Contributions Act, which is the law that authorizes the deduction of Social Security taxes from an employee's pay.

A worker's annual earnings for work covered by Social Security are reported by the employer to the government, which in turn credits the worker's Social Security earnings record. A separate record is maintained for each wage earner.

Before an individual can qualify for benefits, he or she needs credit for a certain amount of work under Social Security. One credit (previously called a "quarter of coverage") is earned for each dollar amount listed below, up to a maximum of four credits per year:

1986	440	**1991**	540
1987	460	**1992**	570
1988	470	**1993**	590
1989	500	**1994**	620
1990	520	**1995**	630

The amount needed to earn a credit increases automatically each year to keep pace with the increase in the average wage.

A person who stops performing work covered by Social Security before earning enough credits will not receive benefits. But the credit already earned will stay on the record and the individual can add to it by returning to work under Social Security any time before or after reaching retirement age.

A worker with enough credit to receive retirement benefits is "fully insured." The amount of credit needed to become fully insured and eligible for a retirement check depends on the year the person will reach age 62, while the amount of the check the person will receive depends on his or her level of earnings over a period of years. The following table shows the amount of credit needed for retirement benefits for persons of different ages.

WORK CREDIT FOR RETIREMENT BENEFITS

Year in which worker reaches age 62, becomes disabled, or dies	Years of credit needed
1987	9 (36 credits)
1988	9¼ (37 credits)
1989	9½ (38 credits)
1990	9¾ (39 credits)
1991 (or later)	10 (40 credits)

A worker who dies before becoming fully insured but who had at least six credits in the three years before death, will be considered "currently insured." This status allows dependent children and their dependent widowed parent to be eligible for benefits.

A wage earner can check with the Social Security Administration to determine whether he or she is receiving credit for earnings by using the postcard shown below. The postcard is available without charge at any Social Security office. Errors in a worker's earnings record can be corrected for up to three years. For further information and instructions on making a rough estimate of a wage earner's Social Security retirement check, see *Your New Social Security and Medicare Fact Sheet*, available from:

BNA Books
P.O. Box 6036
Rockville, MD 20850-9914

SOCIAL SECURITY ADMINISTRATION

Form Approved
OMB No. 0960-0466 ☐ SP

Request for Earnings and Benefit Estimate Statement

To receive a free statement of your earnings covered by Social Security and your estimated future benefits, all you need to do is fill out this form. Please print or type your answers. When you have completed the form, fold it and mail it to us.

1. Name shown on your Social Security card:

First Name　　　　Middle Initial

Last Name Only

2. Your Social Security number as shown on your card:

☐☐☐-☐☐-☐☐☐☐

3. Your date of birth
Month　Day　Year

4. Other Social Security numbers you have used:

☐☐☐-☐☐-☐☐☐☐
☐☐☐-☐☐-☐☐☐☐

5. Your sex: ☐ Male ☐ Female

6. Other names you have used
(including a maiden name):

7. Show your actual earnings for last year and your estimated earnings for this year. Include only wages and/or net self-employment income covered by Social Security.

A. Last year's actual earnings: *(Dollars Only)*

$☐☐☐,☐☐☐.00

B. This year's estimated earnings: *(Dollars Only)*

$☐☐☐,☐☐☐.00

8. Show the age at which you plan to retire:

☐☐ *(Show only one age)*

9. Below, show the average yearly amount you think you will earn between now and when you plan to retire. We will add your estimate of future earnings to those earnings already on our records to give you the best possible estimate.

Enter a yearly average, not your total future lifetime earnings. Only show earnings covered by Social Security. Do not add cost-of-living, performance or scheduled pay increases or bonuses. The reason for this is that we estimate retirement benefits in today's dollars, but adjust them to account for average wage growth in the national economy.

However, if you expect to earn significantly more or less in the future due to promotions, job changes, part-time work, or an absence from the work force, enter the amount in today's dollars that most closely reflects your future average yearly earnings.

Most people should enter the same amount they are earning now (the amount in 7B).

Future average yearly earnings: *(Dollars Only)*

$☐☐☐,☐☐☐.00

10. Address where you want us to send the statement.

Name

Street Address (Include Apt. No., P.O. Box, or Rural Route)

City　　State　　Zip Code

11. ☐ Please check this box if you want to get your statement in Spanish instead of English.

I am asking for information about my own Social Security record or the record of a person I am authorized to represent. I understand that if I deliberately request information under false pretenses I may be guilty of a federal crime and could be fined and/or imprisoned. I authorize you to use a contractor to send the statement of earnings and benefit estimates to the person named in item 10.

Please sign your name (Do not print)

▶

Signature

Date　　(Area Code) Daytime Telephone No.

Form SSA-7004-SM (2-93) Destroy Prior Editions

Special Rules

Most jobs are covered by Social Security. However, there are special rules for coverage for certain types of workers, such as farmers, domestic workers, legal immigrants, and people who receive cash tips. Pamphlets containing information for these persons, as well as information explaining all aspects of the system for any person covered by Social Security, are available at any Social Security office.

Appeals Procedure

A wage earner who disagrees with a decision by the Social Security Administration concerning retirement benefits has the right to appeal the decision through the appeals process explained in Chapter 12.

PRIVATE PENSION PLANS

An employer-provided pension or retirement plan is a means of providing an income to workers after they retire. A pension plan is usually either a defined benefit plan, with a fixed monthly benefit, or a defined contribution plan, with contributions made by an employer under a specified formula. Pension plans can also provide for employee contributions. The majority of current employer-provided pension plans are defined contribution plans.

An employer is not required to provide a pension to its workers. But if it does, the plan must meet minimum standards established by the Employee Retirement Income Security Act (ERISA). An employer may also be subject to the requirements of the Age Discrimination in Employment Act (workers must be allowed to participate in the plan regardless of age and continue to earn benefits after age 65) and the Americans With Disabilities Act, covered elsewhere in this book, as well as meeting the nondiscriminatory requirements of fair employment practice laws, particularly in regard to not distinguishing between men and women in their participation in the plan.

ERISA, a complex law, generally provides that if an employer has a pension plan based on age and length of service, its employees must be allowed to participate in the plan when they reach age 21 and work at least 1,000 hours in 12 months. It prohibits employers from offering retirement and health and welfare plans that discriminate in favor of the highest paid employees. ERISA also requires that a pension "vest" after a worker has participated in the plan for a certain period of time, usually after 10 years. Vesting means that the plan will pay the employee a pension at a specified retirement age even if the worker should leave the job before reaching that age. However, a worker who leaves before the plan vests is not entitled to a benefit from the plan at retirement, although the worker is entitled to a refund of the contributions he or she may have made (but not the contributions made by the employer) to the plan.

ERISA prohibits the discharge of workers to avoid paying them a pension. It also requires employers to give basic information about the plan to their workers and, if workers are entitled to a pension, to tell them how much they can expect to receive at retirement. ERISA, however, does not require the payment of any minimum benefit to persons eligible for benefits under the plan when they retire.

When a worker applies for pension benefits, the plan's administrator must let the worker know within 90 days whether the claim is granted or denied. A worker whose claim is denied must be given a written explanation and must be given 60 days to file an appeal according to the procedures the administrator must explain to the worker. A decision on the appeal must be made in writing within 120 days. If the claim is again turned down, the employee has the right to appeal to a court or to seek assistance by writing to:

Pension and Welfare Benefits Administration
U.S. Department of Labor
200 Constitution Ave., N.W.
Washington, D.C. 20210

TYPES OF PRIVATE PLANS

Simplified Employee Pension Plans (SEPs)

A federal program separate from Social Security encourages workers to establish their own personal retirement program by allowing them to make tax deductible contributions to an Individual Retirement Account (IRA). A worker can contribute up to $2,000 a year into an IRA if neither the worker nor his or her spouse participates in an employer retirement program, or, if either the worker or his or her spouse does participate in an employer retirement program, their combined gross income is less than $40,000. The same rules apply to a single worker except that his or her gross income must be less than $25,000. Money invested in an IRA account cannot be withdrawn before the individual reaches 59½ years of age without paying a penalty, unless the person dies or becomes disabled. An employer also may contribute to a worker's IRA in some circumstances. Banks, savings and loan associations, and employee credit unions will provide information to persons interested in creating an IRA.

401(k) Plans or CODAs

Another means by which employees can create a fund for their later retirement is through what is called a cash or deferred (salary reduction) or 401(k) plan. Federal tax law allows employers to establish an investment fund to which their employees can voluntarily forgo a portion of their salary in favor of a tax-deferred contribution through automatic deductions from their paychecks, with the employees being allowed to contribute more to a "salary reduction" fund than they can to an IRA. The law allows their employers to make matching contributions.

Self-employed persons can establish their own IRA or establish what is called a Keogh plan, which allows larger tax deductible contributions than an IRA. A self-employed person creating a Keogh plan, however, must include his or her employees, if any, in the plan. SEPs are a simplified means for employers to provide retirement benefits for their employees. They do not require the employer to make many of the reports and disclosures of information that it would have to make under an ERISA-type pension plan. They are intended to encourage small employers to set up retirement plans for their employees. An employer may contribute up to $30,000 a year or 15 percent of compensation, whichever is less, to individual accounts for each employee. A bank or other financial institution can provide information on SEPs.

Profit-Sharing Plans

Profit-sharing plans, which are generally not government regulated, involve the sharing of a fixed percentage of profits with employees each year, with a predetermined formula for allocating contributions made to the plan, such as paying the same amount to all workers or basing the payment on an employee's salary or wage rate. If distribution of the funds is deferred, the plan may be regulated under ERISA, with the plan providing that the funds be distributed after a fixed number of years; when the employee reaches a certain age; or upon a layoff, illness, disability, retirement, or death.

Savings or Thrift Plans

Savings or thrift plans involve the voluntary contribution by employees, often through payroll deductions, to an investment fund established by the employer, or by the employees, with a bank or investment company. Employers often make matching contributions up to a predetermined amount.

Stock Plans

Stock bonus and employee stock ownership plans provide benefits similar to profit-sharing plans, although the employer contributions are not necessarily dependent on profits and the benefits are in company stock.

Tax-Sheltered Annuities

Tax-sheltered annuities, available to public school employees and employees of certain tax-exempt organizations, permit those employees to save for retirement on a pretax basis, through salary reduction arrangements.

For more information about pension plans and ERISA, a lawyer or accountant specializing in such matters should be consulted because of the complexities of the law.

Nondiscrimination

Regardless of the type of benefit plan and regardless of whether it is regulated by ERISA, it must in all instances not discriminate against workers in violation of fair employment practice laws.

26

GOVERNMENT EMPLOYMENT

More than 18 million people work for federal, state, and local governments. Each of these levels of government operates its own employment system, with most using some form of "merit" employment, a system that, with certain exceptions, bases the selection and advancement of employees on their job qualifications rather than on their political affiliation. The principal exception to merit employment involves policymaking positions that elected officials can fill with persons whose decisions will reflect those of the official.

Federal Employment

The federal government, the nation's largest employer, employs more than three million persons through its civil service system. Federal employees work in many settings across the country and even around the world in offices, shipyards, laboratories, national forests, and military bases.

The labor relations policies and procedures governing these federal workers are both complex and numerous. In 1993 a study of these policies resulted in a National Performance Review, designed to find ways to make the government more efficient and responsive to citizens. Many of the recommendations in the report that resulted concern human resource management systems in the federal government and, if adopted, would have an impact on the law of the federal government workplace, as described below.

Most federal workers are hired through a "competitive" service procedure, which is a form of a merit employment system administered by the Office of Personnel Management (OPM), formerly called the Civil Service Commission.

A person seeking a federal competitive service job must file an application (Standard Form 171) with OPM. The qualifications for federal jobs are stated in bulletins or announcements that specify the education and/or experience needed and whether a written test is required. This information can be obtained from the agency with the job opening or from OPM.

OPM determines whether an applicant is qualified and, if qualified, gives the applicant a numerical rating based on his or her experience, education and training, or on the results of a written test if one is given for the position. Veterans may receive an additional 5 points and disabled veterans 10 points. The applicant's name is then placed on a list or register with the names of other persons who are also qualified for the same kind of job. Names are listed according to their rating.

When OPM receives a request for the names of qualified applicants from an employing agency, it sends the agency the names of the people highest on the list. The agency's hiring official then makes a choice from among the top three applicants. In some circumstances handicapped persons and disabled Vietnam-era veterans may be hired without competing with other applicants.

New employees in the competitive service serve a probationary period and can be dismissed during this time if they fail to perform satisfactory work. After the probationary period, they become career employees and cannot be dismissed without evidence of misconduct, delinquency, or inefficiency on the job.

Pay Levels

Competitive service jobs are classified by grade levels based on the level of responsibility required for the job. Salaries correspond to the grade level; the higher the grade, the higher the salary. These grade levels are called "General

Schedules" (GS) and apply to most white-collar jobs, starting with GS-1 and going up to GS-18. GS salaries are set by the President with Congressional approval.

Each GS grade has a set range of within-grade increases in salary called "steps." Employees performing adequate work receive step increases based on length of service until the top of the grade is reached. They can also receive step increases for exceptional work. However, step increases for managers and supervisors in grades GS-13, 14, and 15, and Senior Executive Service employees GS-16 and above are based on performance rather than on length of service. Senior Executive Service (SES) employees are those persons who are hired through competitive procedures conducted under the auspices of the employing agency to hold high-level positions in the agency. Career SES executives may be awarded lump-sum payments for performance in addition to regular annual salary adjustments.

Most blue-collar positions are covered by "wage order" pay rates that vary according to the location where the employees work. These prevailing wage rates are determined based on surveys of rates paid by private employers in each local wage area for work similar to that performed by federal wage employees.

Minimum Wage and Overtime

The federal Fair Labor Standards Act's minimum wage and overtime pay provisions apply to federal, state, and local government workers. Generally, federal employers are on a five-day, 40-hour workweek. The workday is 8 hours, and the law provides overtime for work in excess of 8 hours in a day, or in excess of 40 hours in the workweek, with special maximum provisions for general schedule, nonexempt employees at the GS-10, step-one level or higher.

There are provisions for a pay differential for Sunday and holiday work within an employee's basic workweek. Certain general schedule employees are entitled to premium pay for night work.

EXCEPTED SERVICE

Although most federal workers are hired through OPM's competitive service procedures, the Postal Service, Federal Bureau of Investigation, and the Central Intelligence Agency are "excepted" from OPM's procedures.

Certain positions in all agencies are also excepted. These excepted positions fall into one of three "schedules:"

Schedule A applies to attorneys and certain other non-policymaking positions for which it is impractical to hold competitive examinations.

Schedule B covers positions for which competitive examinations are also impractical but for which noncompetitive examinations may be held, such as for student-trainees.

Schedule C applies to positions that are policymaking or positions that involve a close personal and confidential relationship with key policymaking officials who support the President's political aims and practices.

Applications for a job with an excepted agency or for an excepted service position are generally made directly to the employing agency rather than through OPM.

Benefits

Federal workers receive a full range of fringe benefits: annual leave (13 to 26 days a year, depending on length of service), sick leave (13 days a year), 10 paid holidays (plus Presidential Inauguration Day for federal employees working in the District of Columbia), life insurance, medical insurance, workers' compensation, unemployment compensation, and retirement benefits.

Civilian federal employees automatically participate in either the Civil Service Retirement System or the Federal Employees Retirement System, the choice of the particular system generally determined by the employee's date of hire. Employees hired after December 31, 1983, are automatically covered under both the Federal Employees Retirement System and Social Security. All federal employees are eligible to participate in the federal thrift savings plans.

Although federal workers have the right to be represented by unions, the economic benefits they receive are not, for the most part, negotiable.

Promotions

Federal agencies are required to develop merit promotion systems under general OPM guidelines. If an agency's employees are union represented, the agency must develop its merit plan through consultation or negotiation with the union.

When a job vacancy occurs, an agency can fill it in several ways, one of which is by promoting an employee in a lower grade through the agency's merit promotion system. This generally involves posting an "announcement" that the position is vacant and then evaluating the qualifications of the applicants for the position, with the "best qualified" of the applicants being placed on a list from which the selection will be made. The agency's selecting official can choose any of the candidates on the best qualified list. He or she does not necessarily have to select the person at the top of the list or the one with the greatest seniority.

An agency, on the other hand, does not have to fill a position through its merit promotion system. It may fill a position in other ways as well.

- It can reassign an employee to the position.
- It can transfer an employee from another agency.
- It can reinstate a former federal worker with reinstatement rights.
- It can appoint a person from outside the government by obtaining a list of eligible applicants from OPM.

A position may be filled on a temporary basis (120 days or less), or by promoting an employee in a lower grade through a career promotion, provided the employee obtained his or her current position or grade through competitive procedures and the position provides for a "career ladder" promotion to the grade to which the employee is being promoted. An employee who is not eligible for a career ladder promotion to a higher grade, however, cannot be reassigned, transferred, or reinstated by the agency to a higher grade position or to a position with "higher promotional potential" without giving other employees the opportunity to apply and to be considered for the job under the agency's merit promotion system.

An employee who is not selected for promotion can file a grievance with the agency when there were irregularities in the selection process, but cannot file a grievance if the selection was made from among properly ranked applicants.

If the grieving employee proves that there were irregularities in the selection process, the agency will be required to make a new selection based on proper merit promotion procedures.

Unacceptable Performance and Adverse Actions

A career federal employee in the competitive service who does not meet acceptable levels of work performance may be demoted to a lower grade ("reduction in grade") or be terminated ("removed"), while an employee who engages in misconduct is subject to an "adverse action" proceeding that may result in a reduction in grade, a suspension, a furlough of 30 days or less, or a removal.

Before an agency can take action against an employee for unacceptable performance or misconduct, however, it must follow these procedures:

- If the situation involves unacceptable performance, the agency must take corrective action by counseling the employee and giving remedial training and more direct supervision so that the employee is given an opportunity to demonstrate acceptable performance.
- If the agency determines after a period of time that the employee's work performance continues to be unacceptable, or if the situation involves an adverse action, the agency must give the employee 30 days' advance written notice of the action it proposes to take against the employee and specify the reasons for its contemplated action.
- The employee, who is allowed to be represented by an attorney or other representative, must be given a reasonable time to prepare an answer, orally and in

writing (which must be at least seven days when an adverse action is involved).

- The agency then prepares a written decision specifying the reasons for the action it is taking against the employee.

The employee can challenge the agency's decision in one of two ways: either by filing an appeal with the Merit Systems Protection Board within 20 days, or, if the employee is represented by a union, by filing a grievance. The employee, however, cannot do both.

When an adverse action involves a suspension of 14 days or less, the employee can only file a grievance, either through the union-negotiated grievance system, or, if the employee is not union represented, through the agency's administrative grievance system. A suspension of 14 days or less cannot be appealed to the Merit Systems Protection Board.

An employee in the Senior Executive Service being disciplined because of alleged misconduct can appeal the agency's decision to the Merit Systems Protection Board. When the agency's action involves the employee's removal because of poor work performance, however, the employee has no right to a formal appeal to the Board.

An action against an administrative law judge can be instituted by the employing agency by filing a complaint with the Board. The Board then holds a formal hearing on the complaint.

A person dissatisfied with the Board's decision in any of the situations referred to above can appeal either to the U.S. Court of Claims or to a U.S. Court of Appeals. An appeal to either court must be filed within 30 days of the Board's decision.

Reductions in Force

On occasion, such as reorganization or lack of work or funds, an agency may be required to reduce the number of workers it employs. When faced with a reduction in force ("RIF"), the agency must follow prescribed procedures for laying off its employees.

The agency must first determine the geographic area and positions affected. It then places the affected employees in one of three groups.

Group 1—Career employees who have completed their probationary period.

Group 2—Career employees who have not completed their probationary period and career-conditional employees.

Group 3—Employees with an indefinite status, such as temporary employees and employees serving for a specific term.

Employees in each group are then ranked according to their length of service, with the longest-term employees ranked highest and veterans being ranked ahead of nonveterans. An employee with a current outstanding performance rating receives additional years of credit.

Employees are then laid off, after receiving at least a 60-day notice (except under unforseeable circumstances), in reverse order of their ranking, with the lowest ranked employee in Group 3 being the first laid off and the top-ranked employee in Group 1 being the last.

An employee in Group 1 or 2, but not one in Group 3, has the right to "bump" a less senior employee by taking his or her job if the employee doing the bumping is qualified to do the work, or may "retreat" to a lower grade job that the employee had formerly held.

If there are no jobs for the employee to bump into or retreat to, he or she is laid off and placed on a reemployment priority list. Group 1 employees remain on the list for two years; Group 2 employees for one year. Employees in the "excepted" service generally do not have the right to bump or be placed on a reemployment list.

Employees placed in a lower graded position because of a reduction in force may retain their grades for two years. They then receive the grade of the position they are occupying, but at a within-grade pay step that provides a wage comparable to that received before the reduction in force.

An employee separated from government service because of a reduction in force, or for any other reason for which the employee was not at fault, and who is not entitled to immediate retirement benefits may be eligible for severance pay, which is based on years of service but which cannot exceed one year's basic salary.

Laid-off employees (for more than 30 days) may appeal to the Merit Systems Protection Board if they believe that the agency did not follow required reduction-in-force procedures.

Unions

Federal employees have the right to join and participate in union activities. The National Labor Relations Act, the law creating the NLRB and requiring private employers to bargain with unions, does not apply to any level of government, although the U.S. Postal Service, which is a government-owned corporation, is under the NLRB's jurisdiction. The Federal Labor Relations Authority (FLRA), an agency similar to the NLRB, but with less overall authority, oversees federal labor relations. Like the NLRB, the FLRA conducts elections to determine whether employees want union representation and processes unfair labor practice complaints. Government employees, whether union represented or not, generally lack the right to strike and can be discharged if they do.

Agencies and unions are required to negotiate grievance systems covering all matters except those which by law or regulation are excluded from grievance systems. Agencies whose employees are not union represented are also required to provide grievance systems for their workers.

Employees normally must use the grievance procedure first. If a negotiated grievance procedure covers adverse actions and/or performance-based actions, the employee can either pursue the grievance or file an appeal with the Merit Systems Protection Board (MSPB), but cannot do both. A federal executive order provides for arbitration of employee grievances and of disputes over the interpretation or application of collective bargaining agreements with federal agencies. Either party to a dispute may file exceptions to an arbitration award with the FLRA.

State and Local Government Employment

Neither the National Labor Relations Act nor the Federal Labor Relations Act applies to state and local government agency employees. A state or local government agency, therefore, in the absence of other laws requiring it to bargain with a union (which some states and local governments have adopted), can refuse to bargain with a union seeking recognition as the bargaining agent for its employees.

Many states have extended collective bargaining rights to their employees, including Connecticut, Florida, Hawaii, Illinois, Kansas, Maine, Massachusetts, Minnesota, Missouri, Montana, Nevada, New Jersey, New York, North Dakota, Ohio, Oregon, Pennsylvania, Rhode Island, Vermont, Washington, and Wisconsin. Some states limit these rights to police, firefighters, teachers, or other specific groups of employees, while others prohibit these rights altogether.

Provisions for arbitration exist in some states, but the state laws differ as to classes of employees covered, subjects that may be arbitrated, and whether an award is binding or only advisory.

State and local government employees are covered under the federal Fair Labor Standards Act, but are treated differently in that compensatory time may be paid in lieu of overtime, as long as the compensatory time is computed on the basis of time-and-one-half for each hour of overtime worked.

Under a 1990 law, state and local government employees became covered by Social Security if they were not members of the employer's retirement system.

State and local governments are subject to the EEOC's jurisdiction and therefore cannot discriminate against their employees on the basis of race, color, religion, age, disability, or national origin. They are prohibited from discriminating on the basis of age if they receive federal funds. The federal law governing veterans' reemployment rights applies to state and local government employees, thus giving these employees their jobs back when their tour of duty is completed.

Equal Employment Opportunity

It is unlawful for an agency to discriminate against an employee or applicant for employment because of race, color, religion, sex, national origin, age, or disability. The following is the procedure employees use for processing complaints of alleged discriminatory practices:

- A federal worker believing that he or she was discriminated against starts the EEO process by contacting the agency's EEO counselor within 45 days of the alleged discriminatory practice. Ordinarily, counseling must be completed within 30 days.
- If the matter is not resolved, the EEO counselor must notify the employee in writing of the right to file a formal complaint. The employee must file a complaint with the appropriate agency official within 15 days of the notice of the right to file or within 30 days of the first contact of the EEO counselor.
- The agency must acknowledge or reject the complaint. If rejected, the worker must be notified within 30 days of dismissal of the right to appeal to EEOC's Office of Federal Operations. If not dismissed, there will be a fair and complete investigation within 180 days of filing of the complaint.
- The employee can request a hearing or final decision by the agency 180 days after filing the complaint.
- If there is a hearing, the EEOC must issue findings and conclusions within 180 days of request. The final decision, if requested, must be issued within 60 days.
- If the employee is not satisfied with the decision, he or she has 30 calendar days to appeal to the EEOC or 90 calendar days to file suit in a federal district court. If the employee appeals and is dissatisfied with the decision on appeal, he or she may still file a civil action.
- An employee may also file suit after 180 calendar days from the filing of the complaint if the agency

has not issued its final decision, or after 180 days from the appeal to the EEOC when no decision has been made.

The above procedures are available to federal employees in cases of alleged age discrimination or violations of the Equal Pay Act. Direct access to the courts is allowed after a 30-day notice of intent to sue is filed with the EEOC. A local EEOC office or an agency EEO counselor can provide more information on these procedures.

The MSPB can decide an allegation of unlawful discrimination when it is related to an issue (such as one involving adverse action) that the employee has appealed to the Board.

Federal agencies are required by the EEOC to develop affirmative action plans for women, minorities, and disabled individuals to achieve a diversified work force.

Federal employees are entitled to the same protection against sexual harassment that private sector employees are.

AIDS

Almost all federal agencies have developed AIDS policies. Generally, the policies allow AIDS or HIV-infected employees to work as long as their performance is satisfactory and they do not pose a health or safety threat. If unable to work, these employees are entitled to the same rights as other sick employees.

Drug Testing

Under the 1986 Executive Order 12564, all federal employees are prohibited from using illegal drugs. All executive agencies must develop a plan for achieving drug-free workplaces, including drug testing for employees in sensitive positions, a voluntary testing program, and testing where reasonable suspicion exists, such as after an accident, or as follow-up to counseling or rehabilitation through an employee assistance program (EAP). Referral to an EAP, if necessary, will be made, after which appropriate adverse action can be taken.

Prohibited Personnel Practices

Federal agencies are required to observe basic merit principles in the operation of their personnel practices. Among other things federal workers are entitled to fair treatment, protection against arbitrary action or political coercion, protection for nonpolitical appointees against any personnel action based on their affiliation with a political party, and protection against reprisals for lawful disclosures of information, that is, protection for "whistleblowers." These are persons who disclose improper employer practices or policies, including information about an agency's violation of a law, rule, or regulation; mismanagement; gross waste of funds; abuse of authority; or a substantial and specific danger to public health or safety. A whistleblower, however, is not protected if he or she wrongfully discloses information that is classified, required to be kept secret in the interest of national security, or covered by the federal Privacy Act.

The Civil Service Reform Act requires federal employees to report violations of law that may affect the public welfare, under circumstances where the employee can show he or she is acting with a proper motive and that an important public issue is at stake. Protection for whistleblowers was strengthened by the 1988 Whistleblower Protection Act. The Office of Special Counsel was set up to handle all investigations before the MSPB is asked to order corrective action. In certain reprisal cases, the individual employee may seek corrective action directly from the MSPB.

Most state whistleblowing laws cover only state employees, but several, including Pennsylvania's, cover local employees also. Other states' laws cover private sector employees as well. Many states specify that employees will be protected if they report violations of federal, state, or municipal laws, rules, and regulations.

Most states provide for court enforcement, but some require the employee to first exhaust administrative remedies. A few states have established special procedures to handle complaints, while several others provide for injunctive relief.

A federal employee that believes an agency official is violating a merit principle by committing a "prohibited personnel practice" may file a charge with the Special Counsel of the MSPB. The Special Counsel has the authority to investigate the charge and, if he or she believes a violation has occurred, may recommend that the agency take corrective action. If the agency does not comply, the Special Counsel may request that the MSPB take action on the matter. The Special Counsel may also file a charge with the Board against an official who has allegedly committed a prohibited personnel practice and recommend that the official be disciplined or removed. An official against whom a charge is filed has essentially the same rights as a person involved in an adverse action, including the right of court appeal.

Other Provisions

Rules generally restrict work areas where federal employees may smoke. Many federal employees, and to a lesser extent some state employees, are subject to the Hatch Act, which restricts their political activity.

There are prescribed standards of ethical conduct for federal executive branch employees, with restrictions on acceptance of gifts, employee conflict-of-interests, post-employment opportunities, misuse of position/impartiality, and requirements for financial disclosure.

More information about federal employment can be obtained from OPM and the MSPB. The addresses for their national offices are:

Office of Personnel Management
1900 E Street, N.W.
Washington, D.C. 20415-0001

Merit Systems Protection Board
1120 Vermont Ave., N.W.
Washington, D.C. 20419

APPENDIX A

State Labor Departments and Human Relations Commissions*

*Not every state has a Human Relations Commission. If you have a civil rights question and your state has no Human Relations office listed here, ask your state's Department of Labor or the federal Equal Employment Opportunity Commission for assistance.

Alabama:
Department of Labor
1789 Congressman W. L.
  Dickinson Drive
Montgomery 36130

Department of Industrial
  Relations
Industrial Relations Building
649 Monroe Street
Montgomery 36131

Alaska:
Department of Labor
P.O. Box 21149
Juneau 99802

State Commission for
  Human Rights
800 A Street, Suite 202
Anchorage 99501

Arizona:
Industrial Commission
800 West Washington Street
P.O. Box 19070
Phoenix 85005

Civil Rights Division
1275 West Washington Street
Phoenix 85007

Arkansas:
Department of Labor
10421 West Markham Street
Little Rock 72205

California:
Department of Industrial
  Relations
State Building Annex
455 Golden Gate Avenue
San Francisco 94102

Department of Fair
  Employment and Housing
2014 T Street, Suite 210
Sacramento 95814

Employment and
  Development Department
P.O. Box 826880
Sacramento 94280

Colorado:
Department of Labor and
    Employment
600 Grant Street, Suite 900
Denver 80203

Civil Rights Commission
1560 Broadway, Suite 1050
Denver 80202

Connecticut:
Labor Department
200 Folly Brook Boulevard
Wethersfield 06109

Commission on Human
    Rights and Opportunities
90 Washington Street
Hartford 06106

Delaware:
Department of Labor
820 North French Street
Wilmington 19801

District of Columbia:
Department of Employment
    Services
500 C Street, N.W.
20001

D.C. Office of Human Rights
2000 14th Street, N.W.,
    Room 300
20009

Florida:
Department of Labor and
    Employment
Hartman Building
2012 Capitol Circle S.E.
Berkley Building, Suite 206
Tallahassee 32399

Human Relations
    Commission
325 John Knox Road
Tallahassee 32303

Department of Community
    Affairs
2740 Centerview Drive
Tallahassee 32399

Georgia:
Department of Labor
148 International Boulevard
Atlanta 30303

Human Relations
    Commission
100 Peachtree Street, Suite
    350
Atlanta 30303

Hawaii:
Department of Labor and
    Industrial Relations
830 Punchbowl Street
Honolulu 96813

Affirmative Action Office
250 South Hotel Street
Honolulu 96813

Idaho:
Department of Labor and
    Industrial Services
State House Mall
Boise 83720

Department of Employment
317 Main Street
P.O. Box 35
Boise 83735

Commission on Human
    Rights
450 State Street
Boise 83720

Illinois:
Department of Labor
310 South Michigan Avenue
Chicago 60604

Human Rights Department
100 West Randolph Street,
    Suite 10-100
Chicago 60601

Indiana:
Department of Labor
402 West Washington Street
    Room W195
Indianapolis 46204-2287

Civil Rights Commission
100 North Senate Avenue,
    Room N103
Indianapolis 46204

Iowa:
Division of Employment
  Services
100 East Grand Avenue
Des Moines 50319

Iowa Civil Rights Commission
Grimes State Office Building
211 East Maple Street
Des Moines 50319

Kansas:
Department of Human
  Resources
401 Topeka Avenue
Topeka 66603

Commission on Disabilities
  Concern
1430 Southwest Topeka
  Avenue
Topeka 66612

Human Rights Commission
Suite 851 South
900 Southwest Jackson Street
Topeka 66612

Kentucky:
Labor Cabinet
U.S. 127 South, Suite 4
Frankfort 40601

Commission on Human
  Rights
323 West Broadway
Louisville 40202

Louisiana:
Employment and Training
  Department
P.O. Box 94094
Baton Rouge 70804

Maine:
Department of Labor
20 Union Street,
P.O. Box 309
Augusta 04332

Maine Human Rights
  Commission
State House, Station No. 51
Augusta 04333

Maryland:
Division of Labor and Industry
501 St. Paul Place
Baltimore 21202

Department of Human
  Resources
311 West Saratoga Street
Baltimore 21201

Commission on Human
  Relations
20 East Franklin Street
Baltimore 21202

Massachusetts:
Housing and Community
  Development
100 Cambridge Street, Room
  1404
Boston 02202

Department of Labor and
  Industries
100 Cambridge Street, Room
  1100
Boston 02202

Michigan:
Department of Labor
201 North Washington Square
Victor Office Building
Lansing 48933

Civil Rights Department
303 West Kalamazoo
Fourth Floor
Lansing 48913

Minnesota:
Department of Labor and
  Industry
443 Lafayette Road, Fifth
  Floor
St. Paul 55155

Department of Human Rights
500 Bremer Tower
Seventh and Minnesota
  Streets
St. Paul 55101

Mississippi:
Employment Security
  Commission
P.O. Box 1699
Jackson 39203

Missouri:
Department of Labor and
Industrial Relations
3315 West Truman Boulevard
Jefferson City 65103

Montana:
Department of Labor and
Industry
Commissioner's Office
P.O. Box 1728
Helena 59624

Nebraska:
Department of Labor
P.O. Box 94600
550 South 16th Street
Lincoln 68509

Equal Employment
Opportunity Commission
P.O. Box 94934
301 Centennial Mall South,
Fifth Floor
Lincoln 68509

Nevada:
Labor Commission
1445 Hot Springs Road,
Suite 108
Carson City 89710

Nevada Equal Rights
Commission
1515 East Tropicana, Suite
590
Las Vegas 89119

New Hampshire:
Department of Labor
95 Pleasant Street
Concord 03301

Commission for Human
Rights
163 Louden Road
Concord 03301

New Jersey:
Department of Labor
Labor and Industry Building
John Fitch Plaza
Trenton 08625

CN 110 Department of Law
and Public Safety
Civil Rights Division
383 West State Street
Trenton 08625

New Mexico:
Department of Human
Services
PERA Building
P.O. Box 2348
Santa Fe 87503

Human Rights Division
1596 Pacheco Street
Santa Fe 87502

New York:
Department of Labor
State Office Campus,
Building 12
Albany 12240

Division of Human Rights
55 West 125th Street
New York 10027

North Carolina:
Department of Labor
4 West Edenton Street
Raleigh 27601

Human Relations
Commission
121 West Jones Street
Raleigh 27603

North Dakota:
Department of Labor
State Capitol Building
600 East Boulevard
Bismarck 58505

Ohio:
Department of Industrial
Relations
2323 West Fifth Avenue
Columbus 43266

Civil Rights Commission
220 Parsons Avenue
Columbus 43215

Oklahoma:
Department of Labor
4001 Lincoln Boulevard
Oklahoma City 73105

Human Rights Commission
2101 North Lincoln
  Boulevard, Room 481
Oklahoma City 73105

Oregon:
Bureau of Labor and
  Industries
800 Northeast Oregon Street,
  Number 32
Portland 97232

Pennsylvania:
Department of Labor and
  Industry
Labor and Industry Building
Harrisburg 17120

Pennsylvania Human
  Relations Commission
P.O. Box 3145
Harrisburg 17105

Rhode Island:
Department of Labor
610 Manton Avenue
Providence 02903

Commission for Human
  Rights
10 Abbott Park Place
Providence 02903

South Carolina:
Department of Labor
3600 Forest Drive
P.O. Box 11329
Columbia 29211-1329

State Human Affairs
  Commission
P.O. Box 4490
Columbia 29240

South Dakota:
Department of Labor
700 Governors Drive
Pierre 57501

State Commission on Human
  Rights
500 E. Capitol, State Capitol
Pierre 57501

Tennessee:
Department of Labor
501 Union Building, Second
  Floor
Nashville 37243

Tennessee Commission on
  Human Rights
530 Church Street, Suite 400
Nashville 37243

Texas:
Department of Licensing and
  Regulation Standards
P.O. Box 12157
Capitol Station
Austin 78711

Commission on Human
  Rights
P.O. Box 13493
Austin 78711

Utah:
Industrial Commission
P.O. Box 146640
Salt Lake City 84114

Vermont:
Department of Labor and
  Industry
National Life Insurance
  Building
Montpelier 05620

Attorney General
109 State Street
Montpelier 05609

Virginia:
Department of Labor and
  Industry
Power Taylor Building
13 South 13th Street
Richmond 23219

Industrial Commission
1000 DMV Drive
Richmond 23220

Human Rights Council
Washington Boulevard
  Twelfth Floor
Richmond 23219

Washington:
Department of Labor and
Industries
P.O. Box 44000
Olympia 98504

State Human Rights
Commission
711 South Capitol Way
Olympia 98504

West Virginia:
Labor Division
Capitol Complex
Building Three, Room 319
Charleston 25305

State Human Rights
Commission
1321 Plaza East, Room
104–106
Charleston 25301

Wisconsin:
Department of Industry,
Labor and Human
Relations
P.O. Box 7946
Madison 53707

Equal Rights Division
P.O. Box 8928
Madison 53708

Wyoming:
Employment Department
Herschler Building, Second
Floor East
Cheyenne 82002

APPENDIX B

NLRB and Wage and Hour Division Offices

The following is a list of the locations of the regional and resident offices of the National Labor Relations Board and the regional and field offices of the Wage and Hour Division of the U.S. Department of Labor. These offices, covering all or part of the states indicated, are listed in their respective telephone directories.

State	NLRB Offices	Wage and Hour Offices
Alabama	Atlanta, GA Birmingham, AL New Orleans, LA	Atlanta, GA Birmingham, AL Mobile, AL Montgomery, AL
Alaska	Anchorage, AK Seattle, WA	Seattle, WA
Arizona	Albuquerque, NM El Paso, TX Phoenix, AZ	Phoenix, AZ San Francisco, CA
Arkansas	Fort Worth, TX Houston, TX Little Rock, AR Memphis, TN Nashville, TN	Dallas, TX Little Rock, AR
California	Los Angeles, CA Oakland, CA San Diego, CA San Francisco, CA	Glendale, CA Los Angeles, CA Sacramento, CA San Diego, CA San Francisco, CA Santa Ana, CA
Colorado	Denver, CO	Denver, CO

Connecticut	Hartford, CT	Boston, MA
		Hartford, CT
Delaware	Baltimore, MD	Philadelphia, PA
	Philadelphia, PA	
	Washington, DC	
District of Columbia	Baltimore, MD	Baltimore, MD
	Washington, DC	Philadelphia, PA
Florida	Jacksonville, FL	Atlanta, GA
	Miami, FL	Fort Lauderdale, FL
	New Orleans, LA	Jacksonville, FL
	Tampa, FL	Miami, FL
		Orlando, FL
		Tampa, FL
Georgia	Atlanta, GA	Atlanta, GA
	Birmingham, AL	Savannah, GA
	Jacksonville, FL	
	Miami, FL	
	Tampa, FL	
Hawaii	Honolulu, HI	Honolulu, HI
		San Francisco, CA
Idaho	Anchorage, AK	Seattle, WA
	Denver, CO	
	Seattle, WA	
Illinois	Chicago, IL	Chicago, IL
	Peoria, IL	Springfield, IL
	St. Louis, MO	
Indiana	Chicago, IL	Chicago, IL
	Cincinnati, OH	Indianapolis, IN
	Indianapolis, IN	South Bend, IN
Iowa	Des Moines, IA	Des Moines, IA
	Minneapolis, MN	Kansas City, MO
	Mission, KS	
	Peoria, IL	
	Tulsa, OK	
Kansas	Mission, KS	Kansas City, MO
	Tulsa, OK	
Kentucky	Cincinnati, OH	Atlanta, GA
	Indianapolis, IN	Louisville, KY
Louisiana	New Orleans, LA	Baton Rouge, LA
		Dallas, TX
		New Orleans, LA
Maine	Boston, MA	Boston, MA
		Portland, ME
Maryland	Baltimore, MD	Baltimore, MD
	Washington, DC	Hyattsville, MD
		Philadelphia, PA

Massachusetts	Boston, MA	Boston, MA
		Brockton, MA
Michigan	Detroit, MI	Chicago, IL
	Grand Rapids, MI	Detroit, MI
	Milwaukee, WI	Troy, MI
Minnesota	Des Moines, IA	Chicago, IL
	Minneapolis, MN	Minneapolis, MN
Mississippi	Little Rock, AR	Atlanta, GA
	Memphis, TN	Jackson, MS
	Nashville, TN	
	New Orleans, LA	
Missouri	Mission, KS	St. Louis, MO
	St. Louis, MO	Tulsa, OK
	Kansas City, MO	
Montana	Anchorage, AK	Denver, CO
	Denver, CO	
	Seattle, WA	
Nebraska	Denver, CO	Kansas City, MO
	Mission, KS	Omaha, NE
	Tulsa, OK	
Nevada	Albuquerque, NM	San Francisco, CA
	El Paso, TX	
	Las Vegas, NV	
	Los Angeles, CA	
	Oakland, CA	
	Phoenix, AZ	
New Hampshire	Boston, MA	Boston, MA
		Manchester, NH
New Jersey	Newark, NJ	Newark, NJ
	Philadelphia, PA	New York, NY
		Trenton, NJ
New Mexico	Albuquerque, NM	Albuquerque, NM
	El Paso, TX	Dallas, TX
	Phoenix, AZ	
New York	Albany, NY	Albany, NY
	Brooklyn, NY	Bronx, NY
	Buffalo, NY	Buffalo, NY
	New York, NY	Garden City L.I., NY
		New York, NY
		Syracuse, NY
North Carolina	Winston-Salem, NC	Atlanta, GA
		Charlotte, NC
		Greensboro, NC
		Raleigh, NC
North Dakota	Des Moines, IA	Denver, CO
	Minneapolis, MN	

Ohio	Cincinnati, OH Cleveland, OH	Akron, OH Chicago, IL Cincinnati, OH Cleveland, OH Columbus, OH
Oklahoma	Mission, KS Tulsa, OK	Dallas, TX Oklahoma City, OK Tulsa, OK
Oregon	Portland, OR	Portland, OR Seattle, WA
Pennsylvania	Baltimore, MD Philadelphia, PA Pittsburgh, PA Washington, DC	Philadelphia, PA Pittsburgh, PA Wilkes-Barre, PA
Rhode Island	Boston, MA	Boston, MA Providence, RI
South Carolina	Winston-Salem, NC	Atlanta, GA Columbia, SC
South Dakota	Des Moines, IA Minneapolis, MN	Denver, CO
Tennessee	Atlanta, GA Birmingham, AL Little Rock, AR Memphis, TN Nashville, TN Winston-Salem, NC	Atlanta, GA Knoxville, TN Memphis, TN Nashville, TN
Texas	Albuquerque, NM El Paso, TX Fort Worth, TX Houston, TX Phoenix, AZ San Antonio, TX Tulsa, OK	Corpus Christi, TX Dallas, TX El Paso, TX Fort Worth, TX Houston, TX San Antonio, TX
Utah	Denver, CO	Denver, CO Salt Lake City, UT
Vermont	Boston, MA	Boston, MA
Virginia	Baltimore, MD Washington, DC Winston-Salem, NC	Philadelphia, PA Richmond, VA
Washington	Anchorage, AK Portland, OR Seattle, WA	Seattle, WA

West Virginia	Baltimore, MD	Charleston, WV
	Cincinnati, OH	Philadelphia, PA
	Pittsburgh, PA	
	Washington, DC	
	Winston-Salem, NC	
Wisconsin	Des Moines, IA	Chicago, IL
	Milwaukee, WI	Madison, WI
	Minneapolis, MN	
Wyoming	Denver, CO	Denver, CO

APPENDIX C
EEOC Offices

Albuquerque:
505 Marquette, N.W., Suite 900
New Mexico 87102-2189

Atlanta:
75 Piedmont Avenue, N.E., Suite 1100
Georgia 30335

Baltimore:
10 South Howard Street, Third Floor
Maryland 21201

Birmingham:
1900 3rd Avenue, North Suite 101
Alabama 35203-2397

Boston:
1 Congress Street, Tenth Floor
Massachusetts 02114

Buffalo:
6 Fountain Plaza, Suite 350
New York 14203

Charlotte:
5500 Central Avenue
North Carolina 28212-2708

Chicago:
500 West Madison Street, Suite 2800
Illinois 60661

Cincinnati:
525 Vine Street, Suite 810
Ohio 45202-3122

Cleveland:
1660 West Second Street, Suite 850
Ohio 44113-1454

Dallas:
207 South Houston Street, Third Floor
Texas 75202-4726

Denver:
303 East 17th Avenue, Suite 510
Colorado 80203-9634

Detroit:
477 Michigan Avenue, Room 1540
Michigan 48226-9704

El Paso:
The Commons Building C, Suite 100
Texas 79902

Fresno:
1265 West Shaw Avenue, Suite 103
California 93711

Greensboro:
801 Summit Avenue, Room B-27
North Carolina 27045-7813

Greenville:
SCN Building, Suite 530
15 South Main Street
South Carolina 29601

Honolulu:
677 Ala Moana Boulevard,
Suite 404
P.O. Box 50082
Hawaii 96813

Houston:
1919 Smith Street, Seventh
Floor
Texas 77002

Indianapolis:
101 West Ohio Street, Suite
1900
Indiana 46204-4203

Jackson:
207 West Amite Street
Mississippi 39201

Kansas City:
911 Walnut, Tenth Floor
Missouri 64106

Little Rock:
425 West Capitol Avenue,
Sixth Floor
Arkansas 72201

Los Angeles:
255 East Temple, Fourth Floor
California 90012

Louisville:
600 Martin Luther King Jr.
Place, Suite 268
Kentucky 40202

Memphis:
1407 Union Avenue, Suite 621
Tennessee 38104

Miami:
1 Northeast First Street,
Sixth Floor
Florida 33132-2491

Milwaukee:
310 West Wisconsin Avenue,
Suite 800
Wisconsin 53203-2292

Minneapolis:
220 Second Avenue South,
Room 430
Minnesota 55401-2224

Nashville:
50 Vantage Way, Suite 202
Tennessee 37228

Newark:
One Newark Center, 21st Floor
New Jersey 07102

New Orleans:
701 Loyola Avenue, Suite 600
Louisiana 70113-9936

New York:
7 World Trade Center,
Eighteenth Floor
New York 10048-0948

Norfolk:
252 Monticello Avenue, First
Floor
Virginia 23510

Oakland:
1301 Clay Street, Suite 1170N
California 94612-5217

Oklahoma City:
531 Couch Drive
Oklahoma 73102

Philadelphia:
1421 Cherry Street, Tenth
Floor
Pennsylvania 19102

Phoenix:
4520 North Central Avenue,
Suite 300
Arizona 85012-1848

Pittsburgh:
1000 Liberty Avenue, Room
2038A
Pennsylvania 15222

Raleigh:
1309 Annapolis Drive
North Carolina 27608-2129

Richmond:
3600 Broad Street, Room 229
Virginia 23230

San Antonio:
  5410 Fredericksburg Road,
    Suite 200
  Texas 78229-9934

San Diego:
  401 B Street, Suite 1550
  California 92101

San Francisco:
  901 Market Street, Suite 500
  California 94103

San Jose:
  96 North 3rd Street, Suite 200
  California 95112

Savannah:
  410 Mall Boulevard, Suite G
  Georgia 31406

Seattle:
  909 First Avenue, Suite 400
  Washington 98104-1061

St. Louis:
  625 North Euclid Street,
    Fifth Floor
  Missouri 63108

Tampa:
  501 East Polk Street, Tenth
    Floor
  Florida 33602

Washington, D.C.:
  1400 L Street, N.W., Suite 200
  20005

APPENDIX D

Federal Recordkeeping Requirements

Recordkeeping requirements are imposed on employers under a number of federal laws, executive orders, and regulations. Following are summaries of the requirements of the Age Discrimination in Employment Act, the Americans With Disabilities Act, the Davis-Bacon Act, the Employee Polygraph Protection Act, the Employee Retirement Income Security Act, the Equal Pay Act, Executive Order 11246 on Equal Employment Opportunity (applicable to federal contractors), the Fair Labor Standards Act, the Family & Medical Leave Act of 1993, the Federal Unemployment Tax Act, the Federal Insurance Contributions Act (social security), the Immigration Reform and Control Act, the Landrum-Griffin Act, the Occupational Safety and Health Act, Title VII of the 1964 Civil Rights Act, the Service Contract Act, the Toxic Substances Control Act, the Vietnam Era Veterans' Readjustment Assistance Act, the Rehabilitation Act of 1973, and the Walsh-Healey Public Contracts Act. Also included are requirements for OSHA's bloodborne pathogens standard covering health care professionals and Homeworker Employment Regulations. In addition to U.S. Code cites, references are given to tab sections or chapters in the specific volumes of the BNA Policy & Practice Series where more detailed information or text, explanations, or reproductions of specific forms may be found: Personnel Management (PM), Fair Employment Practices (FEP), Compensation (Comp), Wages and Hours (WH), or Labor Relations (LR), or Government Forms, Notices, and Posters (GFNP).

Statute	Records To Be Retained	Period of Retention	Form of Retention
Age Discrimination in Employment Act of 1967 (FEP, Tabs 401 and 403)	a. Payroll or other records containing each employee's name, address, date of birth, occupation, rate of pay, and compensation earned per week b. Personnel or employment records relating to (1) job applications, resumes, or other replies to job advertisements, including applications for temporary positions and records pertaining to failure or refusal to hire; (2) promotion, demotion, transfer, selection for training, layoff, recall, or discharge; (3) job orders submitted to employment agencies or unions; (4) test papers in connection with employer-administered aptitude or other employment tests; (5) physical examination results considered in connection with personnel actions; (6) job advertisements or notices to the public or employees regarding openings, promotions, training programs, or opportunities for overtime work	a. Three years b. One year from date of personnel action to which record relates	a.-b. No particular form specified

Statute	Records To Be Retained	Period of Retention	Form of Retention
Age Discrimination in Employment Act of 1967 (FEP, Tabs 401 and 403)	c. Employee benefit plans, written seniority or merit rating systems d. Personnel records, including the above, relevant to any enforcement action brought against employer	c. Full period that plan or system is in effect, plus one year after its termination d. Until final disposition of the action	c. If plan or system not in writing, summary memorandum to be kept d. No particular form specified
Americans With Disabilities Act (FEP, Tab 401)	Same as for Title VII, a. and b.; no reports required	One year	No particular form specified
Bloodborne Pathogens Standard (OSHA) (PM, Tab 247)	a. Medical records of occupational exposures, including name and social security number of employee; copy of employee's hepatitis B vaccination status (including dates of all hepatitis B vaccinations) and any medical records relative to employee's ability to receive vaccination; a copy of all results of examinations, medical testing, and follow-up procedures, as required; employer's copy of health care professional's written opinion, as required; and a copy of information provided to health care professional, as required. b. Training records, including dates of training sessions; contents or summary of training sessions; names and qualifications of persons conducting training; and names and job titles of all persons attending training	a. For duration of employment, plus 30 years b. Three years from date on which training occurred	a. No particular form specified (Records are required to be kept confidential and must not be disclosed or reported without employee's express written consent to any person within or outside workplace, except as otherwise required. Records must be made available, for examination and copying, upon request of Labor Department and NIOSH.) b. No particular form specified (Training records are required to be made available, for examination and copying, upon request of employees, employee representatives, Labor Department, and NIOSH.)
Davis-Bacon Act (public contracts) (COMP, Tab 305; WH, Tabs 94 and 96)	Payroll records listing name, address, and correct classification of each laborer and mechanic, rate of pay, daily and weekly number of hours worked, deductions made, and actual wages paid	Three years from date of completion of contract	No particular form specified

Statute	Records To Be Retained	Period of Retention	Form of Retention
Employee Polygraph Protection Act (PM, Tab 201; FEP, Tab 401)	a. For the investigation of a workplace theft or other incident or activity resulting in economic loss to the employer: Copy of statement provided to employees setting forth specific incident or activity under investigation and basis for testing	a.-d. Three years from date polygraph test is conducted (or from date examination is requested)	a.-d. No particular form specified (Records must be kept "safe and accessible" at place(s) of employment, or at one or more established central record-keeping offices where records customarily are maintained. All records must be available for inspection and copying by authorized representatives of the Labor Department.)
	b. For an investigation of criminal or other misconduct involving, or potentially involving, loss or injury to the manufacture, distribution, or dispensing of controlled substances: Records specifically identifying the loss or injury in question and the nature of the employee's access to person or property being investigated		
	c. Copy of notice provided to polygraph examiner identifying persons to be examined		
	d. Copies of all opinions, reports, charts, written questions, lists, and other records relating to employee polygraph tests (e.g., records of number of examinations conducted each day, records specifying duration of each test period) that have been furnished to the employer by the polygraph examiner		

Statute	Records To Be Retained	Period of Retention	Form of Retention
Employee Retirement Income Security Act (COMP, Tabs 339 and 343)	a. Records providing basis for all required plan descriptions or reports, or necessary to certify any information therefor, including vouchers, worksheets, receipts, and applicable resolutions	a. Not less than six years after filing date of documents based on information they contain	a.-b. No particular form specified (Records must be in sufficient detail to provide basic information and data by which documents may be verified, explained, or clarified and checked for accuracy and completeness.)
	b. Records pertaining to each employee-participant in the plan for determinations of benefits that are due or may become due	b. As long as relevant	
Equal Pay Act of 1963 (Also see FLSA.) (FEP, Tab 401; WH, Tabs 96 and 97)	Records in accordance with FLSA's basic requirements; records made in regular course of business relating to wage payments, wage rates, job evaluation, job descriptions, merit or seniority systems, collective bargaining agreements, descriptions or explanations of wage differentials for employees of opposite sex; all records relevant to an enforcement action brought against the employer	Retention period for different kinds of records varies, according to regulations	No particular form specified
Executive Order 11246 (FEP, Tab 401)	For federal contractors, subcontractors: Written affirmative action programs and supporting documentation, including required workforce analysis and utilization evaluation; other records and documents relating to compliance with applicable EEO nondiscrimination and affirmative action requirements, including records and documents on nature and use of tests, validations of tests, and test results as required; records pertaining to construction industry EEO plans and requirements	Retention period for different kinds of records varies, according to regulations	No particular form specified

Statute	Records To Be Retained	Period of Retention	Form of Retention
Fair Labor Standards Act (COMP, Tab 375; WH, Tabs 90, 96, and 97; FEP, Tab 401)	a. Basic records containing employee information, payroll records, individual contracts or collective bargaining agreements, applicable certificates and notices of Wage-Hour administrator, sales and purchase records	a. Three years	a.-d. No particular form specified (*Microfilm* is permissible if employer is willing to provide adequate viewing facilities and make any extension, recomputation, or transcript of the film that may be requested. *Punched tape* is permissible if records can be readily converted to reviewable form.)
	b. Supplementary basic records, including basic employment and earnings records; wage rate tables; work-time schedules; order, shipping, and billing records; records of additions to or deductions from wages paid; and documentation of basis for payment of any wage differential to employees of the opposite sex in the same establishment	b. Two years	
	c. Certificates of age	c. Until termination of employment	
	d. Written training agreements	d. Duration of training program	

Statute	Records To Be Retained	Period of Retention	Form of Retention
Family & Medical Leave Act of 1993 (FMLA) (PM, Tab 209; COMP, Tab 335; FEP, Tabs 401, 403, 405, 441; WH, Tabs 95, 96, and 97)	Records pertaining to compliance with FMLA's general requirements for leave (see a.-g., below)	Three years (same as for FLSA)	Employers to make, keep, and preserve records in accordance with §11(c) of Fair Labor Standards Act and as specified in FMLA implementing regulations, §825.500, and to make records available for inspection, copying, and transcription. No particular form specified*; may be maintained and preserved on microfilm or other basic source document of automated dataprocessing memory, provided adequate projection or viewing equipment available, reproductions clear and identifiable, and transcriptions possible and available upon request; computerized records to be available for transcription or copying. (The FMLA restricts DOL's authority to require any employer or plan, fund, or program to submit books or records more than once during any 12-month period, unless DOL is investigating a complaint or has reasonable cause to believe a violation exists. The regulations do not require submission of any records, except at DOL's specific request.)

Statute	Records To Be Retained	Period of Retention	Form of Retention
FMLA, cont.	a. Basic payroll and identifying employee data, including name, address, occupation; rate or basis of pay and terms of compensation; daily and weekly hours worked per pay period**; additions to or deductions from wages; total compensation paid b. Dates FMLA leave taken by employees (e.g., available from time records, requests for leave, etc., if so designated) (Leave must be designated in records as FMLA leave; leave so designated may *not* include leave provided under state law or employer plan not covered by FMLA.) c. Hours of leave, if FMLA leave taken in increments of less than one full day d. Copies of employee notices of leave given employer under FMLA, if in writing; copies of all general and specific notices given to employees as required under FMLA and regulations (e.g., copies may be maintained in employee personnel file) e. Any documents, including written and electronic records, describing employee benefits or employer policies and practices related to taking of paid and unpaid leave f. Premium payments of employee benefits g. Records of any dispute between employer and employee about designation of leave as FMLA leave, including any written statement from employer or employee of reasons for designation and for disagreement	a.-g. Three years	
Federal Unemployment Tax Act (FUTA) (COMP, Tab 356)	Records for each calendar year showing total wages paid to each employee, including withholding; amount of pay subject to tax, and reason, if this amount is not equal to total pay; amount paid into any state unemployment fund, including any amounts deducted or to be deducted from employee pay; data to calculate experience rating	Four years from later of either tax due date or payment	No particular form specified, but must be readily accessible to IRS

Statute	Records To Be Retained	Period of Retention	Form of Retention
Homeworker Employment Regulations*** (Also see FLSA.) (WH, Tab 91)	a. Payroll or other records specifying date on which work given out to or begun by each industrial homeworker, and amount of such work; date on which work turned in by worker, and amount of work; kind of articles worked on and operations performed; piece rates paid; hours worked on each lot of work turned in; and wages paid for each lot of work turned in b. Name and address of each agent, distributor, or contractor through whom homework is distributed or collected, and name and address of each homeworker to whom homework is distributed or from whom homework is collected by the agent, distributor, or contractor	a.-b. Not specified	a.-b. No particular form specified (Upon request, all records must be made available for inspection and transcription by Wage-Hour Division administrator, or for transcription by the employer.)
	c. Homeworker handbook (GFNP, Tab 40) in which each homeworker records daily and weekly hours worked, piece work information, and business-related expenses	c. At least two years after the handbook is filled completely or the homeworker is terminated	c. Not specified (Employers must "keep and preserve" handbook as submitted by each homeworker and, upon request, make handbook available for inspection by Wage-Hour Division of the Labor Department. The handbook must include a statement signed by the employer attesting to the accuracy of the entries.)
Immigration Reform and Control Act (PM, Tab 201; FEP, Tab 401)	INS Form I-9, Employment Eligibility Verification Form (GFNP, Tab 20)	Three years after date of hiring or one year after date of employee's termination, whichever is later	INS Form I-9, signed by new-hire and employer, to be readily available upon request

Statute	Records To Be Retained	Period of Retention	Form of Retention
Internal Revenue Code (COMP, Tab 350)	Employment tax records showing each employee's identification information, remuneration paid, and date of payment; amounts subject to FITW, FICA, and FUTA, and period of services covered; dates on which payments under accident or health plans were made; dates on which cash payments were made for agricultural or domestic services or services outside the course of employer's trade or business. Also, copies of returns, schedules, tip reporting statements, and statements submitted to IRS explaining errors or omissions, or requesting refunds or abatement of payroll taxes and other related documents		
	a. FITW statements by nonresident/resident alien employees, employees working in U.S. territories or foreign countries, or employees authorizing or rescinding additional withholding; non-cash payments made for commission sales on which no FITW taxes withheld; Forms W-4 and W-4E	a. Four years	a. No particular form specified
	b. FICA taxes withheld from cash payments made for agricultural labor or domestic service; amounts deducted as employee tax; the month in which payments made; type of service for which paid; number of days per calendar year that agricultural labor performed	b. Four years	b. No particular form specified
	c. FUTA tax records showing taxable wages; amounts paid into each state unemployment fund, showing amounts deducted or not deducted from employees; copies of FUTA contribution reports	c. Four years	c. No particular form specified

Statute	Records To Be Retained	Period of Retention	Form of Retention
Landrum-Griffin Reform Act (LR, Tab 2)	Records related to required reports on payments, agreements, or arrangements, including vouchers, worksheets, receipts, and applicable resolutions	Not less than five years after filing date of documents based on information they contain	No particular form specified (Records must be in sufficient detail to provide basic information and data by which documents may be verified, explained, or checked for accuracy and completeness.)
Occupational Safety and Health Act (PM, Tab 247; LR, Tab 85)	a. Log & Summary of Occupational Injuries and Illnesses, briefly describing recordable cases of injury and illness, extent and outcome of each incident, and summary totals for calendar year (Effective January 1, 1983, the following industries are exempt: retail trade, finance, insurance and real estate, and services.)	a.-b. Five years following end of year to which records relate	a. OSHA Form 200 (GFNP, Tab 80) (A private equivalent may be substituted.)
	b. Supplemental Record, containing more detailed information for each occurrence of injury or illness		b. OSHA Form 101 (GFNP, Tab 80) (A private equivalent may be substituted.)
	c. Complete and accurate records of all medical examinations required by law	c. Duration of employment, plus 30 years, unless a specific OSHA standard provides different time period	c.-d. No particular form specified (Microfilm storage of employee x-rays, except chest x-rays, is permitted.)
	d. Exposure and medical records of any employee exposed to potentially toxic substances and harmful physical agents required to be monitored or measured	d. Thirty years, except that first-aid records, experimental toxicological research records, and medical records of short-term employees—i.e., workers employed for less than one year—are exempt from the record-retention requirements	

Statute	Records To Be Retained	Period of Retention	Form of Retention
Service Contract Act of 1965 (WH, Tabs 94, 96, and 97)	Basic employee and payroll information, including the name, address, and social security number of each employee; work classification, wage rate and fringe benefits, and total daily and weekly compensation of each employee; number of daily and weekly hours of each employee worked; any deductions from employee's daily or weekly compensation; list of wages and fringe benefits provided service employees not included in wage determination; list of employees who worked for any predecessor contractor	At least three years from termination of contract	No particular form specified
Service Members Occupational Conversion and Training Act (PM, Tab 205)	Records (including certified copies) and accounts of employers pertaining to eligible persons on behalf of whom training assistance has been paid; any other records determined to be necessary to ascertain compliance with statutory requirements	Not specified	No particular form specified; must be made available at reasonable times for examination by authorized government representatives
Social Security Act (FICA) (COMP, Tabs 305 and 353)	Records showing each employee's name, address, and social security number; date, amount, and period of services paid for; amount of pay subject to tax as wages, and reason for any discrepancies between taxable amount and tax actually paid; amount of employee tax collected, and date collected, if not at time the worker was paid; any tips reported by employee	At least four years from later of either tax due date or payment of tax	No particular form specified
Taft-Hartley Act (LR, Tab 2)	NLRB may order employers or unions to keep certain records needed to show compliance with agency orders		

Statute	Records To Be Retained	Period of Retention	Form of Retention
Title VII, 1964 Civil Rights Act (FEP, Tabs 401, 441)	a. Any personnel or employment record made or kept by employer, including application forms and records concerning hiring, promotion, demotion, transfer, layoff or termination, rates of pay or other terms of compensation, and selection for training or apprenticeship	a. One year from date record made or personnel action taken, whichever is later	No particular form specified (Information on racial or ethnic identity may be obtained either by visual surveys of workforce or from post-hire records, where permitted by state law; such post-employment records should be kept separate from employees' basic personnel records or other records available to those responsible for personnel decisions.) Information regarding temporary or seasonal positions must be reported on Standard Form 100 (EEO-1) (GFNP, Tab 30) on September 30 of each fiscal year, in the same fashion as information about permanent employees is reported.
	b. Personnel records relevant to charge of discrimination or action brought by Attorney General against employer, including, for example, records relating to charging party and to all other employees holding similar positions, application forms, or test papers completed by unsuccessful applicants and by all other candidates for same position	b. Until final disposition of charge or action	
	c. For apprenticeship programs: (1) chronological list of names and addresses of all applicants, dates of application, sex, and minority group identification, or file of written applications containing same information; and other records pertaining to apprenticeship applicants (e.g., test papers, interview records); (2) any other record made solely for completing EEO-2 or similar reports	c. (1) Two years from date application received, or period of successful applicant's apprenticeship, whichever is longer; (2) one year from date of report	

Statute	Records To Be Retained	Period of Retention	Form of Retention
Title VII, cont.	d. For employers with 100 or more employees: Copy of EEO-1, Employer Information Report	d. Copy of most recent report filed for each reporting unit must always be retained at each such unit or at company or divisional headquarters (Note: The form is a five-part snap-out form, the last two copies of which may be retained for employer records.	
Toxic Substances Control Act, §8(c), Environmental Protection Agency****	Records of "significant adverse reactions" to health or the environment that may indicate "long-lasting or irreversible damage," "partial or complete impairment of bodily functions," "impairment of normal activities which is experienced by all or most of the persons exposed at one time," and "impairment of normal activities which is experienced each time an individual is exposed" (Records must contain original allegation; abstract of allegation, including name and address of plant site that received allegation, date allegation received, implicated substance, description of alleger, description of health effect(s), and description of environmental effects; results of any self-initiated investigation of allegation; and copies of any required reports or records relating to allegation.)	Thirty years for records of significant adverse reactions to employees' health; five years for all other allegations, including environmental or consumer charges; 30 years for employee health-related allegations arising from any occupational exposure	Signed written and oral allegations (oral allegations must be recorded, unless the alleger has been requested to submit allegation in writing); no specific form to be used for record-keeping or reporting, but required information must be present; OSHA Form 101 (GFNP, Tab 80), or appropriate substitute, where required, for records or reports relating to employee allegation
Vietnam Era Veterans' Readjustment Assistance Act (FEP, Tab 401)	For federal contractors, subcontractors with contracts of $10,000 or more: a. Documentation on number of permanent full-time or part-time Vietnam-era and special disabled employees hired during a 12-month period, to be reported annually to EEOC on Federal Contractor Veterans Employment Report (Form VETS-100) (GFNP, Tab 30) b. Records of complaints and actions taken under Act	b. One year	Numbers required to be listed on annual report form VETS-100 by job category and hiring location

Statute	Records To Be Retained	Period of Retention	Form of Retention
Rehabilitation Act of 1973 (FEP, Tab 401)	For federal contractors, subcontractors: a. For handicapped applicants and employees, complete and accurate employment records required (DOL suggests that this requirement may be met by annotating the application or personnel form of the handicapped employee or applicant to indicate each vacancy, promotion, and training program for which he or she was considered, including a statement of reasons for any rejection that compares the handicapped individual's qualification to those of the person selected, as well as any accommodations considered. Descriptions of accommodations actually undertaken also should be attached.) b. Records of complaints and actions taken under Act	a.-b. One year at minimum (Complete affirmative action program is to be available upon request to any employee or applicant.)	No particular form specified
Walsh-Healey Public Contracts Act (WH, Tabs 94, 96, and 97)	a. Unexpired certificate of age of employed minors	a. Period of employment of such minors	No particular form specified (Records should indicate which employees worked on government contracts and, hence, were covered by the Act.)
	b. Employment records, including name, address, sex, occupation, date of birth of each employee under 19 years of age, and wage and hour records, complete with identifying number of contract on which each employee is working	b. Three years from date of last entry	
	c. Basic employment and earnings records, wage rate tables, and work-time schedules	c. Two years from date of last entry or last effective date, whichever is later	
	d. Supplementary record and annual summary of occupational injuries and illnesses	d. Three years after date of entry (This retention requirement is superseded by the OSHA mandate that the Log and Summary of Occupational Injuries and Illnesses be kept for five years.)	

Notes to Federal Recordkeeping Chart

*   Under FMLA, records and documents relating to medical certifications, recertifications, or medical histories of employees or their family members are to be maintained in separate files or records and be treated (with certain exceptions) as confidential medical records.

**   If employees are not subject to FLSA recordkeeping requirements for purposes of minimum wage or overtime compliance (i.e., are not covered by or exempt from FLSA), employers need not keep a record of actual hours worked, so long as eligibility for FMLA leave is presumed for any employee who has been employed at least 12 months, and, for an employee who takes FMLA leave intermittently or on a reduced leave schedule, the employer and employee agree on the employee's normal schedule or average hours worked each week and reduce that agreement to written record that is maintained in accordance with FMLA requirements.

***   Applies to the gloves and mittens, embroideries, buttons and buckles, handkerchiefs, and jewelry production industries. See Sections 11(c) and 11(d) of the FLSA.

****   Applies primarily to chemical manufacturers.

References

Age Discrimination in Employment Act of 1967, 29 U.S.C. §621

Americans With Disabilities Act of 1990, 42 U.S.C. §12101 et seq.; 47 U.S.C. §225 and §611

Bloodborne Pathogens Standard, 29 C.F.R. Part 1910, Section 1910.1030

Davis-Bacon Act, 40 U.S.C. §276a

Employee Polygraph Protection Act, 29 U.S.C. §2001

Employee Retirement Income Security Act, 29 U.S.C. §1001

Equal Pay Act of 1963, 29 U.S.C. §206(d)

Fair Labor Standards Act, 29 U.S.C. §201 et seq. (For recordkeeping provisions, see §211(c).)

Family & Medical Leave Act of 1993, 107 Stat. 6 (P.L. 103-3) (For recordkeeping provisions, see Title 1, §106(b) of the FMLA and 29 CFR 825.500.)

Federal Unemployment Tax Act, 26 U.S.C. §3304

Homeworker Employment Regulations, 26 U.S.C. §3121

Immigration Reform and Control Act, 8 U.S.C. §1324A

Internal Revenue Code, 26 U.S.C. §6051 et seq; 42 U.S.C. §405 et seq.

Landrum-Griffin Reform Act, 29 U.S.C. §401

Occupational Safety and Health Act, 29 U.S.C. §651

Rehabilitation Act of 1973, 29 U.S.C. § 706; §791

Service Contract Act of 1965, 41 U.S.C. §351

Service Members Occupational Conversion and Training Act of 1992, 10 U.S.C. 1143 (DOD Authorization Act, Subtitle G, §4482 et seq.)

Social Security Act (Federal Insurance Contributions Act), 26 U.S.C. §3101 et seq.

Taft-Hartley Act, 29 U.S.C. §141

Title VII, Civil Rights Act of 1964, as amended, 42 U.S.C. §2000e

Toxic Substances Control Act, 15 U.S.C. §2601

Vietnam Era Veterans' Readjustment Assistance Act, 38 U.S.C. Chap. 42 §4211 et seq.

Walsh-Healey Public Contracts Act, 41 U.S.C. §35

Federal Notice-Posting Requirements

Employers are required to post official notices to employees under the Age Discrimination in Employment Act, the Americans With Disabilities Act, the Davis-Bacon Act, the Employee Polygraph Protection Act, Executive Order 11246 (applicable to federal contractors), the Fair Labor Standards Act, the Family & Medical Leave Act, the Occupational Safety and Health Act, Title VII of the Civil Rights Act of 1964, the Rehabilitation Act of 1973, the Vietnam Era Veterans' Readjustment Assistance Act, and the Walsh-Healey Act. The requirements are summarized below. For reproductions of official forms or detailed information on posting requirements, employers should refer to the cited tab sections in the specific volumes of the BNA Policy & Practice Series: Fair Employment Practices (FEP), Labor Relations (LR), Personnel Management (PM), or Wages and Hours (WH), or to Government Forms, Notices, and Posters (GFNP). A consolidated poster issued by the EEOC and containing the information to be publicly displayed by employers may be obtained by contacting: EEOC, 1801 L St., N.W., Washington, D.C. 20507.

Statute	Coverage	Basic Requirements	Posting Provision	Official Form
Age Discrimination in Employment Act (as amended)	Employers of 20 or more employees and engaged in interstate commerce; unions with 25 or more members	No job discrimination against persons ages 40 and older	In prominent and accessible places where readily observable by employees, job applicants, and union members (FEP 401)	Consolidated EEO Poster (FEP 441; GFNP 95)
Americans With Disabilities Act* (FEP 401)	Employers of 15 or more employees and engaged in interstate commerce; employment agencies; labor organizations with 15 or more members; joint labor-management committees*	Prohibits covered entities from discriminating on basis of disability with respect to hiring and all terms, conditions, and privileges of employment	Notice describing applicable provisions required to be posted in format accessible to applicants and employees, in same manner as is required under Title VII	Consolidated EEO Poster (FEP 441; GFNP 95)
Davis-Bacon Act	Employers on public construction contracts exceeding $2,000	Pay minimum wages found by Labor Secretary to be prevailing in the area	Wage scale to be paid posted in prominent and easily accessible place at worksite (WH 94, 96)	Notice to Employees (WH 98; GFNP 95)
Employee Polygraph Protection Act	Private-sector employers engaged in or affecting commerce, or engaged in production of goods for commerce	Use of lie-detector tests to screen job applicants barred; use of polygraph devices to test current employees restricted	In prominent and conspicuous place in every establishment, where it can be observed readily by employees and job applicants (FEP 401)	Notice of Protection (FEP 441; GFNP 95)
Equal Pay Act (Sec. 206(d) of FLSA)	Employers engaged in interstate commerce	No discrimination based on sex in payment of wages for equal work	In conspicuous places permitting employees to readily observe on way to or from work	Consolidated EEO Poster (FEP 441; GFNP 95)
Executive Order 11246 (as amended)	Federal government contractors and subcontractors; contractors under federally assisted construction contracts	No job discrimination based on race, color, creed, national origin, or sex	In conspicuous places available to employees, job applicants, union representatives (FEP 401)	Consolidated EEO Poster (FEP 441; GFNP 95)

Statute	Coverage	Basic Requirements	Posting Provision	Official Form
Fair Labor Standards Act	Employers engaged in interstate commerce	Pay minimum hourly rate and 1½ hours after 40 hours per week (contains child labor restrictions; addresses equal pay coverage)	Sufficient number in conspicuous places to permit employees to readily observe on way to or from work (WH 96)	FLSA Notice to Employees (WH 98); Consolidated EEO Poster (FEP 441; GFNP 95)
Family & Medical Leave Act (PM 209; COMP 335; FEP 401; WH 95)	Covered employers of 50 or more employees engaged in commerce or any industry or activity affecting commerce	Employers of 50 or more workers required to provide 12 weeks of unpaid, job-protected leave for birth of a child, placement of a child for adoption, serious health condition of a child, parent, or spouse, or employee's own serious health condition	Notice containing pertinent provisions of the Act to be posted in conspicuous places where notices customarily are posted	WH 1420 (FEP 441; WH 98; GFNP 95)**
Occupational Safety and Health Act	Employers engaged in interstate commerce	Requires that a place of employment be free of recognized hazards that might cause serious injury or death (Employers must comply with the specific safety and health standards issued by the Department of Labor. Employees must comply with safety and health standards, rules, regulations, and orders issued under the Act.)	In conspicuous place in each establishment, available to all employees (LR 85) (Injury and illness totals for previous year must be posted during month of February.)	OSHA Poster (LR 85; GFNP 95); Annual Summary, OSHA Form 200 (LR 85; GFNP 80)
Rehabilitation Act of 1973	Federal government contractors and subcontractors (with a contract of $10,000 or more)	Affirmative action to employ and advance in employment qualified persons with disabilities	In conspicuous places, available to employees and job applicants (FEP 403)	Consolidated EEO Poster (FEP 441; GFNP 95)
Title VII, 1964 Civil Rights Act	Employers of 15 or more employees and engaged in interstate commerce; employment agencies; labor unions with 15 or more members	No job discrimination based on race, color, religion, sex, or national origin	In conspicuous places where notices to employees and job applicants customarily are posted (FEP 401)	Consolidated EEO Poster (FEP 441; GFNP 95)
Vietnam Era Veterans' Readjustment Assistance Act	Federal government contractors and subcontractors (with a contract of $10,000 or more)	Affirmative action to employ and advance in employment qualified disabled and Vietnam-era veterans	In conspicuous places, available to employees and job applicants (FEP 403)	Consolidated EEO Poster (FEP 441; GFNP 95)

Statute	Coverage	Basic Requirements	Posting Provision	Official Form
Walsh-Healey Act	Establishments with government contracts exceeding $10,000	Pay minimum hourly rate and 1½ hours after 40 hours per week (contains health and safety requirements and a note on fringe benefits)	In sufficient number of places to permit employees to observe on way to or from work (WH 94, 96)	Notice to Employees (WH 98; GFNP 95)

Notes to Federal Notice-Posting Chart

*   For the first two years following the effective date of ADA's employment title, coverage is limited to employers with 25 or more employees for each working day in each of 20 or more calendar weeks in the current or preceding year and such employers' agents. As of July 26, 1994, Title I applies to businesses with 15 or more employees.

**   The interim final regulations issued on June 4, 1993, by the Wage and Hour Division, Department of Labor (58 *Federal Register* 31794) indicate that the text of the required notice, WH 1420 (see Appendix C of the regulations), may be duplicated by employers, providing the reproduction is no smaller than 8½ by 11 inches.

Federal Reporting Requirements

Various federal labor laws require employers not only to maintain certain records at the workplace and post official notices, but also to file reports with appropriate government agencies. Management's reporting responsibilities, as indicated below, fall into several broad categories. For details on specific required reports, reproductions of report forms, and filing dates, employers should refer to the cited volumes of the BNA Policy & Practice Series.

Reporting Area	Reporting Requirements	Reference
Benefits	The Employee Retirement Income Security Act requires employers to file descriptions of and reports on employee health and welfare plans and pension plans.	Compensation, Tabs 339 and 343
	Beginning in 1995, employers and/or plan administrators are required to report certain group health plan employee information to a Medicare and Medicaid "data bank" administered by the Health Care Financing Administration of the Department of Health and Human Services.	Compensation, Tab 339
Equal Employment Opportunity	Under Title VII of the 1964 Civil Rights Act, employers are required to submit to the Equal Employment Opportunity Commission certain reports indicating compliance with EEO laws. Similar reports are required of federal contractors under Department of Labor regulations.	Fair Employment Practices, Tabs 401, 403, and 441
Payroll	Federal tax withholding laws require reports on income, social security, and unemployment tax payments.	Compensation, Tab 305
Safety & Health	The Occupational Safety and Health Act requires employers to orally report any work-related incident resulting in an employee's death or the hospitalization of three or more employees within 8 hours after the death or multiple-employee hospitalization. Selected employers must participate in an annual injury-and-illness survey. Reports on conditions covered by specific standards may be required.	Labor Relations, Tab 85; Personnel Management, Tab 247
Union Relations	The Labor-Management Reporting and Disclosure Act (Landrum-Griffin) requires reports on employers' financial transactions or arrangements with labor organizations, union officials, or labor relations consultants.	Labor Relations, Tab 46

GLOSSARY

Many words used in describing events occurring in the employer-employee relationship appear in the text of this book. Other terms that have meanings peculiar to employment law, and that are not referred to elsewhere in the book, are defined below. An excellent resource for understanding the host of terms associated with the laws affecting the workplace is BNA's *Roberts' Dictionary of Industrial Relations*, available from BNA Books.

Absenteeism Absence from work. Usually refers to excessive absences.

Across-the-board adjustment Change in the wage rates for workers in a particular group or facility.

Affirmative action A remedial concept involving positive actions taken by an employer in areas such as recruitment, hiring, transfer, upgrading, rates of pay, and selection for training to improve work opportunities of groups considered to have been deprived of these opportunities because of discrimination.

Age certificate A certificate issued by a government or a school official authorizing the employment of a minor.

Agency shop A contract provision requiring nonunion employees represented by a union to pay the union a sum equal to union dues.

Agent A person acting in the interests of another, for whose activities the other may be held responsible.

Annuity Benefits paid to a worker for a given period of time. Usually refers to retirement benefits a worker receives under a pension plan.

Anti-injunction laws Federal and state laws that limit the authority of courts to issue injunctions in labor disputes.

Antitrust laws Federal and state laws that protect trade and commerce from unlawful restraints and monopolies. These

263

laws apply mostly to business activities, but sometimes apply to unions.

Area practice   Prevailing wages and benefits in a geographical area.

Assessments   Special charges levied by a union on its members to meet a financial need.

Assignment   (1) An order to a worker to perform a particular task. (2) A pledge by an employee to have part of his or her wages used to pay a debt or used for some other designated purpose.

Association agreement   A collective bargaining agreement that applies to all members of an employer association that negotiates for them jointly with a union.

Automatic renewal   A provision in a collective bargaining agreement extending it from year to year in the absence of notice by either party to the agreement to modify or negotiate a new agreement.

Automatic wage progression   A system for increasing wages based on length of service.

Award   (1) A ruling (decision) by an arbitrator. (2) A favorable determination on an application for Social Security benefits.

Back pay   Wages required to be paid to workers who have been unlawfully discharged.

Back-to-work movement   Effort by employees opposed to a strike to have striking workers abandon the strike and return to work.

Bartering   Arrangement between two or more persons whereby they agree to exchange services instead of money for the work or services they perform for each other.

Base rate   An employee's regular rate of pay, excluding any premium pay and fringe benefits. Same as "basic hourly rate."

Bidding   An employee's action in seeking a vacant job.

Blacklist   (1) A list of union members circulated among employers. (2) A list of employers barred from federal contracts because of their violations of federal contracting requirements.

Blue-collar workers   A term generally referring to manual laborers.

Board of inquiry   A group of persons appointed to mediate and report to the President in national emergency labor disputes.

Bona fide occupational qualification   An employment standard or job qualification that allows employment on the basis of an individual's sex, religion, national origin, or age, if it is shown to be "reasonably necessary to the normal operation of that particular business of enterprise."

Bonus   A payment in addition to an employee's regular wage.

Bootleg contract   A collective bargaining agreement that attempts to evade working conditions or wages required in other union contracts.

Boycott   A refusal to deal with or buy the products of a business as a means of exerting pressure in a labor dispute.

Bureau of Labor Statistics   A Bureau in the Labor Department that compiles employment-related statistics, including the Consumer Price Index by which some wage adjustments are determined.

Business agent   A paid union official who handles a local union's business matters, organizes workers, negotiates with employers, and generally administers the union's affairs.

"C" cases   A term referring to the NLRB's unfair labor practice proceedings.

Call-back pay   A guarantee to workers that they will receive a minimum number of hours of work if they are called back to work outside their regularly scheduled working hours.

Call-in pay   A guarantee to workers that they will receive a minimum number of hours of work when they are required to report to work. Same as "reporting pay" and "show-up pay."

Captive audience   Employees required to attend a meeting during working hours to hear their employer's views on unions.

Card check   Checking of a union's authorization cards signed by the employees against the employer's payroll to determine whether the union represents a majority of the employees.

Casual Workers   Employees who do not work on a regular basis.

Cease-and-desist order   An order by an administrative agency to a union or an employer, or both, to stop engaging in unlawful conduct.

Ceiling   Upper limit on wages.

Cessation   The termination of a recipient's entitlement to a government benefit.

Challenge   An objection by an employer or a union to the right of an employee to vote in an NLRB-conducted election.

Checkoff   A procedure whereby the employer deducts from the pay of employees who are members of the union in the bargaining unit membership dues and assessments and turns these monies over to the union.

Class action   A court suit in employment discrimination cases brought on behalf of a group of persons similarly affected by the alleged discriminatory practice, but because the number of persons in the group is so large it is impractical to name them all individually as parties to the suit.

Closed shop   An unlawful arrangement between an employer and a union whereby only union members may be hired. A valid union shop agreement must allow workers at least 30 days to join the union.

Coercion   (1) Unlawful pressure exerted by an employer to prevent employees from engaging in concerted or union activities. (2) Unlawful intimidation of employees by a union to compel affiliation with the union. (3) Unlawful pressure exerted on an employer by a union to force it to perform an unlawful act.

Company-dominated union   A union controlled by the employer.

Compensatory time   Time off given instead of overtime pay to employees who work overtime. Compensatory time is generally allowed under the FLSA if time off is given in the same workweek as the one in which the overtime was worked.

Compulsory arbitration   Requiring an employer and a union to submit to arbitration any issues they are unable to resolve in negotiations for a collective bargaining agreement. Also sometimes referred to as "interest" arbitration.

Concerted activities   Action by two or more employees to improve working conditions or for their mutual aid or protection.

Conciliation   A process to help the parties to a labor dispute iron out their differences.

Condonation   An employer's acquiescence in conduct by an employee that normally would be grounds for discipline or discharge.

Consent election   Election held by the NLRB after an informal hearing in which the employer and the union agree on the terms of an election.

Constructive discharge   Treating an employee unfavorably to force him or her to "voluntarily" quit.

Consumer picketing   Picketing a retail store for purposes of urging customers not to patronize the store or not to buy a certain product. If the picketing is in support of a strike against the producer or the supplier, the picketing is legal if it is aimed merely at getting customers not to buy the products of the struck employer. It is unlawful if it is aimed at getting the customers to stop patronizing the store entirely.

Consumer Price Index The Bureau of Labor Statistics' monthly statistical study, which is based on a check of retail prices of selected consumer items and services. *See* Bureau of Labor Statistics.

Contract-bar rules Rules applied by the NLRB in determining when an existing contract between an employer and a union will bar an election sought by the employees or a rival union.

Contracting out The action by an employer in which work performed by its workers is transferred to another company.

Cooling-off period Period during which workers are forbidden to strike.

Cost of living Relationship of the cost of consumer goods and services to wages.

Cost-of-living adjustment (COLA) Increase in wages because of an increase in the cost of living.

Counterproposal An opposing offer made by either a union or an employer following an offer or proposal made by the other party during collective bargaining.

Credit union An organization composed of and operated by the employees of the same employer to provide its employee-members with a means for investing their money and obtaining loans. Credit unions are chartered under either federal or state law.

Damage suits Suits that may be brought in federal courts to recover damages for breach of collective bargaining contracts and for violations of prohibitions against secondary boycotts and other unlawful strike action under the National Labor Relations Act.

Davis-Bacon Act A federal law that fixes the wages that contractors must pay laborers and mechanics engaged in working on federally funded construction projects.

Deadheading Trucks being driven empty or while not in service.

Decertification A union's loss of its right to represent employees in collective bargaining.

Deduction Money withheld from a worker's wages to pay taxes, union dues, or other obligations.

Demotion The transferring of an employee from a higher to a lower job classification.

Disability Insurance Benefits (DIB) Social Security disability benefits.

Disestablishment   An order by the NLRB that an employer-dominated union be dissolved.

Docking   Deducting money from a worker's pay for tardiness or absences.

Domestics   Workers employed to perform household duties in private homes.

Double breasted   An employer, usually a construction firm, that operates two separate businesses performing similar work, with the workers of one being union represented while the workers of the other are not represented.

Double time   A pay rate that is twice the worker's straight-time rate of pay.

Downgrade   Demotion to a job with less pay.

Dual union   Situations where a union signs up workers already claimed by another union.

Early retirement   Arrangement by which the worker may cease employment at an age earlier than the normal retirement age.

Eligibility   Qualification of an employee to vote in an NLRB election.

Employee Stock Ownership Plan (ESOP)   Arrangement allowing workers to own all or part of the business for which they work.

Entitlement   A condition in which an individual meets all the necessary requirements to receive a government-provided benefit.

Entrance rate   The pay a worker receives when first hired.

Escalator clause   A clause in a collective bargaining agreement requiring a wage adjustment at stated intervals as the cost of living changes.

Escape clause   A provision in a collective bargaining agreement that allows union members a period of time in which they can resign from the union.

Exactions   Payments made for work not done and not intended to be done.

Executive order   A directive by the President or a governor, usually addressed to an administrative agency and affecting a government operation and sometimes the public.

Fact-finding boards   Agencies appointed by the government to determine facts and make recommendations in major labor disputes.

Featherbedding   A contract provision requiring that employees be hired even though their services are not needed.

Federal Unemployment Tax Act (FUTA) The law requiring employers to pay taxes to fund the unemployment compensation program.

Flexible benefits The offering of a variety of fringe benefits by an employer to its employees and allowing each worker to select the ones he or she wants with a limit on the number that can be selected. Also sometimes referred to as "cafeteria-style" benefits.

Flextime A policy in which each worker is allowed to set his or her own work schedule within a general time frame established by the employer.

Free riders Union-represented workers who refuse to join or pay dues to the union.

Free speech The right of employers to express their views on unionization to their employees, provided no threats or promises of benefit are made to the employees.

Furlough A layoff because of lack of work.

Garnishment A procedure, usually by court action, whereby a portion of the employee's wages is attached to pay a creditor.

Good standing A union member who is in compliance with all the requirements for membership in the union. Generally means a member whose dues and financial obligations to the union are current.

Goon A person who engages in violence during a labor dispute.

Green card A term commonly used to refer to the Alien Registration Receipt Card (INS Form I-151) and Resident Alien Card (INS Form I-551), which are issued by the Immigration and Naturalization Service to lawful permanent resident aliens and which they can use to establish their identity and employment eligibility when they are seeking work.

Grievance An employee complaint. Under a union contract a grievance is a complaint by the employee that the employer is in violation of some provision of the collective bargaining agreement.

Guard Plant protection employee.

Hearing A formal or informal proceeding at which an arbitrator, a hearing officer, an administrative law judge, or a court listens to all sides of the matter before a decision is made.

Hiring hall Place where workers are recruited for work on construction projects.

Holiday *See* Legal Holiday.

Hot cargo Term applied by unions to products of plants employing nonunion workers or to products of employers with which the union has a dispute. A hot-goods or hot-cargo clause under which a union gets an employer to agree not to require its employees to handle or work on hot goods is an unlawful secondary boycott.

Impartial umpire   An arbitrator.

Impasse   Deadlock in negotiations between management officials and representatives of an employee organization over the terms and conditions of employment.

Incentive wage plan   An arrangement to pay employees extra money for more production.

Incumbent   A union currently serving as the employee's bargaining representative.

Independent contractor   A person who does a job for a price, decides how the work will be done, can hire others to do the work, and generally depends on profits rather than wages for his or her income.

Independent union   A union not affiliated with the AFL-CIO.

Individual contract   An agreement between an employer and an employee covering wages and/or working conditions.

Initiation fee   Fee required by a union as a condition for a worker to become a union member.

Injunction   A court order directing that certain action be taken or not taken.

Inside man   A spy placed in a plant as an employee.

Interference   Unlawful action that infringes on the right of employees to engage or not engage in union or protected concerted activity.

Interim agreement   An agreement setting conditions only for the period from the termination of one contract until a new one is negotiated.

International Labor Organization (ILO)   A United Nations agency that proposes improvements in international labor conditions.

Interstate commerce (or "commerce")   Trade among the states. The U.S. Constitution gives the federal government the power to regulate interstate commerce. The courts have interpreted this to include the power to regulate activities that also "affect" commerce. The federal government has relied upon this authority as a basis for enacting laws creating the NLRB, EEOC, and FLSA.

Job action   Action taken by employees to apply pressure on an employer to force it to accept their demands.

Job analysis Determining a job's requirements by examining its duties and responsibilities.

Job content A job's actual duties and responsibilities.

Job description or classification Evaluation of the nature of the work performed in a job, its relation to other jobs, its responsibilities, and the qualifications needed to do the work.

Job rate Rate of pay for a given job.

Journeyman A craft worker who has completed an apprenticeship and has mastered the type of work he or she was trained to do.

Judicial review Appeal to a court to enforce or set aside an order of an administrative agency.

Jurisdiction (1) Authority of an administrative agency or court to hear and decide a case. (2) A union's authority over certain workers or certain types of work.

Jurisdictional dispute Dispute between two unions over the right to organize a group of workers, or over which union's members are to perform a certain type of work.

Kickback The part of an employee's wages that he or she is forced to refund to the employer or to the person who hired the employee.

Knights of Labor The first national federation of American unions. It was organized in 1869, but no longer exists.

Labor dispute A controversy between an employer and a union.

Labor market A geographic area in which employers seek workers and workers seek employment.

Last-offer ballot A special NLRB-conducted election to give workers involved in a national emergency labor dispute an opportunity to vote on either accepting or rejecting an employer's final offer.

Layoff Usually a temporary separation of an employee from employment because of a lack of work.

Legal holiday A day set apart by law to commemorate a person or an occasion. Employers can require their employees to do any work on a legal holiday that they can require on any other day except for such work as the law may specifically prohibit.

Local union The basic unit of a union organization. The local union has its own constitution and bylaws and elects its own officers. Some unions refer to their locals as lodges.

Longevity Seniority; length of service.

Maintenance of membership A union security agreement that requires employees who are members of a union on a specified date to remain members during the term of the contract.

Make whole   Reimbursement to an unlawfully discharged employee for the difference between what he or she would have earned if not discharged and what the employee did earn.

Mandates   Government requirements that employers pay for or contribute to such employment-related benefits as Social Security, unemployment compensation, workers' compensation, or medical plans.

Mandatory injunction   A term applied to injunctions the NLRB's General Counsel is required to seek from a court when certain types of unfair labor practices are allegedly being committed.

Mandatory subjects for bargaining   Items that are by agreement, law, court or administrative ruling subject to negotiations between employers and the union representing the employees and required to be bargained in good faith by both parties.

Master agreement   A multiemployer or a national agreement that settles major issues, but does not settle those matters that are left to negotiation between individual companies or plants and local unions.

Maximum hours   The number of hours that can be worked at straight-time rates before overtime rates have to be paid.

Medicaid   A program providing medical assistance to persons who are eligible for benefits under a welfare program established under the Social Security Act.

Medicare   A program providing medical assistance to persons eligible for retirement benefits under the Social Security Act.

Members-only contract   A collective bargaining agreement that recognizes a union as the bargaining agent only for those employees who are members.

Merit increase   Wage increase based on performance rather than on length of service.

Migratory workers   Persons who move regularly from one work site to another, usually doing the same type of work, such as farm workers who follow a harvest from one farm area to another.

Minority union   A union that has some members in a bargaining unit but not a majority.

Moonlighting   Holding down two or more jobs.

Multiemployer unit   A bargaining unit consisting of workers employed by more than one employer.

Multiplant unit A bargaining unit consisting of employees of the same employer but working at separate locations.

National Mediation Board An agency created by the Railway Labor Act to mediate labor disputes in the railroad and air transport industries and to conduct elections to allow workers to choose a bargaining representative.

National Railroad Adjustment Board An agency set up under the Railway Labor Act to settle disputes in the railroad industry arising out of grievances or the application of contracts.

Nepotism Giving jobs, promotions, and other benefits to relatives.

No-raid agreement An agreement by a union not to try to displace another union as a bargaining agent.

Norris-LaGuardia Act Federal anti-injunction law that limits the circumstances in which courts can issue injunctions in labor.

No-solicitation rule A company rule prohibiting the solicitation of union dues, memberships, or authorization cards on company time and property.

Old-Age, Survivors and Disability Insurance (OASDI) The Social Security program providing benefits to retired and disabled workers.

Open shop A plant, office, or facility in which workers are free to join or not to join a union.

Operating employees Workers whose activities involve the driving or operation of a bus, truck, or construction equipment.

Order The directive by an administrative agency or court to an employer or a union to comply with its decision.

Organizational picketing Picketing an employer in an attempt to induce its employees to join the union.

Outside union A union seeking to organize and represent workers who are already represented by another union. *See* Incumbent.

Paper local A local union that is issued a charter by its parent organization before any workers have joined the local.

Past service credits The credit a worker is given toward a pension for the work he or she performed prior to the creation of the pension plan.

Paternalism A system in which an employer decides what is best for its workers.

Patrolling Picketing by employees.

Payment in kind   Remuneration other than money (for example, meals, housing, or reciprocal services) for work performed. *See* Bartering.

Payroll period   The period of time from one payday to the next.

Period of Disability (POD)   A continuous period of at least five months during which a worker is unable to work and is considered to be disabled under the Social Security Act because of a severe physical or mental impairment.

Perquisite ("Perk")   An extra benefit or special consideration usually given to higher levels of management.

Picketing   Advertising by union members with signs or handouts to publicize the existence of a labor dispute.

Piecework   Wages based on the number of units produced rather than on time spent in producing them.

Pirating   Encouraging workers to change jobs by offering them higher wages.

Plant closing   Termination of operations as employer relocates or goes out of business.

Posting   (1) Announcing a job vacancy. (2) Displaying for workers copies of laws, orders of administrative agencies, or other material that an employer by law must display where it can be seen by its workers.

Premature extension   An attempt by a union and employer to extend an existing collective bargaining agreement prior to its automatic renewal or expiration date to bar a petition for an election filed by the employees or by a rival union.

Premium pay   Pay that a worker receives above his or her straight-time rates, such as overtime pay.

Primary Insurance Amount (PIA)   The amount of monthly Social Security benefits a worker receives when he or she retires or becomes disabled. It is based on the worker's average monthly wage.

Profit-sharing   An arrangement under which a worker receives a share of the employer's profits.

Protected class   Any of the classes of persons protected from job discrimination under equal employment opportunity laws.

Protected concerted activity   Activity that the National Labor Relations Act allows employees to engage in without interference from an employer or union.

"R" cases   NLRB representation (election) cases. "RC" indicates a union-filed petition for election; "RD" a decertification petition; "RM" an employer-filed petition.

Railway Labor Act A federal law providing procedures for the settlement of disputes between the railroads, the airlines, and the unions representing their employees.

Rank and file Union members who are not officers.

Rat A stronger word for "scab."

Rate range The pay range from minimum to maximum for a given job.

Reasonable accommodation Under federal laws prohibiting discrimination on the basis of religion or disability, employers are required to accommodate the religious needs, beliefs, and practices, or physical and mental disabilities of employees or prospective employees, so long as the accommodations do not impose an undue hardship on business operations.

Recognition An employer's act in accepting and dealing with a union as its employees' bargaining representative.

Recognition picketing Picketing an employer to force it to recognize the union.

Red circle A contract provision allowing an employer to pay wages higher than the contract provides for certain positions.

Reduction in force Synonymous with layoff, the term is commonly used in the public sector to denote the abolition of a position or positions, necessitated by reductions in workload, reorganization, or changes in the numbers of employees caused by a reduction in funds or other similar reasons.

Reinstatement Returning a job to an unlawfully discharged worker.

Remedial order An order by an administrative agency to an employer or a union to take corrective action for engaging in unlawful conduct.

Reopening clause A clause in a collective bargaining agreement providing for the reopening of the contract for renegotiations during the term of the contract.

Replacements Workers hired to do the work of strikers.

Representation proceeding *See* "R" cases.

Representative payee A person designated by the Social Security Administration to receive a beneficiary's monthly benefits when such action appears in the beneficiary's best interests.

Restraint and coercion Action by an employer or union that unlawfully hinders the right of employees to engage in, or not engage in, union or concerted activity.

Right to know Workers' right to be informed of hazards they may encounter on the job.

Right to work law   Provisions in state laws that prohibit or make illegal arrangements between an employer and union that require membership in a union as a condition of obtaining or retaining employment.

Roving pickets   Pickets who follow a struck employer's trucks.

Runaway shop   A plant or an operation that has been moved so the employer can avoid bargaining with a union.

Runoff election   Second employee election directed by the NLRB when three or more choices were presented to the employees in the first election and none of the choices received a majority of the votes. A runoff election is usually limited to the two choices receiving the greatest number of votes in the first election.

Saving clause   A provision in a contract that if any part of the contract is held illegal the rest of the contract will remain binding on the parties.

Scab   A term striking union members use to refer to nonstriking workers.

Scale   The rate of pay union-represented workers receive.

Schism   An internal split in a union resulting in one group breaking away and forming another union.

Seasonal workers   Workers hired regularly each year but for only part of the year.

Self-employment   Work that an individual does for clients or customers rather than for an employer.

Self-organization   Employee action in forming a union.

Seniority   Preference given to employees in promotions or pay based on their length of service.

Service Contract Act   A federal law fixing the wages that employers providing services to the government must pay their employees.

Settlement agreement   A term usually applied when parties to a legal dispute agree to compromise their differences to avoid further litigation.

Set-up man/woman   A worker who makes adjustments on machinery for the machine's operator.

Severance pay   A payment to a worker who is being terminated.

Shadowing   Keeping a person under surveillance.

Shape-up   Selecting casual workers from a group or pool of workers.

Share-the-work plan   Plan in which, when work falls off, the available work is spread among all the workers to avoid a layoff.

Sheltered workshop   A nonprofit workplace employing handicapped workers.

Shift   An employee's regularly scheduled period of working hours. Usually refers to an operation where two or more groups of workers performing the same work have different working hours.

Shift differential   A premium pay that a worker on a shift other than a day shift receives in compensation for the inconvenient working hours.

Shop steward   Person designated by a union to present grievances of fellow workers to a foreman or supervisor.

Showing of interest   The employee support a union must have in a bargaining unit and which it must show to the NLRB before the NLRB will process the union's election petition.

Sit-down strike   A strike in which the employees refuse to leave the employer's premises.

Situs   The location of a labor dispute. Also a test used by the NLRB to determine whether a union is engaging in an unlawful secondary boycott.

Slowdown   A form of strike in which the employees continue to work but at a slower pace.

Soldiering   Deliberately working at a slower pace.

Sole bargaining representative   A union representing all employees in a bargaining unit as their exclusive bargaining representative.

Speedup   Quickening the work pace.

Statute of limitations   A provision in most laws that bars legal action on a claim or dispute if the required action (e.g., filing a complaint or charge with an agency or a court) is not taken within a specified period of time.

Straight-time pay   Regular or basic hourly rate of pay.

Stranger picketing   Picketing by persons who are not employees of the picketed employer.

Straw boss   A subforeman.

Stretch out   Increasing an employee's work quotas.

Strikebreakers   A term used by union members to refer to persons who accept work that had been performed by striking employees.

Struck work Work performed by a company for an employer whose employees are on strike.

Subcontracting Farming out part of a company's work to another company.

Submission agreement Agreement of the parties to submit a dispute to an arbitrator.

Subsistence allowance Payment of a worker's expenses while he or she travels on company business.

Successor company An employer who takes over another's business.

Superseniority Seniority granted by contract to certain employees in addition to the seniority they have because of their length of service. Union stewards are sometimes given superseniority.

Supplemental unemployment benefits Employer-provided payments to laid-off employees to supplement their government-provided unemployment benefits.

Surveillance Keeping a watch on employees to detect union activity.

Sweat shop A low-paying operation with poor working conditions.

Sympathetic strike Strike called to influence the outcome of a strike at another employer's facility.

Take-home pay The actual amount in a paycheck after all deductions are made.

Temporary employee A worker hired with the understanding that his or her employment will not be permanent.

Tenure Status given an employee, usually after serving a probationary period, assuring the employee of the permanency of his or her job.

Termination (1) The permanent separation of an employee from a job either by the employer discharging the employee or by the employee quitting. (2) Cessation of the payment of a government-provided benefit when the beneficiary is no longer entitled to receive that type of benefit.

Three-year rule NLRB rule that the first three years of a valid collective bargaining agreement will bar a petition for an election by a rival union or any attempt to decertify the union.

Traveling card A card issued by a local union to a member who will be working in another area under the jurisdiction of another local union.

Turnover The number of workers who quit or are terminated in a given period of time.

Two-tier wages A pay system that allows an employer to pay lower wages to recently hired workers than it paid to new employees hired in the past.

Umpire (1) An arbitrator. (2) An official who hears and decides workers' compensation cases.

Unauthorized strike A strike by a local union without the parent international union's consent.

Unconditional offer Stated willingness of a union to call off a strike without any qualifications.

Underemployed Persons who work in low-wage jobs or work less than full-time who would like to work more or at better paying jobs.

Under-the-table pay Payments to worker for which no records are kept.

Unfair employment practice Discrimination in employment based on race, color, religion, sex, disability, or national origin.

Unfair labor practice (ULP) Employer or union workplace conduct that the National Labor Relations Act prohibits.

Unfair list Names of employers publicized by unions as "unfair" because of disputes the unions have with them.

Unilateral action Action taken by one party to a collective bargaining agreement without consulting the other concerning a matter that is negotiable. Such action is usually an unfair labor practice.

Union insignia Buttons or other signs worn by employees to indicate that they are union members.

Union label A mark placed on goods indicating that they have been made by union-represented workers.

Vacation Authorized annual period of leave.

Vested rights Rights of workers to pension or profit-sharing plan benefits upon satisfying the conditions in the plan for receiving benefits.

Wage Payment for the performance of work or services.

Wage and hour law The Fair Labor Standards Act.

Waiver Surrendering of a claim.

Walk out A strike.

Welfare plan A plan that provides insurance and other benefits to employees and their families.

Whistleblower An employee who discloses improper employer practices or policies.

White-collar workers Generally refers to employees who work in offices.

Wildcat strike A strike by employees without their union's consent.

Work restriction Union-imposed limitation on the kind or amount of work union members will perform.

Work time The time spent by employees for which they are entitled to be paid under the Fair Labor Standards Act.

Workfare programs Federal programs under which welfare benefits are paid to recipients based on participation in federal training programs.

Work-to-rule Doing no more work than the minimum required.

Yellow-dog contract An unlawful agreement under which an employee agrees not to join a union while working for the employer.

Zipper clause A contract clause that seeks to prevent any further negotiations for the term of the contract.

INDEX

281